MODERN INTERPRETATIONS OF MARX

MODERN INTERPRETATIONS OF MARX

Edited with an Introduction by

Tom Bottomore

BASIL BLACKWELL · OXFORD

First published in 1981 by
Basil Blackwell Publisher
108 Cowley Road
Oxford OX4 1JF
England

British Library Cataloguing in Publication Data

Modern interpretations of Marx.
1. Marx, Karl – Addresses, essays, lectures
I. Bottomore, Thomas Burton
335.4'092'4 HX39.5

ISBN 0–631–18040–0
ISBN 0–631–12708–9 Pbk

Photoset by Nene Phototypesetters Ltd, Northampton
Printed in Great Britain by
Billing and Sons Limited
Guildford, London, Oxford, Worcester

Contents

INTRODUCTION *Tom Bottomore* 1

1 Marx's Concept of Man *Gajo Petrović* 22

2 Sociology and the Philosophy of Praxis *Antonio Gramsci* 29

3 Philosophy and Sociology in Marx's Early Writings *Lucien Goldmann* 42

4 Critique of Marx's Positivism *Albrecht Wellmer* 56

5 Marx's New Science *Louis Althusser* 68

6 Structuralism and Marxism *Maurice Godelier* 84

7 Marx's Political Economy *Meghnad Desai* 95

8 Towards a Sociological Analysis of Property Relations *Andras Hegedus* 110

9 The Materialist Conception of History *Rudolf Hilferding* 125

10 Social Classes and the State *Nicos Poulantzas* 138

11 Ideology *Jürgen Habermas* 155

12 The Ethical Potential of Marx's Thought *Svetozar Stojanović* 170

13 Labour and Human Needs in a Society of Associated Producers *Agnes Heller* 188

BIBLIOGRAPHICAL REFERENCES 202

CONTRIBUTORS 207

INDEX 211

Introduction

THE PRESENT WORK is intended as a sequel to the volume of essays on Marx which I edited some years ago.[1] In that book I brought together expository and critical accounts, by Marxists and non-Marxists, of the basic conceptions of Marx's social theory; and in the introduction I considered briefly the formation of Marx's ideas, as well as indicating some of the controversies to which they had given rise. During the past twenty-five years, however, there has been a notable revival of Marxist thought and scholarship, and new formulations and critical reassessments of the theory have proliferated.

This new collection of essays is designed to show the nature and implications of the principal 'modern interpretations'. By 'modern' is meant here those interpretations which have followed – though often with a considerable cultural lag – the profound changes in economic and political conditions, and in international relations, since the world depression of the 1930s, the rise of Fascism and the Stalinist dictatorship, the Second World War, and the postwar reorientation of social policies in capitalist welfare states, state socialist societies, and newly independent nations. Undoubtedly one of the major factors in the revival of Marxist thought has been the decay of 'orthodox Marxism', or the 'Bolshevik ideology', following Kruschev's revelations about the Stalinist regime at the 20th Congress of the Communist Party of the Soviet Union, and the revolts in Eastern Europe in 1956. From these upheavals sprang the new radical movements of the 1960s, international in their scope, which were the bearers of a renaissance of Marxist theory in a more critical form. But the radical movements, and the

[1] Tom Bottomore (ed.), *Karl Marx*. Originally published by Prentice-Hall, Inc., Englewood Cliffs, NJ, 1973. Republished in a revised edition by Basil Blackwell, Oxford, 1979.

intellectual reawakening, were not simply responses to events in Eastern Europe. They also reflected those changes in the world social situation since the 1930s which I have just mentioned, and they addressed themselves to such problems as the increasing centralization of capital in large transnational corporations, the emergence of new forms of imperialism, the growth of state power and bureaucratic administration accompanying the development of the 'interventionist state', changes in class structure and in the political orientations of different classes, and the 'authoritarian' and 'elitist' tendencies in various types of socialist movement, not only, and obviously, in Stalinism. Many of these themes had been discussed, in fact, by earlier Marxist thinkers, and it is not surprising, therefore, that one feature of the recent revival has been the rediscovery, and the diffusion (especially in the English-speaking world, where Marxist scholarship was notoriously impoverished) of styles of Marxist thought which had been submerged during the period of Bolshevik hegemony: the Marxism of Korsch and Lukács, of Gramsci, of the Frankfurt School and of the Austro-Marxists.

Two principal, and more or less opposed, currents of thought can be identified in recent formulations of Marxist theory. The first emphasizes its humanist, democratic or emancipatory content, while the second focuses attention upon its scientific character and seeks to elicit the distinctive conceptual scheme and epistemology upon which it is based. As a matter of convenience I shall refer to these two interpretations as the 'humanist' and the 'scientific'. Both are directed in large measure, though in very different ways, against the orthodox Marxism of the Stalinist era: in one case, against its inhumane and autocratic orientation, manifest in the practice which it guided; and in the other, against its crude and dogmatic theoretical stance.

The humanist current in Marxist thought has taken a number of different forms, but it is characterized in general by a pre-eminent concern with the conscious actions of individuals and groups, with cultural studies and historical interpretation, rather than with the analysis of economic structure and processes. An early manifestation of this tendency is to be found in the writings of Korsch and Lukács, who initiated, in the view of many critics,[2] a re-Hegelianizing of Marx's thought which probably attained its greatest influence in the works of the later Frankfurt School in the 1960s. Korsch, in *Marxism and Philosophy*, and Lukács, in *History and Class Consciousness* (both published in 1923) reintroduced into Marxist theory distinctly Hegelian concepts, such as that of 'totality',[3] and more broadly, represented Marxism as a critical philosophy of history, indissolubly linked with the historical situation and role of the proletariat, rather than any kind of social science. Korsch, in particular, argued that Marxism, as a materialistic dialectic, is the revolutionary philosophy of the working class, standing in the same relation to the working-class revolutionary movement as did German idealist philosophy to the bourgeois revolutionary movement.[4]

Korsch and Lukács both played a part in the creation of the Institute for Social Research (the institutional basis of the Frankfurt School). They participated in the 'First Marxist Work Week' held in the summer of 1922, where the idea of the Institute was first conceived, and much of the time at this conference was spent in discussing the manuscript of Korsch's *Marxism and Philosophy*.[5] It is evident that the ideas of some of

[2] See, for example, George Lichtheim, *From Marx to Hegel*, especially in the title essay, pp. 1–49. [*Note*. Details of the principal works referred to in this introduction, and in the texts, will be found in the Bibliographical References at the end of the volume.]

[3] Lukács, *History and Class Consciousness*, p. 27. 'It is not the primacy of economic motives in historical explanation that constitutes the decisive difference between Marxism and bourgeois thought, but the point of view of totality. The category of totality, the all-pervasive supremacy of the whole over the parts is the essence of the method which Marx took over from Hegel and brilliantly transformed into the foundations of a wholly new science.' Similarly, Korsch refers to the 'totality of the historico-social process', and says of Marxism that it is 'a theory of *social development* seen and comprehended as a living totality; or, more precisely, it is a theory of *social revolution* comprehended and practised as a living totality.' *Marxism and Philosophy*, p. 52.

[4] Korsch later changed his views, and rejected what he regarded as the 'distortion of the strongly empirical and critical sense of the materialistic principle', and the elaboration of Marxism as 'a general philosophical interpretation of the universe'. 'The main tendency of historical materialism', he concluded, 'is no longer "philosophical", but is that of an empirical scientific method.' *Karl Marx*, rev. German edn, 1967, p. 203.

[5] For details see Martin Jay, *The Dialectical Imagination*, ch. 1.

the leading members of the Frankfurt School, at the outset and subsequently, were very close to those of Korsch and Lukács, notably in their emphasis upon the philosophical sources of Marx's thought and especially its direct and crucial relationship with Hegel's dialectic. This is apparent, for example, in Horkheimer's essays on critical theory[6] published in 1937, and in Marcuse's *Reason and Revolution* (1941). Nevertheless, there were important differences between Korsch and Lukács on one side, and the Frankfurt School thinkers on the other. The former were active in political life (in 1923 both were leading members of Communist parties, and Lukács remained a party member throughout his life except for the period 1957–69), and they saw the critical function of Marxist theory as one which is carried on by a revolutionary party. In *History and Class Consciousness* Lukács conceives Marxism as 'the expression in thought of the revolutionary process itself', and goes on to refer to 'the correct class consciousness of the proletariat and its organizational form, the communist party'. The Frankfurt School thinkers, on the other hand, were largely detached from political activity,[7] and they came to regard the critical reason embodied in Marx's social theory as being borne along, not by a party or a political movement, but by an intellectual group – a view not unlike that of the Young Hegelian 'critical critics', as Lichtheim noted.[8]

This difference is particularly significant in respect of the connection between theory and practice, which all these thinkers emphasized as a vital element in the dialectical thought of authentic Marxism. Whereas Korsch and Lukács took the inherently plausible view that the unity of theory and

[6] The term 'critical theory' has come to be used as a general description of the ideas of the Frankfurt School, though it perhaps refers more particularly to the later views of members of the School, and also to the views of thinkers who were not, in a strict sense, members at all.

[7] See Jay, *The Dialectical Imagination*, pp. 13–15.

[8] Lichtheim, *From Marx to Hegel*. This outlook is most fully expressed, at a much later date, in the pessimistic concluding pages of Marcuse's *One-Dimensional Man*, where the critical thinker is represented as an isolated individual swimming hopelessly against the torrent of technological rationality; the critical theory of society no longer finds in society 'real forces' which are moving toward more rational and freer institutions, and it becomes 'incapable of translating its rationality into terms of historical practice'.

practice is achieved in a revolutionary party or movement, and can themselves be said to have lived this unity, the Frankfurt School thinkers expressed a purely theoretical conception of theory and practice, engaged in no political practice, and proposed no way in which theory and practice could be brought into a valid and fruitful relation with each other. It is partly for this reason, I think, that much of the later writing of these thinkers is characterized by a preoccupation with the development of knowledge and culture, and a lack of attention to economic, and especially political, phenomena.[9]

This is not to say, however, that the difference can be summed up by concluding that Korsch and Lukács were consistent and correct in the position they adopted, while the Frankfurt School thinkers were inconsistent and mistaken. The matter is more complex than that. In the first place, it may be noted that both Korsch and Lukács, in the particular historical context of the postwar revolutionary movements in Europe, gave their allegiance to a party which eventually proved to be, not a liberating force, but, on the contrary, the instrument of a new despotism. Second, the ground of this allegiance, their conception of the proletariat as the subject of a historical process which can be cognized infallibly by dialectical reason (that is to say by Marxism, which is represented as being only the expression in thought of the process itself, or in other words the adequate, 'correct' self-consciousness of the subject) helped to transform Marxism into a dogmatic ideology and to exclude, as Korsch himself later recognized, those elements in Marx's own thought which gave it the character of an empirical, hence corrigible, social science.

The Frankfurt School thinkers, on the other hand, though they also grounded their thought on the idea of Marxism as dialectical reason, confronted more directly the disjunction between the pronouncements of reason (as they understood them) and the actual conditions and tendencies of social life, among which the non-revolutionary outlook and practice of the Western working class had a prominent place. In this sense it

[9] For some critical comments on Adorno from this point of view, see Gillian Rose, *The Melancholy Science: An Introduction to the Thought of Theodor W. Adorno*, ch. 7.

may be said that their thought was more 'critical', and that their detachment from the existing political parties and movements had a certain justification. But still there is something contradictory in accepting such a disjunction between the actual state of affairs (which can be known, presumably, only through some kind of scientific inquiry) and the judgements of critical reason (which seem to assume more and more the character of disguised or undisguised value judgements, where they are not concerned with purely epistemological questions) on the basis of an interpretation of Marxism which sees its uniqueness precisely in its overcoming of the dualism of fact and value, theory and practice.[10]

One way out of this contradictory position is, of course, to abandon Marxism as an adequate social theory in the new historical circumstances, and to look for some other form of dialectical theory. This is a path which seems to have been taken not only by some critical theorists of the later Frankfurt School, but also by Korsch, who wrote, towards the end of his life, in 'Ten Theses on Marxism Today' (1950), that '. . . all attempts to re-establish the Marxist doctrine as a whole in its original function as a theory of the social revolution of the working class are a reactionary utopia,' and then went on to speak of 're-establishing a revolutionary theory and practice', presumably in a new form. But Korsch gave no indication of how this was to be done, of the possible content of such a theory and practice, or whether it corresponded in any way with the social reality of the time. In this respect his thought resembles that of many radical sects over the past two decades, for whom 'revolutionary theory and practice' became simply an article of faith.

But there is, evidently, another way of escape from this contradiction. This involves accepting the dualism of fact and value, and seeing in Marx's thought both a science of society (sociology or political economy) *and* a normative social theory (the assertion and grounding of definite values and ends) which are distinct but related. Along these lines I have argued

[10] See especially the discussion of this unique character by Lucien Goldmann, ch. 3 below. I have examined the relation between theory and practice more fully in *Marxist Sociology*, ch. 4.

elsewhere that '. . . in Marx's lifetime his theoretical analysis and his allegiance to the labour movement were congruent and, in a sense, mutually supporting. . . . Thus Marx's theory could find empirical confirmation, and its empirical testing provided at the same time a degree of rational and factual support for Marx's moral convictions.'[11] Many recent Marxist thinkers, as well as some earlier ones, have interpreted Marx broadly in this way,[12] while differing widely in their accounts of the relation between judgements of fact and judgements of value, or more specifically between theoretical analysis and political practice; and they have done so whether they have devoted their attention mainly to the revision and development of a science of society, or to the philosophical investigation of normative questions.

Let us first consider the ideas of the humanist Marxists. The principal concepts underlying much recent humanist thought are no longer those of 'historical totality', or a privileged 'historical subject' (the working class), but those of 'human nature' and 'human needs'. This is apparent, for example, in a major collection of essays published in 1965 under the title *Socialist Humanism*,[13] and in the general orientation of one of the best-known Marxist journals of the past two decades, *Praxis*, which was published in Yugoslavia from 1964 to 1974 in Serbo-Croat and international editions.[14] Two of the contributors to

[11] Bottomore, *Sociology as Social Criticism*, p. 83.

[12] It is worth noting here that Lucien Goldmann, although he argues strongly in favour of a dialectical theory which purports to overcome the dualism of fact and value, himself makes some concessions to the opposed view; see note 1 in ch. 3 below.

[13] Erich Fromm (ed.), *Socialist Humanism*.

[14] For a brief account of the history of *Praxis*, and of the philosophical and sociological debates which it encouraged, see Mihailo Marković, 'Marxist Philosophy in Yugoslavia: The Praxis Group', part I of M. Marković and R. S. Cohen, *Yugoslavia: The Rise and Fall of Socialist Humanism*. See also Mihailo Marković and Gajo Petrović (eds.), *Praxis: Yugoslav Essays in the Philosophy and Methodology of the Social Sciences*. One particularly important feature of the contributions made by Yugoslav thinkers to these discussions is that they embodied serious and critical reflection upon the experiences, problems, needs and opportunities of a functioning socialist society which still presents today, as it has done for a quarter of a century, the most attractive model available for the future development of a democratic socialist system. This is not to say that it is by any means a perfect model; the fate of *Praxis*

the present volume, Petrović and Stojanović, were closely associated with the *Praxis* group, and it will be clear from the excerpts from their writings reprinted below[15] that their concern is not to construct an empirical science of human nature from which values could then be immediately derived, but to develop a normative theory, and in particular a Marxist ethics, which would formulate individual and social ideals as objectives of policy decisions. In the same way, one of the contributors to *Socialist Humanism*, Marek Fritzhand, expounds Marx's normative 'ideal of man', within which he distinguishes three related conceptions: that of the 'complete', rather than fragmented or limited, human being; that of the 'harmonious individual'; and that of the 'freely acting', creative individual.[16]

A similar dualism is apparent – although it shows itself in a less obvious way – in the thought of some recent 'critical theorists'. Thus Jürgen Habermas, in the course of his epistemological critique of positivism, distinguishes three human 'cognitive interests' (which are presumably, in some sense, components of 'human nature'): an interest in technical control which manifests itself in scientific knowledge; an interest in social interaction and self-understanding which manifests itself in hermeneutic knowledge; and an 'emancipatory' interest which is conceived as bringing together, in some way, theoretical and practical reason. Certainly, as Habermas' discussion of the emancipatory interest shows, his analysis is intended to lead to a monistic, rather than a dualistic, conception; but it remains doubtful whether this unity of reason is convincingly established. Kolakowski, in a critical assessment,[17] has argued that:

> Habermas does not clearly define his key concept of 'emancipation'. It is evident that, in the spirit of the whole tradition of

itself, which was obliged to cease publication in 1974, because its critical stance offended important political leaders and bureaucrats, shows that democracy and self-management are still far from being securely established in Yugoslavia.

[15] Ch. 1 and ch. 12.

[16] Fromm, *Socialist Humanism*, pp. 157–65.

[17] Leszek Kolakowski, *Main Currents of Marxism*, vol. III, pp. 387–95.

> German idealism, he is seeking for a focal point at which practical and theoretical reason, cognition and will, knowledge of the world and the movement to change it, all become identical. But it does not appear that he has actually found such a point or shown us how to arrive at it. . . . It may be that, in some cases, acts of self-understanding by individuals or societies are themselves part of the practical behaviour leading to 'emancipation', whatever this term means. But the question will always remain: by what criteria are we to judge the accuracy of that self-understanding, and on what principle do we decide that 'emancipation' consists in one state of affairs rather than another? On the second point we cannot avoid making a decision that goes beyond our knowledge of the world.

In Habermas' thought, then, the identity of theoretical and practical reason appears to be less successfully established than their separateness as distinct forms of reason. This distinctiveness is also recognized implicitly by another critical theorist, greatly influenced by Habermas, when he writes that:

> In order to reformulate Marx's supposition about the prerequisites for a successful revolution in the case of the capitalist countries, it would be necessary to include socialist democracy, socialist justice, socialist ethics and a 'socialist consciousness' among the components of a socialist society to be 'incubated' within the womb of a capitalist order.[18]

The dualism expressed by the writers I have mentioned is certainly not intended to erect an impassable barrier between a realm of facts and a realm of values; nor to assert that the activity of reason is confined to the former, whereas will, or 'decisionism' (to use the term which Habermas applies to Max Weber's position), prevails in the latter. None of them would accept the view that in the sphere of practical activity reason is, and can be, only 'the slave of the passions'. Their aim is, rather, to demarcate the proper sphere and methods of scientific and philosophical inquiry, and to determine the role of philosophy within Marxist thought as a whole, especially in relation to the social sciences. Habermas, as we have seen, formulates a

[18] Albrecht Wellmer, *Critical Theory of Society*, pp. 121–2. See also the excerpt below, ch. 4.

conception of the essential unity of reason, but this is best interpreted, I think, in a weak sense as a claim concerning the *relatedness* of the different forms of reason which he distinguishes. Such an interpretation seems to be warranted by some of Habermas' own presentations of his argument, as for example in *Legitimation Crisis* (p. 10) where he says that: 'To the truth claims that we raise in empirical statements there correspond claims of correctness or appropriateness that we advance with norms of action and evaluation.'

The Yugoslav thinkers, on the other hand, accept more fully the idea that reason has distinct, irreducible (but not unrelated) forms – that its procedures differ in diverse spheres, and that its scope and effectiveness are perhaps more restricted in some spheres than in others – and hence they are more inclined to formulate the specific problems of the social sciences, of the philosophy of value, or of the philosophy of science, as separate and distinct issues. The following passage from Marković's exposition of the research programme of the *Praxis* group illustrates this tendency:

> How to explain the fact that socialist revolutions did not occur in developed industrial countries of the West but in backward rural societies of the East? What really is a revolution if, after an apparent revolution, a bureaucratic society can emerge? How build up socialism in a relatively under-developed country? What does it mean for the state to wither away? How is a non-market modern economy possible? What is *Marxist* logic, ethics, aesthetics? Is there a Marxist anthropology? What is the essence of man with respect to which one speaks about alienation? If that essence is universal, how is history possible? If it is particular, how can we escape relativism? If man is a being of *praxis*, and *praxis* is (among other things) labour and production, how can the standpoint of *praxis* be a standard of critical evaluation? How reconcile the principle of determinism, according to which historical processes are governed by laws independent of human consciousness and will, with the principle of freedom according to which it is men who make their own history?[19]

In many respects the outlook of the humanist Marxists has

[19] Marković and Petrović, *Praxis*, Introduction, pp. xxii–xviii.

affinities with the views of Gramsci, formulated in his prison notebooks,[20] and expressed particularly in his claim that

> . . . the philosophy of praxis is 'sufficient unto itself', that it contains in itself all the fundamental elements needed to construct a total and integral conception of the world, a total philosophy and theory of natural science, and not only that but everything that is needed to give life to an integrated practical organisation of society, that is, to become a total integral civilization.[21]

Any such outlook, however, confronts a major difficulty; for whereas a Marxist sociology or political economy can be, and has been, developed on the basis of Marx's own analysis and investigation of modes of production and social formations, there is no real starting-point in Marx himself – in the sense that he provided any systematic and comprehensive treatment of philosophical issues – for the elaboration of a Marxist conception in any of the principal fields of philosophical inquiry. In short, Marx was *not* a German philosopher.[22] Hence the fact that every attempt to construct a Marxist philosophy tends to depart from Marx's own work, and to draw heavily upon some non-Marxist scheme of philosophical thought: that of Hegel in the case of Lukács, Gramsci (partly through the influence of Croce), and the Frankfurt School; of neo-Kantian and positivist philosophy of science in the case of the Austro-Marxists; of French rationalism, especially in the form given to it by Bachelard, and structuralist epistemology in the case of Althusser.

What is present in Marx's own work, philosophically considered, is only a sketch of a normative social theory,

[20] See Antonio Gramsci, *Selections from the Prison Notebooks*, section III, 'The Philosophy of Praxis'.

[21] Ibid., p. 462.

[22] See the contrary assertion on page 1 of Kolakowski, *Main Currents*, vol. I. It may indeed be argued, as it was by Korsch in his later work, that the elaboration of Marx's thought into 'a comprehensive materialist philosophy embracing both nature and society, or a general philosophical interpretation of the universe' was a 'distortion of [its] strongly empirical and critical sense'. Karl Korsch, *Karl Marx*, rev. German edn, p. 145.

expounded most fully in the *Economic and Philosophical Manuscripts*,[23] from which, as Stojanović observes, a Marxist ethics '. . . has yet to be constructed'.[24] Even here it might be more appropriate to speak of a 'socialist ethics', as does Wellmer, since the construction of such an ethical theory – requiring a systematic analysis and elaboration of such concepts as 'emancipation', 'human needs', 'justice', a 'good society' – must evidently draw upon the work of many thinkers besides Marx, go far beyond Marx's own fragmentary observations, and probably, in some important respects, fundamentally revise his conceptions.[25] Outside the sphere of ethical theory it is clear that Marx's contribution to philosophical inquiry was even more slight, or non-existent: there is in his work no attempt to develop in a systematic way an ontology, an epistemology, a logic, a philosophy of science, or an aesthetic theory (as distinct from his sporadic reflections upon a possible sociology of art and literature).[26] Thus, any elaboration of a 'Marxist' view in these spheres is, in a strict sense, non-Marxist, involving subsequent interpretation and elaboration of fragmentary observations and notes (which, in the case of Marx's occasional comments upon his own scientific method, can easily give rise to contradictory accounts), or of what are taken to be implicit philosophical orientations discoverable in Marx's texts; and relying to a very great extent, as I have indicated, upon ideas derived from quite varied philosophical traditions.

This poverty of Marxist philosophy is in sharp contrast with the substantial and largely autonomous development of Marxist social science on the foundation of Marx's own major

[23] So that Hendrik de Man quite rightly claimed, in an essay written when the manuscripts were first published, that they showed '. . . more clearly than any other work the ethical-humanist themes which lie behind Marx's socialist convictions and behind . . . his whole scientific work.' *Der Kampf* (1932).

[24] See p. 170 below.

[25] The view expressed here would be accepted by many humanist Marxists; see, for example, some of the contributions, and Erich Fromm's introduction, to *Socialist Humanism*.

[26] On the latter see the illuminating study by S. S. Prawer, *Karl Marx and World Literature*.

investigations. In these circumstances it is scarcely surprising that one main current of Marxist thought should always have held that Marxism is primarily, or exclusively – and certainly most fruitfully – a science of society.[27] But this conception raises two distinct kinds of questions. First, we may inquire into the nature of this science: is it political economy, sociology, or historiography, or is it some quite distinctive kind of thought which incorporates and transcends these specialized disciplines? In other words, what are its fundamental concepts, and how are they connected in a theoretical model or paradigm? And further, what are its distinctive methods of research and of proof? Second, we may ask how the science should actually be developed substantively in diverse fields of inquiry.

The first of these questions poses general issues in the philosophy of science, and 'scientific Marxists' have taken very different positions in their attempts to establish the scientific character of Marx's theory, and to distinguish it from non-science, pseudo-science, or ideology. Such positions have been influenced primarily, as I have already indicated, by developments in the post-Marxian philosophy of science itself, and they take the form of meta-theoretical reflections upon Marx's thought. Max Adler, who provided the epistemological and methodological foundations of the Austro-Marxist conception of Marxism as a scientific sociology, with the aid of a

[27] This view has also been taken by many non-Marxist commentators. Croce, for example, argued in his essay on 'The Scientific Form of Historical Materialism' that Marx's conception of history was not philosophical – 'within its limited field the elements of things are not presented in such a way as to admit of a philosophical discussion' – and in another essay, that historical materialism is 'simply a *canon* of historical interpretation', that is, 'an aid in seeking for [results] . . . entirely of empirical origin'. See Benedetto Croce, *Historical Materialism and the Economics of Karl Marx*, pp. 1–21, 77–8. Similarly, Schumpeter, while recognizing what he calls the 'prophetic' element in Marxism, says of Marx that 'Nowhere did he betray positive science to metaphysics,' and further that '. . . his theory of history is not more materialistic than is any other attempt to account for the historic process by the means at the command of empirical science. It should be clear that this is logically compatible with any metaphysical or religious belief – exactly as any physical picture of the world is.' See J. A. Schumpeter, *Capitalism, Socialism and Democracy*, pp. 9–11.

neo-Kantian and positivist philosophy of science,[28] recognized this clearly when he argued that just as Kant's question about nature as an object of thought followed the emergence of Newtonian physics, so the neo-Kantian question about society as an object of thought followed the construction of Marx's social theory.

More recently, Louis Althusser has also attempted, from an entirely different perspective, to establish the character of Marxism as a science.[29] In this case, the external influences upon Marxist thought are those of French rationalism,[30] and more particularly of structuralism, also largely French in inspiration, through the work of Lévi-Strauss. Hence the two fundamental ideas propounded by Althusser are his conception of science as a theoretical activity which consists above all in the construction of a 'problematic' (a conceptual scheme or theoretical system), and his assertion that the key concept of Marxist science, which is implicit, but not explicitly formulated, in Marx's work, is that of 'the effectivity of a structure on its elements'.

In the past two decades structuralism has had a considerable influence, not only in the philosophy of science,[31] but in the social sciences and humanities generally. Thus, while Althusser's work has been mainly confined to the philosophy of science, other Marxist structuralists such as Poulantzas[32] and Godelier[33] have undertaken empirical studies from this standpoint. Further, it is arguable that the diffusion of

[28] See the selections from Adler's writings in Tom Bottomore and Patrick Goode (eds.), *Austro-Marxism*, section II. See also the critical discussion of Adler in Kolakowski, op. cit. *Main Currents*, vol II, pp. 258–76.

[29] See the texts below, ch. 5.

[30] Especially that of Bachelard, who is the source of one of Althusser's most important ideas: that of the 'epistemological break' which divides pre-science (or ideology) from science, and in the case of Marx is held to separate the young Marx as a humanist philosopher sharply from the mature Marx (after 1845) who was a social scientist.

[31] For example, the new 'transcendental realism', as expounded by Roy Bhaskar in *A Realist Theory of Science* and *The Possibility of Naturalism*, conceives causal explanation as comprehension of the deep structures of the world – both physical and social – which lie behind, and produce, patterns of events.

[32] See ch. 10 below.

[33] See ch. 6 below.

structuralist ideas has been largely responsible for an important shift of emphasis within recent Marxist thought towards the analysis of modes of production, which is evident not only in the general revival of Marxist political economy, but more specifically in the field of development studies.[34]

This last example is also significant as indicating that the present debates within Marxism are far from being limited to general discussions of epistemology and methodology. Many Marxist scholars, in fact, have been principally concerned with the second question that I posed earlier: namely, how should this science of society be developed substantively in specific fields of research? Besides the extensive work on development and underdevelopment to which I have just referred, there have been major studies of the historical development of the capitalist economy[35] and of social formations;[36] of kinship and the social relations of production;[37] of the family (greatly influenced by radical feminist criticisms of traditional Marxism);[38] of social classes;[39] of property;[40] of the state;[41] and of culture and ideology.[42] It is not the case, of course, that all

[34] For a general review and criticism of sociological theories of development and underdevelopment, and an outline of a theory of modes of production, see John G. Taylor, *From Modernization to Modes of Production*. There is an excellent comprehensive account of the revival of Marxist political economy in Karl Kühne, *Economics and Marxism*.

[35] See Immanuel Wallerstein, *The Modern World System*.

[36] See, for example, the two works by Perry Anderson, *Passages From Antiquity to Feudalism* and *Lineages of the Absolutist State*.

[37] See the discussion and references in M. Godelier, *Perspectives in Marxist Anthropology*.

[38] For a general account of recent work and discussion of some of the theoretical issues, see the essays in A. Kuhn and A. M. Wolpe (eds.), *Feminism and Materialism*.

[39] See Nicos Poulantzas, *Classes in Contemporary Capitalism*, and the text below, ch. 10.

[40] See Andras Hegedus, ch. 8 below.

[41] See Ralph Miliband, *The State in Capitalist Society*; Claus Offe, *Strukturprobleme des kapitalistischen Staates* and 'The theory of the capitalist state and the problem of policy formation'; and J. O'Connor, *The Fiscal Crisis of the State*.

[42] See Goldmann, *The Hidden God*, and various essays in his *Marxisme et sciences humaines*. Much of the work of the Frankfurt School was, of course, devoted to cultural analysis; among the later works which deal particularly with ideology see Habermas, *Legitimation Crisis*, and also ch. 11 below. The

the recent substantive studies in economics, sociology or anthropology have been undertaken by 'structuralists', or by scholars who would consider themselves 'scientific Marxists' even in a very broad sense; nevertheless, it seems to me that the most important work of the past two decades has been produced in an intellectual context which emphasizes the idea of Marxism as a social science, in whatever way the relation of science to philosophy or other modes of thought may be conceived.

It is clear that the general view of the scientific Marxists is dualistic, drawing a sharp distinction between science and other forms of knowledge; but the ways in which science is conceived to be related to these other forms are quite diverse. Max Adler examined this question at length in his first major work,[43] where he seems to argue that there are different perspectives on the world, of which science is only one. The task of a science of society is to provide causal explanations, but it reveals only one aspect of life, and 'the complete reality of our being' is to be found in practical, conative activity. He returned to the problem in later writings, where he argued that the causal mechanism of history is transformed into a teleology by the scientific illumination of it, since this scientific knowledge itself becomes a cause; and in one of his last works he embarked upon a fresh analysis of motives as causes.[44] The Austro-Marxists – with the exception of Otto Neurath, if he can properly be counted as a member of the school – were not

essay by Althusser, 'Ideology and Ideological State Apparatuses', in *Lenin and Philosophy and Other Essays* has provoked much critical debate, and some investigations of ideology from a Marxist structuralist standpoint (for instance, by Godelier, in *Perspectives*).

[43] Max Adler, *Kausalität und Teleologie im Streite um die Wissenschaft*. The view he expounds here is similar to that of other neo-Kantians, including Max Weber, who was also concerned to delimit the sphere of science as a distinct 'realm of value'. It also appears to be close to the ideas of some recent philosophers of science; thus Roy Bhaskar, in *The Possibility of Naturalism*, while arguing that it is *sometimes* possible to pass directly from a scientific explanation to a value judgement, concludes that 'science, although it can and must illuminate, cannot finally "settle" questions of practical morality and action, just because there are always – and necessarily – social practices besides science, and values other than cognitive ones.' (pp. 82–3)

[44] Max Adler, *Lehrbuch der materialistischen Geschichtsauffassung*.

positivists in the manner of the Vienna Circle, for they did not explicitly argue that only the statements of empirical science and logic are meaningful; but in a wider sense they were undoubtedly positivists. They gave primacy to scientific knowledge, the philosophy in which they were interested was the philosophy of science, not ethics or social philosophy,[45] and they regarded Marxism as being pre-eminently, if not exclusively, a science of society.[46]

Althusser and other structuralist Marxists similarly assign primacy to science, but they dismiss in a more radical way any form of non-scientific thought – subsumed under the concept of 'ideology' – including the pre-scientific thought of Marx himself, expressed in the 'humanism' and 'historicism' of his early works. Althusser's view presents a number of difficulties. One is that of defining and explaining ideology.[47] Another concerns the epistemological status of Althusser's own philosophy of science (or more precisely, his philosophical reading of Marxism as science).[48] These questions, however, only pose in a particularly acute form problems which are inherent in any project to ground securely a scientific Marxism, or indeed any scientific sociology: (i) how, if at all, can science be

[45] The Austro-Marxists paid relatively little attention to these subjects, and both Adler and Bauer rejected the ideas of those thinkers – influenced by another form of neo-Kantianism – who claimed that Marxism needed to be supplemented by an explicit ethical doctrine. However, in his essay on 'Marxism and ethics' Bauer recognized the value of Kant's doctrine in combating 'ethical scepticism' and in examining 'the question of which of the contending maxims (of practical reason) is supposed to guide us'. Only, he argued, 'science must come first, before we can successfully pose the moral question.' It is also worthy of note that *Der Kampf* (the theoretical journal of the Austro-Marxists) published a long essay by Hendrik de Man emphasizing the ethical-humanist themes in Marx's *Economic and Philosophical Manuscripts* (see note 23 above).

[46] This view is set out very forecefully by Hilferding in his preface to *Finance Capital*.

[47] See pp. 72–7 below. On the variations, and contradictions, in Althusser's accounts of ideology, see Jorge Larrain, *The Concept of Ideology*, pp. 154–64. See also the discussion of ideology by Godelier, in *Perspectives in Marxist Anthropology*, pp. 169–85, where a Marxist analysis of ideology is closely related to Lévi-Strauss' structural analysis of myth.

[48] This is similar to the well-known problem of the status of the verification principle in logical positivism.

demarcated from non-science; (ii) if so demarcated, what kind of relation is held to exist between science and non-science; and (iii) are the problems that arise in the non-scientific domain – in ethics, let us say – capable in principle of solution by reason and/or by reference to experience.

The Austro-Marxists, as we have seen, took a less extreme view of the primacy of science than do the Marxist structuralists. They did not intend to establish an impassable gulf between the spheres of cognitive/theoretical reason and practical reason; and they held that science can illumine, and profoundly influence, even if it cannot ultimately decide, matters of practical (especially political) conduct. For them, moreover, practical reason is still reason; their view was not that values are the result of arbitrary choices or decisions, set in a framework of determination by 'interests' – as for instance Max Weber's value theory asserted – but rather, as Bauer's essay indicates, that there can be universally valid reasons, such as are formulated in Kant's maxims, for choosing one course of action rather than another.

It is true, none the less, that the Austro-Marxists, like other scientific Marxists, devoted little of their intellectual effort to the problems of ethics and social philosophy; and it has been a major contribution of the humanist Marxists, exemplified in several of the following texts, to revive the discussion of ethical questions, of the Marxist conception of human nature, and of the theory of needs. In his eleventh thesis on Feuerbach Marx set 'changing the world' above 'interpreting' it; in his life work, I would say, he gave equal importance to 'explanation' and 'action', to theory and practice, or in other terms, to theoretical and practical reason. Recent Marxist thought has been developing, and needs to develop further, in both these spheres, taking up the kind of problems – some scientific, some ethical – outlined by Marković in the passage cited earlier.[49]

But let us not be deceived either about the extent of the revisions that may be needed in the Marxist theory of society, or about the difficulty of elaborating a Marxist theory of practice. I do not agree entirely with Kolakowski's argument that '. . . the concept of Marxism as a separate school of

[49] See p. 10 above.

thought will in time become blurred and ultimately disappear altogether. . . . What is permanent in Marx's work will be assimilated in the natural course of scientific development';[50] for it may also happen that Marxism, in a revised but still distinctive form, will provide the main elements of this scientific development, and become the most widely accepted and acceptable paradigm among the competing paradigms in theoretical sociology. But even if there were such an outcome, as I think is certainly possible, the kind of Marxist theory which eventually attained such a pre-eminent position would have been considerably affected by other methodological and theoretical orientations in the social sciences, as it has already been influenced, most recently by structuralism; some important specific propositions in the theory – for example, those concerning the basic classes of capitalist society and their political role, or the relations of dependence or reciprocity between the economy and the political system – would have been replaced or at the least profoundly modified, as the content of recent critical debates within Marxism clearly indicates; and the scope of the theory would have been extended to provide, in particular, a more adequate analysis of the social structure and the historical significance of the various forms of 'post-capitalist' society which now exist in the world.

On the other hand, the difficulties to be faced in advancing Marxist social science still appear to me far less formidable than those involved in working out an adequate Marxist theory of practical action, that is to say, an ethical and political doctrine. Marxism does not have anything like the same pre-eminence, or offer the same prospects, in the analysis of ethical and social philosophical questions as in the scientific study of social life. This is due above all, as I suggested earlier, to the fact that there is only a very limited basis in Marx's own work for the development of such an analysis; for not only did he devote little sustained attention to these questions, but he showed far less originality in this field than in his scientific investigations, remaining content for the most part to adopt – and then express in his own way – the radical humanism and

[50] Leszek Kolakowski, *Marxism and Beyond*, p. 204.

naturalism of the Enlightenment philosophers, the Saint-Simonians, and Feuerbach.

I have considerable doubts, therefore, about the possibility of developing a specifically Marxist, rather than broadly socialist ethics, or a Marxist, as distinct from a socialist, humanism, except in the rather limited sense that the ethical theory or humanist outlook would necessarily be influenced by the findings of Marxist social science. For contrary to a widely held view I do not consider that science cannot tell us anything at all about how we should live. In so far as science discloses the reality of the physical world, of human nature, and of human societies, it does undoubtedly offer *some* guidance in the conduct of practical life, at the very least perhaps in telling us how we should *not* live. But it is also evident that science cannot finally decide questions of conduct and morality, and we are obliged therefore to ask what kind of thought or knowledge can provide answers to such questions, and can do so with anything like the precision or reliability of science. As Ulrich, the 'man without qualities', reflected: '. . . science has developed a conception of hard, sober intellectual strength that makes mankind's old metaphysical and moral notions simply unendurable.'[51] Whether such intellectual strength is likely to emerge in the field of ethics and social philosophy may be a matter of doubt. What is certain is that these questions constitute a major intellectual problem for Marxist thinkers, but also that we still await the appearance of a great Marxist moral philosopher.

A NOTE ON THE SELECTIONS

As in the previous volume I have selected here only texts which discuss directly Marx's own work. I have not, therefore, included anything from the very large body of writing which is intended to develop independently a particular version of Marxism; that would provide the material for an interesting volume of quite a different kind.

I have also taken a broad view of what is to be regarded as a

[51] Robert Musil, *The Man Without Qualities*, vol. I, p. 48.

'modern interpretation' of Marx. Thus I have included a text from Gramsci's *Prison Notebooks*, written between 1929 and 1935: first, because his writings did not become widely known and influential until the 1950s; and second, because this text discusses a question of great current interest concerning the relation between Marx's thought and sociology. Similarly, I have included a text (here translated into English for the first time) from Hilferding's *Das historische Problem*, written in the few years preceding his death in 1941, because it examines critically Marx's conception of the state in relation to the economy, and this too is a matter of considerable controversy at the present time.

In general, I have chosen those texts which seem to me to examine in a particularly enlightening way crucial aspects of Marx's thought, from the perspective of present-day controversies and intellectual movements, whether the authors are principally concerned to extend Marx's work in certain areas, or to revise it (and reject parts of it) in the light of subsequent historical changes in social life and reorientations of social thought.

I

Marx's Concept of Man

GAJO PETROVIĆ

People often doubt the legitimacy of the question 'What is man?' in its general form. This question, they say, is sometimes posed by certain philosophies, but it is a false question, and it cannot be asked by Marxism. Different special sciences explore different aspects of man's activity; no aspect remains unexplored; and all 'special' sciences together give a complete picture of man. On the other hand, man in general, man as such, does not exist; there is only a concrete man of a concrete society; slave owner or slave, landlord or serf, bourgeois or worker.

Man is not, however, the sum of his parts or aspects, but an integral being; and no special science does or can answer the question of what he is as an integral being, that is, what makes him man and each of his activities or aspects human. Although man is not always and everywhere the same, although he historically changes, there is something that allows us to call a proletarian as well as a capitalist, a landlord as well as a slaveowner, a man.

What makes a man – man? What, if anything, makes somebody more and somebody less a man?

If Marx had bypassed these questions, they would still demand an answer. But nothing is more false than the assumption that Marx condemned discussions about man in general.

It is unnecessary to quote texts from *Economic and Philosophical Manuscripts* because it is well known that Marx speaks there about man as man. But it is sometimes held that Marx later came to the conclusion that all general speculations about man are inadmissible. In support of this assumption some passages from *German Ideology* can be quoted. But is *German Ideology* Marx's last word in philosophy? Did not he also write *Capital*?

According to *Capital*, the labour process is

> human action with a view to the production of use-values, appropriation of natural substances to human requirements; it is the necessary condition for effecting exchange of matter between man and Nature; it is the everlasting nature-imposed condition of human existence, and therefore is independent of every social phase of that existence, or rather, is common to every such phase. It was, therefore, not necessary to represent our labourer in connection with other labourers; man and his labour on one side, Nature and its materials on the other, sufficed. As the taste of porridge does not tell you who grew the oats, no more does this simple process tell you of itself what are the social conditions under which it is taking place, whether under the slave-owner's brutal lash, or the anxious eye of the capitalist, whether Cincinnatus carries it on in tilling his modest farm or a savage in killing wild animals with stones.[1]

Marx in *Capital*, then, stresses that we can speak not only about labourer, capitalist and slave-owner, but also about man, labour and nature in general.

In another place in *Capital* Marx writes against the Utilitarian Bentham:

> To know what is useful for a dog, one must study dog nature. This nature is not to be deduced from the principle of utility. Applying this to man, he who would criticize all human acts, movements, relations, etc., by the principle of utility, must first deal with human nature in general, and then with human nature as modified in each historical epoch. Bentham makes short work of it. With the driest naïveté he takes the modern shopkeeper, especially the English shopkeeper, as the normal man. Whatever is useful to this queer normal man, and to his world, is absolutely useful. This yardstick, then, he applies to past, present and future.[2]

[1] Marx, *Capital*, vol. I, pp. 204–5.
[2] Marx, *Capital*, vol. I, p. 668.

Marx thinks that a dog has its dog nature and man his human nature, but that man differs from a dog by having a 'human nature in general' as well as one 'modified in each historical epoch'. He reproaches Bentham for regarding the modern shopkeeper as a normal man, ignoring in this way general human nature and its historical development.

Marx not only 'permits' discussion of human nature in general, in *Capital* he criticizes bourgeois society precisely because in it universal human nature cannot express itself, because in it 'a general or a banker plays a great part, but mere man [man as man], on the other hand, a very shabby part.[3]

In accordance with this, Marx in the third volume of *Capital* opposes to capitalism a society in which the socialized man, the associated producers, will produce under conditions 'most adequate to their human nature and most worthy of it'.[4]

Marx thus without any hesitation speaks about human nature and about man as man. [. . .] Just as the sense of Marx's question about man has been misunderstood, so has his answer to this question.

Expounding different conceptions of man, Max Scheler mentions as one of the five basic conceptions the positivistic, according to which man is an instinctive being, and as one of three sub-classes of positivistic conception the 'Marxist' or 'economic' conception, according to which man is determined by his impulse for food. He obviously does not know that, according to Marx, animals 'produce only under the compulsion of direct physical need, while man produces when he is free from physical need and only truly produces in freedom from such need.'[5]

A view similar to Scheler's is also found in some 'Marxists' who attribute to Marx Benjamin Franklin's definition of man as a tool-making animal. It is true that Marx quotes Franklin's definition with a certain sympathy in the first volume of *Capital*. But those who have noticed this often overlook the fact that in the same volume Marx characterizes this definition not as his, but as typically American. Of Aristotle's definition of

[3] Ibid., p. 51.
[4] Ibid., vol. III, p. 954.
[5] Fromm, *Marx's Concept of Man*, p. 102.

man as a political animal he comments: 'Strictly, Aristotle's definition is that man is by nature a town-citizen. This is quite as characteristic of ancient classical society as Franklin's definition of man as a tool-making animal is characteristic of Yankeedom.'[6]

Marx believes that Aristotle's and Franklin's definitions of man are important – like Hegel, he thinks that no fundamental philosophical thought can be either simply false or worthless – but neither Aristotle's nor Franklin's definition is his.

When he rejects the traditional conception of man as a rational animal Marx does not do so simply because this gives reason the primary place, but first of all because he considers that neither reason nor political activity, neither production of tools nor any other special activity or property can be man's essence. Man is not a mechanical sum of his 'spheres' (economic, political, moral, artistic, etc.), and even in so far as it is possible to distinguish such 'spheres' they do not maintain for eternity the same relationships. Therefore, what makes a man man is not his 'main sphere', but his whole way of Being, the general structure of his relationship toward the world and toward himself. This way of Being, which is peculiar to man, Marx designates by the word 'praxis'. Man for Marx, is, the being of 'praxis'.

When we define man as praxis all questions are not answered; many only begin. First of all, what is praxis? Praxis is human activity. But a certain kind of activity is also peculiar to all animals. What is it that distinguishes praxis as human activity from animal activity? In answering this question people often lose what they gained in defining man as a being of praxis. Difficulties in answering the question are seen in Marx also.

About the activity of man and animal we read in Marx's *Economical and Philosophical Manuscripts* of 1844:

> The animal is one with its life activity. It does not distinguish the activity from itself. It is *its activity*. But man makes his life activity itself an object of his will and consciousness. He has a conscious life activity. It is not a determination with which he is

[6] Marx, *Capital*, vol. I, p. 358.

> completely identified. Conscious life activity distinguishes man from the life activity of animals.[7]

One can agree that man's life activity is conscious, whereas animals' is not. But can one agree that it is first of all consciousness (or perhaps even only consciousness) that distinguishes man's activity (praxis) from animal activity? If man differs from animal by praxis, and if praxis differs from animal activity by being conscious, then man differs from animal by his consciousness and we are back to the traditional definition of man as a rational animal.

Is this unavoidable, or is it possible to give an interpretation of praxis that would determine its general structure and also contain its determination as a conscious and free activity?

I think that such is the interpretation of praxis as a universal-creative self-creative activity, activity by which man transforms and creates his world and himself. Exactly such an interpretation prevails in Karl Marx.

In *Economic and Philosophical Manuscripts* he writes, for example:

> Animals construct only in accordance with the standards and needs of the species to which they belong, while man knows how to produce in accordance with the standards of every species and knows how to apply the appropriate standard to the object. Thus man constructs also in accordance with the laws of beauty.

It is precisely in his work upon the objective world that man proves himself as a *species-being*. This production is his active species life. By means of it nature appears as *his* work and *his* reality.

> The object of labour is, therefore the *objectification of man's species life*; he no longer reproduces himself merely intellectually, as in consciousness, but actively and in a real sense, and he sees his own reflection in a world that he has constructed.[8]

[7] Fromm, *Marx's Concept of Man*, p. 101.
[8] Ibid., p. 102.

The interpretation of praxis as a universal-creative self-creative activity contains its determination as a free, conscious activity. From this conception, the conception of man as a social history also follows. If man is a creative self-creative being that constantly creates and changes himself and his world, he is necessarily not always the same.

Animal species are also not always the same. But whereas an animal changes by adapting to and transforming its environment without any plan or purpose, man can by his creativity change purposefully his world and himself. 'In short,' says Engels, 'the animal merely *uses* external nature and brings about changes in it simply by his presence; man by his changes makes it serve his ends, masters it.'[9]

Therefore only man has a history. One can speak only figuratively of a 'history' of the animal kingdom. But man's history is not only the history of the transformation of nature; it is also and in the first place the history of man's self-creation: 'Since, however, for socialist man, *the whole of what is called world history* is nothing but the creation of man by human labour, and the emergence of nature for man, he therefore has the evident and irrefutable proof of his *self-creation*, of his own *origins*.'[10]

Just because man is praxis and history, he is also the future. If man's essence is universal-creative and self-creative activity by which he historically creates his world and himself, then, if he does not want to cease being man, he can never interrupt the process of his self-creation. This means that man can never be completely finished, that he is not man when he lives only in the present and in the contemplation of the past, but only in so far as he in the present realizes his future. Man is man if he realizes his historically created human possibilities.

At this point one can see clearly the difference between Marx and Hegel. For Hegel, man is also an active being, but he conceives man's activity primarily as an activity of self-consciousness, the final goal of which is the absolute knowledge of the absolute reality, a definitive completion of man and absolute. Absolute, which without man is only *an sich*, becomes

[9] F. Engels, *Dialectics of Nature*, Foreign Publishing House (Moscow, 1954) p. 241.

[10] Fromm, *Marx's Concept of Man*, p. 139.

through man *für sich*. Man's philosophical knowledge, which is at the same time the self-knowledge of the Absolute, means the end of human history. Man can be completed, and in Hegel's philosophy he is completed. For that reason he can also be fully described.

For Marx, man is an active being, but his activity is not the self-knowledge of the Absolute, but the transformation and creation of the world and of man himself. Therefore for Marx man can be never completed and never finally defined.

For that reason Marx's conception of man can never remain only a conception. Only to conceive man would mean only to conceive what man already was. But man is not only what he has been; he is in the first place what he can and ought to be. Marx's turn to praxis follows from this in the sense that his conception of man cannot remain a mere conception, but is also a criticism of alienated man who does not realize his human possibilities and a humanistic programme of struggle for humanness. Marx's conception of man can thus not be separated from his humanistic theory of alienation and de-alienation.

2

Sociology and the Philosophy of Praxis

ANTONIO GRAMSCI

HISTORICAL MATERIALISM AND SOCIOLOGY

One preliminary observation to be made is this: that the title does not correspond to the content of the book.[1] 'Theory of the philosophy of praxis' ought to mean a logical and coherent systematic treatment of the philosophical concepts generically known under the title of historical materialism (many of which are spurious and come from other sources and as such require to be criticized and eliminated). The first chapters should treat the following questions: What is philosophy? In what sense can a conception of the world be called a philosophy? How has philosophy been conceived hitherto? Does the philosophy of praxis renew this conception? What is meant by a 'speculative' philosophy? Would the philosophy of praxis ever be able to have a speculative form? What are the relationships between ideologies, conceptions of the world and philosophies? What is or should be the relationship between theory and practice? How do traditional philosophies conceive of this relationship?

Excerpt from Antonio Gramsci, *Selections from the Prison Notebooks*. Edited and translated by Quintin Hoare and Geoffrey Nowell Smith (London: Lawrence & Wishart Ltd., 1971) pp. 425–36. Reprinted by permission of Lawrence & Wishart Ltd.

[1] The title [of a book by Nikolai Bukharin] is *Theory of Historical Materialism*, and the sub-title *A Popular Manual of Marxist Sociology*. Gramsci goes on to argue below that only the sub-title is in any way an exact description of the content of Bukharin's work, and even then only 'on condition that one gives an extremely restricted meaning to the term "sociology"'. It should be noted that Gramsci himself vacillates slightly in his notion of what sociology is. His main targets would appear to be empiricism and positivism applied to the science of society, and the reflection of these doctrines, in the guise of 'materialism', in Bukharin's *Manual*. [Tr.] Bukharin's book was published in English under the title *Historical Materialism: A System of Sociology*. [Ed.]

etc. The answer to these and other questions constitutes the 'theory' of the philosophy of praxis.[2]

In the *Popular Manual* there is not even a coherent justification offered of the premise implicit in the exposition and explicitly referred to elsewhere, quite casually, that the *true* philosophy is philosophical materialism and that the philosophy of praxis is purely a 'sociology'. What does this assertion really mean? If it were true, then the theory of the philosophy of praxis would be philosophical materialism. But in that case what does it mean to say that the philosophy of praxis is a sociology? What sort of thing would this sociology be? A science of politics and historiography? Or a systematic collection, classified in a particular ordered form, of purely empirical observations on the art of politics and of external canons of historical research? Answers to these questions are not to be found in the book. But only they could be a theory. Thus the connection between the general title *Theory of Historical Materialism* and the sub-title *Popular Manual of Marxist Sociology* is unjustified. The sub-title would be a more exact title, on condition that one gave an extremely restricted meaning to the term 'sociology'. In fact the question arises of what is 'sociology'. Is not sociology an attempt to produce a so-called exact (i.e. positivist) science of social facts, that is of politics and history – in other words a philosophy in embryo? Has not sociology tried to do something similar to the philosophy of praxis?[3] One must however be clear about this: the philosophy of praxis was born in the form of aphorisms and practical criteria for the purely accidental reason that its founder dedicated his intellectual forces to other problems, particularly economic (which he treated in systematic form); but in these practical criteria and these aphorisms is implicit an entire conception of the world, a philosophy.

Sociology has been an attempt to create a method of

[2] These questions are effectively those to which Gramsci himself attempts to give an answer in his own philosophical writings. [Tr.]

[3] What Gramsci has in mind at this point is less the empiricism which is his most usual target than the attempts, notably by Max Weber but also by Pareto and Michels, to construct a general and comprehensive theory of man and society, under the general title (first coined by Auguste Comte) of 'sociology'. [Tr.]

historical and political science in a form dependent on a pre-elaborated philosophical system, that of evolutionist positivism, against which sociology reacted, but only partially. It therefore became a tendency on its own; it became the philosophy of non-philosophers, an attempt to provide a schematic description and classification of historical and political facts, according to criteria built up on the model of natural science. It is therefore an attempt to derive 'experimentally' the laws of evolution of human society in such a way as to 'predict' that the oak tree will develop out of the acorn. Vulgar evolutionism is at the root of sociology, and sociology cannot know the dialectical principle with its passage from quantity to quality. But this passage disturbs any form of evolution and any law of uniformity understood in a vulgar evolutionist sense. In any case, any sociology presupposes a philosophy, a conception of the world, of which it is but a subordinate part. Nor should the particular internal 'logic' of the varying forms of sociology, which is what gives them a mechanical coherence, be confused with general theory, that is to say philosophy. Naturally this does not mean that the search for 'laws' of uniformity is not a useful and interesting pursuit or that a treatise of immediate observations on the art of politics does not have its purpose. But one should call a spade a spade, and present treatises of this kind for what they really are.

All these are 'theoretical' problems, while those that the author of the *Manual* considers as such are not. The questions which he poses are all of an immediate political and ideological order (understanding ideology as an intermediate phase between philosophy and day-to-day practice); they are reflections on disconnected and casual individual historical and political facts. One theoretical question arises for the author right at the beginning, when he refers to a tendency which denies that it is possible to construct a sociology of the philosophy of praxis and which maintains that this philosophy can be expressed only through concrete historical works. This objection, which is extremely important, is not resolved by the author except on the level of phrasemongering. Certainly the philosophy of praxis is realized through the concrete study of past history and through present activity to construct new history. But a theory of history and politics can be made, for even if the facts are always unique and changeable in the flux of movement of history, the concepts can be theorized. Otherwise one would not even be able to tell what movement is, or the dialectic, and one would fall back into a new form of nominalism.[4]

The reduction of the philosophy of praxis to a form of sociology has represented the crystallization of the degenerate tendency, already criticized by Engels (in the letters to two students published in the *Sozial. Akademiker*),[5] and which consists in reducing a conception of the world to a mechanical formula which gives the impression of holding the whole of history in the palm of its hand. This has provided the strongest incentive to the 'pocket-geniuses', with their facile journalistic improvisations. The experience on which the philosophy of praxis is based cannot be schematized; it is history in all its infinite variety and multiplicity, whose study can give rise to 'philology'[6] as a method of scholarship for ascertaining particular facts and to philosophy understood as a general methodology of history. This perhaps is what was meant by those writers who, as is mentioned in rather summary fashion in the first chapter of the *Manual*, deny that one can make a sociology of the philosophy of praxis and maintain rather that this philosophy lives only in particular historical essays (this

[4] It is because he has not posed with any exactitude the question of what 'theory' is that the author has been prevented from posing the further question of what is religion and from offering a realistic historical judgement of past philosophies, all of which he presents as pure delirium and folly.

[5] F. Engels. Letters to Josef Bloch and to Heinz Starkenburg, 21 September 1890 and 25 January 1894, published in *Der Sozialistischer Akademiker*, 1 and 15 October 1895. In the letter to Bloch, Engels writes: 'According to the materialist conception of history the determining moment in history is *ultimately* the production and reproduction of real life. More than this neither Marx nor I have ever asserted. If therefore somebody twists this into the statement that the economic moment is the only determining one, he transforms it into a meaningless, abstract and absurd phrase.' Both letters are in fact intended as correctives to the pseudo-Marxist reductionism which Gramsci is also concerned to attack. [Tr.]

[6] 'Philology': Gramsci uses the word here partly in its conventional sense of the study of linguistic and historical documents (i.e. the primary sources of historiography and literary history) but partly in the sense resuscitated by Croce from the writings of Vico, which divides knowledge into philosophy as the science of the True and philology as the pursuit of the Certain. [Tr.]

assertion, in such a bald and crude form, is certainly erroneous and seems like a new and curious form of nominalism and philosophical scepticism).

To deny that one can construct a sociology, understood in the sense of a science of society, that is a science of history and politics, which is not coterminous with the philosophy of praxis itself, does not mean that one cannot build up an empirical compilation of practical observations which extend the sphere of philology as traditionally understood. If philology is the methodological expression of the importance of ascertaining and precising particular facts in their unique and unrepeatable individuality, one cannot however exclude the practical utility of isolating certain more general 'laws of tendency' corresponding in the political field to the laws of statistics or to the law of large numbers which have helped to advance various of the natural sciences. But the fact has not been properly emphasized that statistical laws can be employed in the science and art of politics only so long as the great masses of the population remain (or at least are reputed to remain) essentially passive, in relation to the questions which interest historians and politicians. Furthermore the extension of statistics to the science and art of politics can have very serious consequences to the extent that it is adopted for working out future perspectives and programmes of action. In the natural sciences the worst that statistics can do is produce blunders and irrelevances which can easily be corrected by further research and which in any case simply make the individual scientist who used the technique look a bit ridiculous. But in the science and art of politics it can have literally catastrophic results which do irreparable harm. Indeed in politics the assumption of the law of statistics as an essential law operating of necessity is not only a scientific error, but becomes a practical error in action. What is more it favours mental laziness and a superficiality in political programmes. It should be observed that political action tends precisely to rouse the masses from passivity, in other words to destroy the law of large numbers. So how can that law be considered a law of sociology? If one thinks about it even the demand for a planned, i.e. guided, economy is destined to break down the statistical law understood in a mechanical sense, that is statistics produced by the fortuitous putting together of an infinity of arbitrary individual acts. Planning of this kind must be based on statistics, but that is not the same thing. Human awareness replaces naturalistic 'spontaneity'. A further element which, in the art of politics, leads to the overthrow of the old naturalistic schema is the replacement by political organisms (parties) of single individuals and individual (or charismatic,[7] as Michels calls them) leaders. With the extension of mass parties and their organic coalescence with the intimate (economic-productive) life of the masses themselves, the process whereby popular feeling is standardized ceases to be mechanical and casual (that is produced by the conditioning of environmental factors and the like) and becomes conscious and critical. Knowledge and a judgement of the importance of this feeling on the part of the leaders is no longer the product of hunches backed up by the identification of statistical laws, which leaders then translate into ideas and words-as-force. (This is the rational and intellectual way and is all too often fallacious.) Rather it is acquired by the collective organism through 'active and conscious co-participation', through 'compassionality', through experience of immediate particulars, through a system which one could call 'living philology'. In this way a close link is formed between great mass, party and leading group; and the whole complex, thus articulated, can move together as 'collective man'.

Hendrik de Man's book,[8] if it has any value, has it precisely in this sense, in that he invites us to 'inform' ourselves in more detail about the real feelings of groups and individuals and not those that are assumed on the basis of sociological laws. But de Man has made no original discoveries, nor has he found any original principle which goes beyond the philosophy of praxis or scientifically proves it to be sterile or mistaken. He has elevated to the status of a scientific principle an empirical criterion of the art of politics which was already well known

[7] The notion of 'charisma' as a quality which causes leaders to be followed in spite of their lack of legitimate or institutional authority derives in fact not from Michels but from Max Weber, who in turn took it from the jurist and church historian Rudolf Sohm. [Tr.]

[8] *Au delà du Marxisme*. 1929. [Tr.]

and had been applied, although it had perhaps been insufficiently defined and developed. But de Man has not even been able to establish the exact limits of his criterion, for he has finished up by just producing a new statistical law and, unconsciously and under another name, a new method of social mathematics and of external classification, a new abstract sociology.

Note. The so-called laws of sociology which are assumed as laws of causation (such-and-such a fact occurs because of such-and-such a law, etc.) have no causal value: they are almost always tautologies and paralogisms. Usually they are no more than a duplicate of the observed fact itself. A fact or a series of facts is described according to a mechanical process of abstract generalization, a relationship of similarity is derived from this and given the title of law and the law is then assumed to have causal value. But what novelty is there in that? The only novelty is the collective name given to a series of petty facts, but names are not an innovation. (In Michels' treatises[9] one can find a whole catalogue of similar tautological generalizations, the last and most famous being that about the 'charismatic leader'.) What is not realized is that in this way one falls into a baroque form of Platonic idealism, since these abstract laws have a strange resemblance to Plato's pure ideas which are the essence of real earthly facts.

THE CONSTITUENT PARTS OF THE PHILOSOPHY OF PRAXIS

A systematic treatment of the philosophy of praxis cannot afford to neglect any of the constituent parts of the doctrines of

[9] See in particular 'Political Parties' (*Zur Soziologie des Parteiwesens*, 1911. English translation, from the Italian, 1915). Robert Michels (1876–1936) was a German sociologist of (originally) Social-Democratic leanings who emigrated first to Switzerland and then to Italy, where he became a naturalized citizen under the Mussolini regime. Michels is most famous for his 'iron law of oligarchy' and together with Mosca and Pareto is an originator of the theory of political *elites*. Despite Gramsci's evident contempt for Michels' method and distaste for his politics, it has been argued that there was a certain indirect influence of Michels and elite theory on his own theory of social and political structures in non-revolutionary periods. (See G. Galli, 'Gramsci e le teorie delle elites', in *Gramsci e la cultura contemporanea*, vol. II, pp. 201–17.) [Tr.]

its founder [Marx]. But how should this be understood? It should deal with all the general philosophical part, and then should develop in a coherent fashion all the general concepts of a methodology of history and politics and, in addition, of art, economics and ethics, finding place in the overall construction for a theory of the natural sciences. One widespread conception is that the philosophy of praxis is a pure philosophy, the science of dialectics, the other parts of it being economics and politics, and it is therefore maintained that the doctrine is formed of three constituent parts, which are at the same time the consummation and the transcending of the highest level reached around 1848 by science in the most advanced countries of Europe: classical German philosophy, English classical economics and French political activity and science. This conception, which reflects rather a generic search for historical sources than a classification drawn from the heart of the doctrine itself, cannot be set up in opposition, as a definitive scheme, to some other definition of the doctrine which is closer to reality. It will be asked whether the philosophy of praxis is not precisely and specifically a theory of history, and the answer must be that this is indeed true but that one cannot separate politics and economics from history, even the specialized aspects of political science and art and of economic science and policy. This means that, after having accomplished the principal task in the general philosophical part, which deals with the philosophy of praxis proper – the science of dialectics or the theory of knowledge, within which the general concepts of history, politics and economics are interwoven in an organic unity – it would be useful, in a popular manual, to give a general outline of each moment or constituent part, even to the extent of treating them as independent and distinct sciences. On close examination it is clear that in the *Popular Manual* all these points are at least referred to, but casually and incoherently, in a quite chaotic and indistinct way, because there is no clear and precise concept of what the philosophy of praxis itself actually is.

STRUCTURE AND HISTORICAL MOVEMENT

This fundamental point is not dealt with: how does the

historical movement arise on the structural base? The problem is however referred to in Plekhanov's *Fundamentals*[10] and could be developed. This is furthermore the crux of all the questions that have arisen around the philosophy of praxis and without resolving this one cannot resolve the corresponding problem about the relationship between society and 'nature', to which the *Manual* devotes a special chapter. It would have been necessary to analyse the full import and consequences of the two propositions in the Preface to *A Contribution to the Critique of Political Economy* to the following effect:

> 1. Mankind only poses for itself such tasks as it can resolve; . . . the task itself only arises when the material conditions for its resolution already exist or at least are in the process of formation.
> 2. A social order does not perish until all the productive forces for which it still has room have been developed and new and higher relations of production have taken their place, and until the material conditions of the new relations have grown up within the womb of the old society. Only on this basis can all mechanism and every trace of the superstitiously 'miraculous' be eliminated, and it is on this basis that the problem of the formation of active political groups, and, in the last analysis, even the problem of the historical function of great personalities must be posed.

THE INTELLECTUALS

It would be worth compiling a 'reasoned' catalogue of the men of learning whose opinions are widely quoted or contested in the book, each name to be accompanied by notes on their significance and scientific importance (this to be done also for the supporters of the philosophy of praxis who are certainly not quoted in the light of their originality and significance). In fact there are only the most passing references to the great intellectuals. The question is raised: would it not have been better to have referred only to the major intellectuals on the enemy side, leaving aside the men in the second rank, the regurgitators of second-hand phrases? One gets the impression

[10] G. Plekhanov, *Fundamental Problems of Marxism*, 1908. [Tr.]

that the author wants to combat only the weakest of his adversaries and the weakest of their positions (or the ones which the weakest adversaries have maintained least adequately), in order to obtain facile verbal victories – for one can hardly speak of real victories. The illusion is created that there exists some kind of more than formal and metaphorical resemblance between an ideological and a politico-military front. In the political and military struggle it can be correct tactics to break through at the points of least resistance in order to be able to assault the strongest point with maximum forces that have been precisely made available by the elimination of the weaker auxiliaries. Political and military victories, within certain limits, have a permanent and universal value and the strategic end can be attained decisively with a general effect for everyone. On the ideological front, however, the defeat of the auxiliaries and the minor hangers-on is of all but negligible importance. Here it is necessary to engage battle with the most eminent of one's adversaries. Otherwise one confuses newspapers with books, and petty daily polemic with scientific work. The lesser figures must be abandoned to the infinite casebook of newspaper polemic.

A new science proves its efficacy and vitality when it demonstrates that it is capable of confronting the great champions of the tendencies opposed to it and when it either resolves by its own means the vital questions which they have posed or demonstrates, in peremptory fashion, that these questions are false problems.

It is true that an historical epoch and a given society are characterized rather by the average run of intellectuals, and therefore by the more mediocre. But widespread, mass ideology must be distinguished from the scientific works and the great philosophical syntheses which are its real cornerstones. It is the latter which must be overcome, either negatively, by demonstrating that they are without foundation, or positively, by opposing to them philosophical syntheses of greater importance and significance. Reading the *Manual* one has the impression of someone who cannot sleep for the moonlight and who struggles to massacre the fireflies in the belief that by so doing he will make the brightness lessen or disappear.

SCIENCE AND SYSTEM

Is it possible to write an elementary book, a handbook, a 'popular manual', on a doctrine that is still at the stage of discussion, polemic and elaboration? A popular manual cannot be conceived other than as a formally dogmatic, stylistically poised and scientifically balanced exposition of a particular subject. It can only be an introduction to scientific study, and not an exposition of original scientific researches, since it is written for young people or for a public which, from the point of view of scientific discipline, is in a condition like that of youth and therefore has an immediate need for 'certainties', for opinions which, at least on a formal level, appear as reliably true and indisputable. If the doctrine in question has not yet reached this 'classical' phase of its development, any attempt to 'manualize' it is bound to fail, its logical ordering will be purely apparent and illusory, and one will get, as with the *Popular Manual*, just a mechanical juxtaposition of disparate elements which remain inexorably disconnected and disjointed in spite of the unitary varnish provided by the literary presentation. Why not therefore pose the question in its correct theoretical and historical terms and rest content with a book in which each of the essential problems of the doctrine receives separate monographic treatment? This would be more serious and more 'scientific'. But the vulgar contention is that science must absolutely mean 'system', and consequently systems of all sorts are built up which have only the mechanical exteriority of a system and not its necessary inherent coherence.

THE DIALECTIC

The *Manual* contains no treatment of any kind of the dialectic. The dialectic is presupposed, in a very superficial manner, but is not expounded, and this is absurd in a manual which ought to contain the essential elements of the doctrine under discussion and whose bibliographical references should be aimed at stimulating study in order to widen and deepen understanding of the subject and not at replacing the manual itself. The absence of any treatment of the dialectic could have two origins. The first of these would be the fact that philosophy of praxis is envisaged as split into two elements: on the one hand a theory of history and politics conceived as sociology – i.e. one that can be constructed according to the methods of natural science (experimental in the crudest positivist sense); and on the other hand a philosophy proper, this being philosophical alias metaphysical or mechanical (vulgar) materialism.

Even after the great debate which has taken place against mechanicism, the author of the *Manual* does not appear to have changed very much his way of posing the philosophical problem. It would appear from the contribution presented at the London Congress on the History of Science that he continues to maintain that the philosophy of praxis has always been split into two: a doctrine of history and politics, and a philosophy, although he now calls the latter dialectical materialism. But if the question is framed in this way, one can no longer understand the importance and significance of the dialectic, which is relegated, from its position as a doctrine of knowledge and the very marrow of historiography and the science of politics, to the level of a sub-species of formal logic and elementary scholastics. The true fundamental function and significance of the dialectic can only be grasped if the philosophy of praxis is conceived as an integral and original philosophy which opens up a new phase of history and a new phase in the development of world thought. It does this to the extent that it goes beyond both traditional idealism and traditional materialism, philosophies which are expressions of past societies, while retaining their vital elements. If the philosophy of praxis is not considered except in subordination to another philosophy, then it is not possible to grasp the new dialectic, through which the transcending of old philosophies is effected and expressed.

The second origin would appear to be psychological. It is felt that the dialectic is something arduous and difficult, in so far as thinking dialectically goes against vulgar common sense, which is dogmatic and eager for peremptory certainties and has as its expression formal logic. To understand this better one can think of what would happen if in primary and secondary schools natural and physical sciences were taught on the basis of Einsteinian relativity and the traditional notion of a 'law of nature' was accompanied by that of a statistical law or of the law of large numbers. The children would not understand anything at all and the clash between school teaching and family and popular life would be such that the school would become an object of ridicule and caricature.

This motivation seems to me to act as a psychological brake on the author of the *Manual*; he really does capitulate before common sense and vulgar thought, since he has not put the problem in exact theoretical terms and is therefore in practice disarmed and impotent. The uneducated and crude environment has dominated the educator and vulgar common sense has imposed itself on science rather than the other way round. If the environment is the educator, it too must in turn be educated,[11] but the *Manual* does not understand this revolutionary dialectic. The source of all the errors of the *Manual*, and of its author (who does not seem to have changed his position, even after the great debate which apparently, or so it would appear from the text presented at the London Congress, resulted in his repudiating the book), consists precisely in this pretension to divide the philosophy of praxis into two parts: a 'sociology' and a systematic philosophy. Separated from the theory of history and politics philosophy cannot be other than metaphysics, whereas the great conquest in the history of modern thought, represented by the philosophy of praxis, is precisely the concrete historicization of philosophy and its identification with history.

[11] Cf. the third of Marx's *Theses on Feuerbach*. [Tr.]

3
Philosophy and Sociology in Marx's Early Writings

LUCIEN GOLDMANN

Although it is obvious that Marx's thought is centred upon the idea of the unity of theory and practice there have not been wanting thinkers, ever since the time of Vorländer, Max Adler and Werner Sombart . . . who have insisted upon Marx's 'sociologism'; that is, upon the existence in his work of a positivist sociology, complemented by an ethical or political theory, which is no doubt based upon this sociology but nevertheless remains relatively autonomous.

Equally, there are to be found at the other extreme important thinkers such as the young Lukács, or Karl Korsch in his early writings, who affirm the strictly philosophical character of Marx's thought and his refusal to separate, even in a relative fashion, thought and practice.

Given this situation the most appropriate solution might appear to be an attempt to show that Marx actually adopted the third standpoint,[1] which does in fact seem to me to correspond both with his own thought and with the real situation of research in the social sciences. But this would also

Excerpt from Lucien Goldmann, *Marxisme et sciences humaines* (Paris: Éditions Gallimard, 1970) pp. 133–50. Translated by Tom Bottomore. Published by permission of Éditions Gallimard.

[1] Goldmann begins his essay by outlining three possible conceptions of the relation between philosophy and sociology, the third of which is 'the standpoint according to which it is indeed impossible to separate factual judgements from value judgements, positive investigations from a world view, science from philosophy, theory from practice . . .', but which also recognizes that the two poles of investigation and action do not stand in a constant and immutable relation to each other, and that scientific inquiry may require, depending upon the context, either a more objective or a more committed approach. [Ed.]

involve an undue simplification, for Marx's thought was not born in an instant like Minerva from the head of Jupiter, but was formed gradually, in a process which we can find expressed in his early writings. It would be valuable one day to undertake a thorough study of the way in which the problem that concerns us here was posed successively in Marx's writings between 1842 and 1845, or even 1847, before he had achieved a comprehensive formulation of his basic standpoint; a standpoint, moreover, which itself displays a number of variations in its application to specific research problems. In short, a genetic study of the problem of the relations between philosophy and sociology in Marx's early writings is an important task for future Marxological studies. Needless to say, I do not pretend to treat the subject exhaustively in the present essay, and at most I would like to propound some reflections . . . which may indicate a number of major issues and thus contribute to further research. . . .

Here, however, it is essential to make an additional comment. Even if the philosophical standpoint which explicitly asserts the impossibility of making a radical separation between factual judgements and value judgements is *not* philosophy in general but a specific philosophy which we call dialectical, it is still the case that if this dialectic conforms, as I believe, with reality, then all philosophical systems, including those which explicitly affirm the possibility, and even the necessity, of separating the theoretical from the normative, assertions in the indicative mood from hypothetical or categorical imperatives, contain within themselves a body of closely and intimately related factual assertions and valuations. That is to say that even if one finds in all Marx's early writings factual assertions and scientific analyses along with valuations and political or practical orientations, this does not mean in the least that these works had from the outset a dialectical character. The latter requires in effect an awareness of the inseparability of the two attitudes, a *consciousness* which is only to be found explicitly expressed in *The German Ideology* and above all in the *Theses on Feuerbach*. And it is striking that only when Marx has attained this awareness of the central core of dialectical thought do we find explicitly posed in his work the problem of the connection between theory and practice, and of the circular relation between social conditions and that which is conditioned by them. . . .

Terminology is undoubtedly very difficult to establish definitively in the social sciences, because of the dynamic character of the reality which they study and the impossibility of any non-genetic definitions. If however, taking this into account, we designate *sociology* as a science of society which aims to be objective and independent of the practical orientations of the investigator, and *historical materialism* as the dialectical conception which asserts the impossibility of separating these two kinds of human activity (one might equally well distinguish between 'historical sociology' and 'sociological history', but the double use of the term 'sociology' could lead to confusion), then it can be said that there is a highly important study to be made of the relations between sociology, morals or natural law, politics, and historical materialism in the various works in which the young Marx elaborated his ideas, up to *The German Ideology* and the *Theses on Feuerbach*.

In the present essay . . . I intend only to indicate four important aspects of this development, or more precisely to draw attention to Marx's fundamental standpoint on this problem in four texts: his articles in the *Rheinische Zeitung*, the *Critique of Hegel's Philosophy of the State*, the *Introduction to Hegel's Philosophy of Right*, and the *Theses on Feuerbach*.

Let me observe at once that it is in the articles in the *Rheinische Zeitung* that Marx comes closest to the dualist position, which many interpreters have regarded as characterizing his work as a whole, a position which recognizes the existence of two more or less autonomous, though closely related, types of analysis: namely, on one side, a purely theoretical, sociological analysis, and on the other side, a normative analysis, dealing with political or moral questions. In fact, at the time when he was editing the *Rheinische Zeitung* Marx, like many Young Hegelians, had moved away from Hegel's dialectical approach and drawn closer to a rationalist style of thought, related to the philosophy of the Enlightenment. Lukács, and later historians, have already analysed this movement of the Hegelian Left from dialectics to rationalism, or to use Lukács' expression, 'the return from Hegel to Fichte'.

The most important historical factor which can explain this development is probably that all dialectical thought has to base itself upon reality, and the German reality of that period was not sufficiently revolutionary to justify a radical orientation. It was only the discovery of a real and effectively revolutionary force in the shape of the English and French proletariat which made it possible for Marx and Engels (and perhaps also Moses Hess to some extent, though this needs to be examined more fully) to return to a dialectical standpoint.

Be that as it may, the *political* positions taken by the young Marx in his articles in the *Rheinische Zeitung*, it must be said bluntly, are not particularly original. They only express, though in a brilliant style, the ideas of democratic radicalism and individualistic rationalism. The state should represent society as a whole, and such representation is only possible if freedom of expression – which means freedom of the press – is assured. The collusion between the state and private interests with their established privileges is a real evil which must be unceasingly denounced as one of the most dangerous abuses of political power.

The real originality of these articles seems to me to lie, on the contrary, in their extremely subtle and penetrating sociological analyses, which are of course closely interwoven with Marx's political views, but still retain an independent value. Considering that the articles were written in 1842, and that many of them are still of great interest today, one must recognize that they are the work of a thinker who demonstrated already, at that time, his exceptional quality.

The first series of articles, concerned with the debates in the Rhenish Diet on the freedom of the press, and the publication of these debates, embodies an extremely subtle analysis, of great methodological interest, of the relation between the structure of the arguments presented by various speakers and the social groups which they represent. Marx is not content, in fact, merely to note that the speakers oppose the freedom of the press, or advocate a very limited freedom, and to criticize their views in the name of his democratic rationalism. He also notes – and it is in this respect that his articles retain their interest today – that the arguments invoked by each speaker to support his view are characteristic of the specific categories of thought of his group. Thus, in the case of the speaker representing the princely order, Marx observes that he justifies censorship in terms of the existing state of affairs, a specious argument perhaps, but one which is characteristic of the general outlook of this order; though it must be added that the validity of the 'existing state of affairs' is not, for this speaker or for the group which he represents, a universal principle, but is valid only when it is a matter of asserting the authority of governments and restricting the liberties of the people. That is why this same speaker, after having observed that censorship is good because it already exists, and is even developing in the German federation generally, feels obliged to add that the existence of freedom of the press in England, Holland and Switzerland, far from providing a sound argument for the validity of such freedom is, on the contrary, a doubtful argument to the extent that this freedom, where it exists, has 'arisen from particular circumstances', or has had 'pernicious' consequences.

The speaker representing the nobility begins by affirming that he is in favour of freedom to publish the debates in the Diet, on condition, however, that the decision on whether to publish them should be left to the Diet itself, so that there will be the maximum freedom of debate, without any 'external' pressures. Marx justly remarks that in this argument the notion of liberty, far from being the universal liberty of rationalism, becomes that of 'liberties', which is the term that the aristocracy of the sword or of the robe has always used to characterize its privileges. The speaker does not regard the Diet as an assembly of representatives of the provinces, and subject to their control, but rather – in the manner of the early French parliaments – as a privileged corporation similar to the body which he himself represents, which has to defend its 'liberties', that is to say, the free exercise of its privileges. Turning to the question of the freedom of the press, the same speaker expresses his opposition to it, giving as his specific, and specious, reason that since, according to him, human beings are by nature wicked, any kind of freedom of expression which allowed the 'bad' press as well as the 'good' press to appear freely would incur the risk of ensuring the triumph of the former, which would have a much stronger influence on public opinion; it being understood, of course, that for him the 'good' press is that which ensures the defence of individual privileges. In effect, he defines an 'ill-disposed outlook' as 'the arrogance which does not recognize authority in the church and in the state' and 'the envy which preaches the suppression of what the people call aristocracy'.

As Marx says,

> these gentlemen who do not regard liberty as a natural gift of the spread of universal reason, but only as a supernatural gift resulting from a particularly favourable conjunction of the stars, because they want to recognize liberty only as the individual attribute of certain people or certain estates, are obliged in consequence to put universal reason and universal liberty in the category of those ill-disposed ideas and fantasies which characterize 'logically constructed systems'. In order to safeguard special liberties, i.e. privileges, they are led to proscribe the universal liberty of human nature.

Marx concludes his analysis with a quotation which expresses in a striking way the aristocratic perspective and its limitations. The speaker adds to his other arguments the view that 'to be able to speak and to write are purely mechanical talents.' It is well known indeed to what extent, for the aristocracy, writing and speaking were subsidiary activities.

The third speaker, finally, representing the bourgeoisie, declares himself in favour of the freedom of the press, but in a very particular fashion, since he explains that journalism is an occupation like any other and must be given the same freedom which is granted to all other professions. Thus he proposes to grant this freedom with the same restrictions as are imposed upon other occupations: namely, to accord the right of being a journalist only to a certain number of individuals whose competence will have been attested and who will have been granted a licence.

It is no exaggeration, I think, to say that, in the history of sociology, this study by Marx is one of the first examples of a sociological theory of knowledge, and that its methodological importance can scarcely be overestimated. It bears upon a central issue in any sociological study of human phenomena – namely, the general categories of thought which are specific to different social groups – which is, regrettably, either misunderstood or ignored in many sociological investigations, not only in the nineteenth century but even today.

Marx's articles on 'The leading article in No. 179 of the *Kölnische Zeitung*' formulate the basic principles of the sociology of thought in general, and of philosophical thought in particular. The following passage seems to me exceptionally striking:

> Philosophies do not spring up from the ground like mushrooms; they are the product of their age and of their people, whose most subtle, precious and hidden essence flows into philosophical ideas. The same spirit constructs philosophical systems in the heads of philosophers and railways with the hands of workers. Philosophy is not outside the world any more than the brain is outside man, even though it is not located in the stomach.

In his articles devoted to the thefts of wood Marx sketches, though certainly in an inadequate, undialectical fashion, the elements of the theory of reification, by showing how human relationships are transformed, in a society based upon private property, into qualities of objects; and in the particular case considered, how wood becomes more important than the men it oppresses and destroys. In these same articles there is a remarkable sociological analysis of the juridical sanctioning of recent social transformations, by means of an interpretation in terms of Roman law of the relationships inherited from the middle ages, when the notions of possession and property had an entirely different social content. I shall not discuss these last two studies further here, for the simple reason that the theory of reification, and also the justification of the expropriation of the customary rights of the peasants by the interpretation of the right of overlordship as an absolute property right, are now well understood in the sociological literature.

The last series of articles, concerned with defending the correspondence from a wine grower of the Moselle region which the paper had published, and on which the authorities were demanding explanations, is again a noteworthy sociological analysis of the bureaucratic mentality, and of the structural reasons which necessarily incline it to misunderstand the nature of any protest against administrative measures and to support the administrative authority. Let me quote here Marx's comment that even when the administration desires to examine complaints objectively it is likely to confide the investigation to an official who is familiar with the problem, which means in most cases an official who has worked in the department concerned even if he is no longer employed there. Such an official is usually of fairly high rank; hence, the person who is to evaluate the complaint is not only a member of the department, and so tends to approve its actions, but also, very frequently has to assess measures which were taken either by himself or by one of his superiors.

The foregoing account shows the extent to which, in the period when Marx's thought was not very dialectical, but was close to the rationalism of the Enlightenment, there is to be found that dualism in his thought which some interpreters have claimed to discover in his later work; and equally, how far Marx, at that time, showed himself to be not only a militant supporter of radical democracy and a brilliant disciple of Enlightenment philosophy, but also a notable empirical sociologist. Let me add here that the value of all these sociological studies which I have mentioned consists, among other things, in the fact that they are studies in the sociology of knowledge, focused upon the mental categories specific to various social groups, and for that reason are capable of being incorporated later on, to a great extent, into a dialectical perspective. It is from this aspect, even at the time when Marx's thought is most remote from the dialectic, that it foreshadows, by its concentration upon the relation between structures of consciousness and social reality, its subsequent development.

The nature of the sociological studies in the *Rheinische Zeitung* can be characterized roughly in the following way. There exists for Marx a natural law and a natural morality upon which his political judgements are founded, and in the name of which he conducts his struggle. But this natural law and morality is confronted by a social reality which is full of abuses and errors, a reality which has to be explained sociologically; and Marx studies it in a *determinist*, not a *genetic* way, focusing his analyses upon a *causal* explanation of the mental categories which form the consciousness of diverse social groups. Whether Marx is aware of it or not, this standpoint, like that of most of the

Young Hegelians of the period, is at the opposite pole from dialectical thought.

It is in his next work, the *Critique of Hegel's Philosophy of the State*, that Marx is again confronted with the basic standpoint of dialectical thought. This is an extremely complex work, and there is no question of undertaking a detailed analysis of it here; what interests us for the present is the problem of the relations between theory and practice, sociology and politics, factual judgements and value judgements. But in approaching Hegel's thought, and regardless of the criticisms that he brings against it – which I shall consider later – Marx confronts a body of thought in which valuations are not formulated in terms of natural law or morality, but in terms of what is conceived as *reality*, even if this reality is not that which is directly and empirically given but the development of objective spirit and its advance toward the realization of freedom. It is important to note (and this is perhaps largely explicable by the historical context, in which *all the radicals wanted to be more or less Hegelian* even though opposing Hegel on political grounds) that Marx does not criticize Hegel from a political standpoint based upon natural law and morality, but asks what is the flaw in a system which bases its value judgements not upon the 'ought' but upon existing reality and arrives, in its philosophy of the state, at conclusions which are so strongly opposed to those of democratic radicalism, and are indeed a mere apologia for the existing social and political conditions in Germany. The central problem of the book, beyond all its particular analyses, is therefore that of an *immanent criticism* of the Hegelian system, and for that reason Marx is led to make an important step from Enlightenment rationalism toward dialectical thought.

In fact, from the very first pages of the book Marx points to the central issue which distinguishes Hegel's idealist dialectic from the future materialist dialectic of Marx and Engels, and makes the former an apologia for the existing state, the latter a revolutionary ideology. Marx's principal objection to Hegel is that he has inverted the real relation between subject and predicate by making spirit, which is above all a predicate, the subject of history, while reducing real human beings and the institutions created by their interrelations (the family, civil society, the state) to the status of predicates. This procedure, for reasons internal to it, is bound to reach a conservative conclusion, even if it is used in the most critical way and with the best intentions. There is, in fact, no way of gaining direct and immediate knowledge of objective spirit or of its short- or medium-term developmental tendencies (the thinker knows only the ultimate goal of its development). Thus the philosopher can only establish his political standpoint by means of a detour, by basing himself upon the so-called predicates, or in other words upon the existing institutions. That is why any honest use of an idealist dialectic, if it takes itself seriously and desires to avoid the dualism of 'being' and 'what ought to be', is bound to result in a conservative standpoint and an apologia for the existing social and political order. If value judgements have to be based upon the real subject of history, and if the latter can only be known through its empirical predicates which are conceived as *lacking any dynamism of their own*, then value judgements can only be a vindication of what is known positively about absolute spirit, that is to say, an apologia for what exists, which eliminates any valuation of possible change.

This fundamental criticism of the Hegelian system seems to me valid, and I do not see any objection which could be brought against it. At most, it might be added that a vindication of the existing reality may be progressive, and even revolutionary, when this reality is itself manifestly progressive or revolutionary, as was the case, for example, when it took the form of the Jacobin dictatorship or the Napoleonic empire; whereas it is necessarily reactionary during periods of conservative stabilization, as it was at the time when Hegel wrote his *Philosophy of Right* or when Marx wrote the work which we are engaged in studying.

Marx opposes to Hegel's error of inverting the real relation between subject and predicate the need for a scheme of thought which would be both positive and radical, and would see in real human beings and their social institutions (the family, civil society, the state) the genuine subject of historical action. But this requirement, pressed to its limit, was bound to lead Marx from the sociological/political dualism of his articles in the *Rheinische Zeitung* to historical materialism, for the idea of real human beings as the subjects of history, if it is conceived in a rigorous way, implies: (1) the need for a *genetic* study of social facts and social institutions, and; (2) the need to regard the theory itself as an element in human historical action, and to conceive the human beings and institutions which are studied as having a part, more or less directly, in the elaboration of the theory. In short, the need to reconstitute the relation between subject and predicate implied a kind of thought, both dialectical and positive, focused upon the close connection between theory and practice, and upon the total or partial identity of the subject and the object of thought and action.

Very frequently, however – indeed almost always – there is a considerable lag between the requirements immanent in the development of a theoretical standpoint and the effective realization of this development in the historical process and in the life of a thinker. The *Critique of Hegel's Philosophy of the State* already required the elaboration of a dialectical form of thought. But like most of the Young Hegelians Marx was too strongly attached to his radical, democratic and oppositional standpoint to be able to accept the requirements of dialectical thought, and particularly that of basing valuations exclusively upon the objective tendencies of the existing historical structures, so long as he had not discovered in these structures an objectively revolutionary force which would make it possible to reconcile the requirements of dialectical thought with the political attitudes of the Young Hegelians. In short, between the implicit requirement of a critique of Hegel's philosophy and the working out of dialectical materialism, there stood necessarily *the discovery of the English and French proletariat as revolutionary forces*.

Even so, it must be remembered that the discovery of the proletariat as the subject and driving force of the socialist revolution did not result immediately in the elaboration of a monist and consistent form of dialectical thought. It is usual to locate the beginnings of historical and dialectical materialism in Marx's writings of 1843 and the first part of 1844, published in the *Deutsch-Französische Jahrbücher*; and especially in the *Critique of Hegel's Philosophy of Right. Introduction*. There is, however, an error in this interpretation which is not without interest for the development of Marxism after Marx. For although it is undeniable that this *Introduction* is the first of Marx's texts in which the idea of the proletariat as the class which is decisive for the achievement of a socialist revolution appears, it is far from being dialectical and takes a strictly dualist position.[2] Essentially, it is an attempt to synthesize the writings of 1842, which based the hopes for social and political reform upon the power of reason, supported by a natural morality and natural rights, with the dialectical requirements of the *Critique of Hegel's Philosophy of the State*, which sought to discover the active subject of history and progress in the real structures of society, not in the heaven of ideologies. Schematically expressed, the basic standpoint adopted in the *Introduction* asserts a duality between rational thought, which is the active force of history but remains powerless and ineffectual as long as it does not succeed in embodying itself in some material reality, and on the other side, this material reality, which is in itself, and in isolation, passive but may become, and does become, active when it is penetrated by rational thought. It will be enough to cite here a few passages: 'Revolutions need a *passive* element, a *material* basis. Theory is only realized in a people so far as it fulfils the needs of the people.' 'It is not enough that thought should seek to realize itself; reality must also strive towards thought.' 'It is clear that the arm of criticism cannot replace the criticism of arms. Material force can only be overthrown by material force; but theory itself becomes a material force when it has seized the masses.' 'The *emancipation of Germany* will be an *emancipation of man*. *Philosophy* is the *head* of this emancipation and the *proletariat* is its *heart*. Philosophy can only be realized by the abolition of the proletariat, and the proletariat can only be abolished by the realization of philosophy.'

It remains to ask why, not withstanding the passages just cited and the clearly dualist structure of the work as a whole, its transitional character, as a text which is dualist and not dialectical, has been so little emphasized in the later literature on Marx. It seems to me that the reason is to be found mainly in the fact that this literature itself had a dualist, non-dialectical character, and that what was called Marxism was essentially much closer to the standpoint of the *Introduction* than to that of

[2] On this matter see the unpublished thesis of Michael Loewy, 'Revolution communiste et auto-émancipation du prolétariat dans l'oeuvre du jeune Marx.'

the *Theses on Feuerbach*. In fact, it is enough to replace the word 'philosophy' in the *Introduction* by the word 'party' (and in both cases it is really a matter of the group which elaborates an ideology) in order to arrive at a standpoint very close to that which Lenin formulated in *What is to be Done?*, but also close to the theoretical views, more or less clearly expounded, which corresponded with the actual practice of both German Social Democracy and the Bolsheviks; that is to say, of the two major sources of the development of Marxist theory.

The *Theses on Feuerbach* constitute, in the whole corpus of Marx's work, the first text which is rigorously monist and dialectical. In the history of European philosophy these two or three pages seem to me equal in importance to the most famous philosophical works, and I have no hesitation in comparing them with the *Discourse on Method*, the *Critique of Pure Reason*, and the *Phenomenology of Mind*. It is evident that an exhaustive analysis of this text would probably require a whole volume or more, and nothing of the kind can be attempted here. Let me simply note, in concluding this essay, that the *Theses on Feuerbach* pose in an uncompromising fashion the problem of the relations between theory and practice, factual judgements and valuations, knowledge of human phenomena and the transformation of the world; and that on this occasion Marx's response is strictly *monist* and *genetic*, asserting that the real subject of history is not the individual but the social group oriented toward identification with the species. The first thesis, subsequently confirmed by experimental studies, and notably by those of Jean Piaget, is one of the most radical affirmations of the unity of theory and practice, of knowledge and action, because it locates this unity not only at the level of consciousness and thought, but also at the more elementary level of sensation and perception: 'The chief defect of all previous materialism (including that of Feuerbach) is that things (*Gegenstand*), reality, the sensible world, are conceived only in the form of *objects (Objekt) of observation*, but not as human sense activity, not as *practical activity*, not *subjectively*.'

The third thesis asserts the impossibility of any determinist, or even simply objective, conception of social reality, given that such a standpoint always results in attempting to explain human thought and behaviour by social circumstances, whereas these circumstances themselves are created by human thought and behaviour. Every kind of thought and every theory is located within the historical process, and involves both cognitive endeavour and a practical intervention. As for the pretensions of an objective sociology, they correspond with the attempt 'to divide society into two parts, one of which is superior to society'.[3]

The sixth thesis reproaches Feuerbach, and by implication any objective sociology, with the lack of a genetic perspective. Finally, this same sixth thesis, and the ninth and tenth theses, underline the fact that the static and dualist standpoint results necessarily from the fundamental error of regarding the isolated individual as the subject of praxis, an error which leads to obscuring the historical character of praxis. The real subject is the collectivity, the human species. This is no doubt too general an assertion, but one which Marx will soon make precise by substituting for the abstract generic collectivity a more definite empirical reality, namely that of social classes.

[3] It is easy to see the connection between sociological objectivism and any fundamental division of society, or of the party, into two different groups: the passive masses and the active militants or theorists.

4
Critique of Marx's Positivism
ALBRECHT WELLMER

My critique of the objectivism of Marx's philosophy of history was directed at a latently positivistic misconception, which, according to Habermas's thesis, arises from the part played in Marx's theory by the concept of labour. Of course it would be a basic misunderstanding of this thesis to suppose that Habermas's concept of 'instrumental behaviour' could conceal Marx's notion of production. It is well known that when Marx talks of 'production' in his economic analyses, he also means 'distribution', 'forms of intercourse' – which corresponds to 'communicative behaviour'.[1] Habermas also makes a distinction between the level of material analyses, on which Marx makes use of a concept of social practice incorporating labour *and* interaction,[2] and the level of historico-philosophical interpretation, on which Marx comprehends the self-production (that is, creation) of the human species solely on the basis of the logic of its activity in the production of objects:

> For his analysis of the development of socio-economic formations Marx uses a concept of the system of social labour containing more elements than are declared in the concept of the self-creating human species. Self-constitution through social work is conceived *on the categorical level* as a production process; and instrumental behaviour, work in the sense of productive activity, characterizes the dimension in which natural history runs its course. *On the level of his material investigations*, on the other hand, Marx always takes into account a social *praxis* in-

Excerpt from Albrecht Wellmer, *Critical Theory of Society* (New York: Herder & Herder, 1971) pp. 67–75, 94–9. Reprinted by permission of The Seabury Press.

[1] Cf. Marx, *Grundrisse der Kritik der politischen Ökonomie* (Berlin, 1953), Introduction, pp. 16 ff.

[2] Cf. Jürgen Habermas, *Erkenntnis und Interesse*, 1968, p. 71.

corporating work *and* interaction; the natural-historical processes are intermediated by the productive activity of the individual and the organization of its intercourse.[3]

The epistemological implications of Marx's understanding of history lead to the misconception of ideology-critical social theory as a 'science' in the same sense as the natural sciences, which Marx in fact favoured.[4] The camouflaging of the difference between 'strict experimental science' and 'criticism',[5] between 'productive knowledge' and 'reflective knowledge', would necessarily have consequences in regard to the apprehension of the interplay of critical theory and revolutionary practice: Marx's self-conception provides the starting-points for an erroneously technocratic interpretation of his theory, which was then to become practical reality in the hands of the omniscient administrators of historical necessity.[6]

[3] Ibid., p. 71.

[4] In his Preface to the second edition of *Capital* (vol. I), for example, Marx quotes (with approval) a Russian reviewer who compares Marx's method of economic analysis with a biology oriented to the history of evolution: 'Marx views the social movement as a process of natural history, governed by laws which are not only independent of the will, consciousness and intelligence of men, but on the contrary determine their volition, consciousness and intelligence' (*MA* [*Karl Marx–Ausgabe*, ed. H. J. Lieber, Darmstadt: 1962.] vol. 4, p. xxix). Marx acknowledges the reviewer's description as a representation of his dialectical *method* (ibid., p. xxx); this is fatal in view of the following, far-reaching assertion by the reviewer: 'Consequently, Marx is concerned with only one thing: to show, by precise scientific investigation, the necessity of successive definite systems of social conditions, and to establish, as impartially as possible, the facts that serve him as starting-points and grounds. For this purpose it is wholly adequate if he proves, at one and the same time, the necessity of the present order and the necessity of another order into which the first must inevitably pass over, quite oblivious of whether men believe or do not believe it, are conscious or unconscious of it' (ibid., p. xxix). These statements already show that a positivistic self-misconception cannot fail to affect even the material contents of the theory – here in particular the interpretation of the world-historical transition to the classless society. Subsequently, I try to demonstrate the inner context of theory that allowed Marx – not quite by accident – to let pass these statements by his St Petersburg reviewer.

[5] Cf. Habermas, *Erkenntnis und Interesse*, p. 62.

[6] Cf. Oskar Negt, Introduction to A. Deborin and N. Bukharin, *Kontroversen über dialektischen und mechanistischen Materialismus* (Frankfurt, 1969).

Of course the two levels of material analysis and categorical interpretation are not related as object- and meta-level. The categorical framework already includes an historico-philosophical articulation which allows the production of basic statements about the 'mechanism' of historical development. These pronouncements however have, as it were, no merely meta-theoretical status;[7] consequently, one might suppose that the contradiction between theory *qua* criticism and its objectivistic self-misconception has an inner-theoretical correlative in the form of a contradiction between the historical interpretation of historical materialism and the criticism of political economy. Of course this supposition, formulated in this global way, is *prima facie* implausible: historical materialism enters into the approach proper to the criticism of political economy, just as much as it is the result of that approach.[8]

In addition, the criticism of political economy becomes a *criticism of ideology*, inasmuch as it turns into what Lukács calls an 'historical criticism of economy'.[9] When Marx criticizes commodity-fetishism, he discovers behind the apparent natural qualities and the apparent social relations of things, the social relations of men, produced historically and both mediated and repressed from consciousness by coercive conditions; and behind the 'natural' characteristics of capital an historically produced class relationship.[10] Therefore there is a reciprocally consolidated relationship between historical materialism as a theory of socio-economic development mediated through class struggle, and the criticism of political economy. But if a 'modification' of Marx's interpretation of

[7] Otherwise one would only need to disengage Marx's statements about the scientific status of his theory and his 'meta-theory' of history from the body of the theory, and to allow them to speak for themselves as against their positivistic misinterpretations. It should soon become apparent that the matter is more complex than this.

[8] For the first part of the assertion cf. K. Marx, *Grundrisse der Kritik der politischen Ökonomie* (Berlin, 1953) Introduction, esp. sections 2 and 3. The most effective evidence for the second part is the connection between the beginning and the end of *Capital*; cf. K. Kosik, *Dialektik des Konkreten* (Frankfurt, 1967) pp. 174 ff.

[9] Cf. Georg Lukács, 'Klassenbewusstsein', in *Geschichte und Klassenbewusstsein* (Amsterdam, 1967) p. 60.

[10] Cf. *MA*, vol. 4, pp. 47 ff.

history actually becomes available and if this modified construct is not merely to have the status of a meta-theory of history (unauthoritative in regard to the material contents of the theory), then an inner-theoretical contradiction between the 'historical' and the 'ideology-critical' theoretical approaches nevertheless has to be established – unless criticism of the objectivistic traces in Marx's philosophy of history, especially his conception of the transition to the classless society, is to mean the total conception of theory. I believe it can be shown that, even to the extent of specific economic analyses, there is an unresolved contradiction between the 'modified' historical materialism (that is, that which traces the 'dialectics of morality' back to the dialectics of production) and the ideology-critical theoretical approach; and that, in particular, in contrast to this theoretical approach, 'modified' historical materialism results in an objectivistic concept of revolution that Marx has at some points explicitly acknowledged as his own.

I shall first of all indicate where this alleged contradiction is to be found. If, on this construction, the human *praxis* which constitutes and transforms society, and with it 'production' and the transformation of men's societal consciousness, appear ultimately as derivations and functions of their work in transforming nature, then the dialectical interplay between the world-historical process of formation of consciousness and social institutions on the one hand, and the historical development of productive forces on the other, must be misconceived as a functional relationship. Conditions of production, and ideologies that legitimize domination, then tacitly become second-order productive forces; their history can no longer be reconstructed in practical terms as that of a progressive emancipation from the pressures of naturally effective social repression, instead their sole logic is that of another history: that of the technical conquest of external nature, that is, of the emancipation of men from the natural pressures that restrict them – but emancipation by means of the progressive reification of their 'essential powers' in material production. The dissolution of a false social consciousness of a kind that stabilizes domination (for Marx a constitutive aspect of the dissolution of relations of domination in the class struggle) cannot then be conceived as the result of a practical 'process of formation'; instead, it must itself reappear as the *product* of social work, that is, as the necessary by-product of socio-economic changes, which for their part were exacted solely by processes of technical innovation. But if the determining relationship between the development of productive forces, the transformation of forms of domination, and transformation of social consciousness, is constructed in this way, there are distinct consequences amounting to the establishment of an objectivistic theory of revolution. *Firstly*, the immanent logic of a progressive technological self-objectification of men provides both the goal and the necessary result of human 'prehistory', namely, the complete rationalization of the process of social reproduction; *secondly*, the theoretical reconstruction of the prehistorical determining relationship between productive forces, conditions of production, and ideologies, becomes a task for strict experimental science; *thirdly*, there is the result that, in the capitalist process of production, the *subjective* conditions for a revolutionary transition to the classless society must be 'produced' at the very same time as the objective conditions; *fourthly*, and finally, the 'correct' proletarian consciousness can utlimately be none other than the consciousness of positive science: the freedom of proletarian men is attenuated and blunted to become insight into historical necessity, and their revolution can merely reduce and alleviate the 'birth pangs' of the new society.

Of course this theoretical relationship is not to be found in *this* form anywhere in Marx. But if the more or less evident 'distortions' of Marx's philosophy of history are seen in the perspective of decisions made in advance on the level of categorization, then they can be presented in terms of that theoretical relationship as their ideal limit value. This means, however, that the modification of Marx's construction of history potentially removes the basis of his critical social theory *qua* ideology-*criticism*. For this theory can only be a *critique* of ideology as a socially necessary illusion, if, as an historically explicative theory, it simultaneously reveals the contradiction between society as it is, and what it could and must be in terms of its technical possibilities and of the interpretations of the 'good life' acknowledged within it. This means that critical theory does not wish to replace an ideological consciousness with a scientific consciousness, but – of course by means of empirical and historical analyses – to assist the practical reason existing in the form of ideological consciousness to 'call to mind' its distorted form, and at the same time to get control of its practical-utopian contents. Ultimately, therefore, critical theory can prove itself only by initiating a reflective dissolution of false consciousness resulting in liberating *praxis*: the successful dissolution of false consciousness as an integrative aspect of emancipatory practice is the proper touchstone for its truth, because only in the process of this dissolution and resolution can it exist as the *acknowledged* truth of false consciousness. The truth of critical social theory is a *vérité à faire*; in the last resort it can demonstrate its truthfulness only by successful liberation: hence the hypothetico-practical status peculiar to the theory.

This hypothetico-practical status (and this is my thesis) is challenged by the basic assumptions of Marx's interpretation of history. In those basic assumptions, technical progress, the abrogation of 'dysfunctional' social repression and the dissolution of false consciousness are so indissolubly joined that the irresistible advance of technical progress, which starts with the capitalist mode of production, has to be interpreted as the irresistible advance towards the commonwealth of freedom. The building of the realm of freedom is therefore shifted back into the same continuum of historical necessity in which, for Marx, the prehistory of the human species had advanced. But on this assumption, the reasonableness of liberating practice can no longer be measured according to the degree to which it has already liberated from the existing coercive context those active individuals who have been enlightened as to their true interest, but only according to the extent to which they act on the basis of insight into the scientifically detectable regularities of the course of history. In this way, there is a potential elimination from the concept of liberating practice of that aspect of a reflective dissolution of false consciousness, which allows the practical realization of critical theory to be distinguished from the practical realization of a strictly experimental scientific theory: insight into the history and meaning of experienced social bondage and constraint, at which critical theory aims as the precondition of a process of collective emancipation, is indissolubly bound up with the transformation of attitudes, modes of behaviour and possibilities of experience; the dissolution of false consciousness mediated through practice *and* self-reflection is therefore at one and the same time transformation of consciousness and transformation of men.[11] Against this, a critical social theory which is misconceived as a strict experimental scientific theory can no longer anticipate the necessary transformation of men who want to transform society, in the dimension of a self-enlightening *praxis*; instead it must rigorously distinguish between the transformation of consciousness and the transformation of attitudes and modes of behaviour: the first becomes knowledge of the economic law of movement of capitalist society, the second must be comprehended as the necessary result of the process of material production.

The basic thesis that I shall now try to establish in greater detail may be provisionally formulated thus: the union of historical materialism and the criticism of political economy in Marx's social theory is inherently contradictory. In particular, the basic assumptions of Marx's interpretation of history suggest, in contrast to the ideology-critical approach of the theory, an 'objectivistic' concept of revolution in a twofold sense: on the one hand, they determine the revolutionary *function* of critical theory as that of a post-ideological, 'positive' science, whereas on the other hand they lead to the camouflaging of the distinction between the *inevitable* and the practically necessary transformation of capitalist society, thus allowing the transition to the classless society to appear as the

[11] It is possible to interpret in this sense those statements of Marx's in which he anticipates the necessary transformation of the proletarians as the result of their liberating *praxis*. E.g., in the *Revelations about the Cologne Communist Trial*: 'Whereas we say to the workers: You have fifteen, twenty, or even fifty years of civil wars and national wars to endure, not only in order to change conditions, but in order to change yourselves and to fit yourselves for political rule, you say, on the contrary: "We must come to power immediately, or else lay ourselves down to rest"' (*MA*, vol. 3, i, p. 454). Significantly, in this *political* document Marx stresses the emancipatory function of the class *struggle*. On the other hand, in so far as a modified historical materialism is brought to bear in his theory, precisely this liberating function of the class struggle is neglected in favour of the system-breaking function of objective class *antagonism*.

enforced result of the solution of problems proper to the capitalist system.

If this thesis is correct, then two misconceptions of Marx's theory which have certain practical consequences may depend on a theoretical relationship which is more or less latent in this theory itself; I shall call them the 'technocratic' and the 'evolutionist' misconceptions. According to the first misconception, under certain historic initial conditions socialism would have to be brought about by an exclusive, theoretically trained, revolutionary minority ruling by authoritarian measures; according to the second, it would have to be the enforced result of the development of capitalist society. In fact, as can easily be seen, there is only one misconception: namely, a 'mechanistic' misunderstanding of historical materialism, according to which the revolution becomes the mere question of more or less expenses on the bill of history – since the end-result of history is already settled. If, however, this error can find support in a theoretical relationship latent in Marx's theory, then a meta-criticism of Marx's critique of political moralism is also requisite; at any rate to the extent that this critique, which struck at the Young Hegelians, early socialists and anarchists with equal severity, understood itself to be precisely the result of the development of socialism from utopia to *science*. . . .

'All collisions in history', says *The German Ideology*,[12] '. . . originate, in our view, in the contradiction between the productive forces and the form of intercourse.' 'This contradiction . . . had on every occasion to break out in a revolution, assuming at the same time various subsidiary forms: comprehensive collisions, collisions of different classes, contradiction of consciousness, battle of ideas, and so on, class warfare, and so on.' Marx distinguishes a basic form of social contradiction from its 'subsidiary forms'; the mistake of written history in the past was that in any particular case it made one of these subsidiary forms the basis of social upheavals and historical development in general. 'From a restricted viewpoint one can isolate one of these subsidiary forms and see it as the basis of these revolutions – this is all the easier because the very individuals who started the revolutions had illusions about their own activity

[12] *MEW*, [Karl Marx and Friedrich Engels, *Werke*, Berlin; Dietz Verlag, 1958 onwards.] vol. 3, p. 73.

according to the extent of their education and the stage of historical development.'

In what sense can it be said now that a 'collision' between classes is the 'subsidiary form' of a contradiction between productive forces and forms of intercourse? Does it mean that this contradiction can be detected independently of the social conflicts in which it manifests itself, that is, as the dysfunctionality of a form of domination in regard, say, to the systematic goal of a development of the productive forces? Or does it mean only that the calling in question of a dominant order, manifest in class conflict, would only be possible and could only be resolved through the development of the productive forces? In one case, class conflict would be the necessary *consequence* of an 'objective' contradiction; in the other case, it would constitute it only *as* contradiction in the general sense. The incompatibility of these two possible interpretations, which are still left open here, is the incompatibility of two different versions of historical materialism made plain in the well-known formulations of the Preface to *A Contribution to the Critique of Political Economy*:

> In the social production of their life, men enter into certain necessary relations that are independent of their will, relations of production which correspond to a certain stage of development of their material productive forces. . . . At a certain stage of their development, the material productive forces of society come into conflict with the existing relations of production, or – what is only a legal expression for those same relations – with the property relations within which they have acted until now. These relations turn from forms of development of productive forces into their fetters. Then an epoch of social revolution commences. With the transformation of the economic basis, the whole immense superstructure is more slowly or more speedily transformed. When considering such transformations, one must always make a distinction between the material transformation of the economic conditions of production, which can be determined with natural scientific exactitude, and the legal, political, religious, artistic or philosophical, or, in short, the ideological forms in which men become conscious of this conflict and fight it out. Just as one does not judge an individual by what he thinks of himself, so such an epoch of transformation

> cannot be judged by its consciousness; instead, this consciousness must be explained on the basis of the contradictions of material life, of the existing conflict between the social productive forces and relations of production.[13]

Here Marx states clearly that social revolutions solve social systematic problems which are reflected in men's consciousness but which are defined – independently of the interpretations of the individuals concerned – as conflicts 'of material life'; hence there are necessary solutions (independent of human volition) to such systematic problems in the shape of a transition to the next, higher mode of production, which in each particular case guarantees the further reproduction of society and the possibility of further development of the productive forces. Each stage of development of the productive forces allows, so to speak, only *one* definite institutionalization of the social reproduction process; hence the class struggle is necessary in order to carry out these institutionalizations, but it is at the same time merely the vehicle of an historical progress which advances to completion behind the backs of the warring classes, and whose unique logic is that of a progressive conquest of external nature by means of a species subject only apparently split into classes.

That is the first of the alternative possible interpretations proposed above; it appears irreconcilable with Marx's intentions. But the second possible interpretation, which takes into account the ideology-critical approach of the theory, is for its part equally incompatible with the text just cited. It would mean that a 'conflict' between the productive forces and forms of intercourse was always to be understood *also* as the protest of repressed individuals against forms of domination whose legitimations had become questionable, and against the burdens and deprivations demanded by such forms of dominations and experienced as capricious and unjust. It would be a conflict between the *possibility* of a 'good life' anticipated by these very individuals (admittedly on the basis of a definite stage of development of productive forces), and the social constraint that they experience in reality; between the demands of

[13] *MA*, vol. 6, pp. 838 ff.

an inherited (that is, traditional) form of domination and the realizable demands of repressed classes. The social conflicts would be those of *material life*, because they would be grounded in the discrepancy between the possible fulfilment and the actual suppression of real needs; but they would be *conflicts* only because, through the interpretation and legitimation of their needs, social groups would put themselves in conflict with the traditional interpretations and legitimations of existing relations of domination. This would mean, however, that the forms in which men became conscious of their social conflicts, and in which they fought them out, would be not only an epiphenomenon of 'objective' conflicts between productive forces and conditions of production, but their constitutive aspect (*Moment*). The ideology-critical tracing back of these forms as forms of a distorted ethical context of relations could not be carried out solely by recourse to the 'transformation[s] of the economic conditions of production, which can be determined with natural scientific exactitude'; on the contrary, it would first of all require recourse to an immanently critical dissolution of their false consciousness.

Marx's formulations feature an ambiguity which is difficult to resolve, inasmuch as they can be interpreted according to differing theoretical approaches. Hence the programme of a transition from ideology to science, already indicated in the confrontation of an ideological consciousness requiring enlightenment with an explicative theory on the basis of facts 'which can be determined with natural scientific exactitude', as described by Marx in *The German Ideology*, also appears ambivalent. Nevertheless it is to be interpreted here in the perspective of our ideal-typical reinterpretation of a modified historical materialism.

The fact that Marx believes that the time has come for a transition from the 'ideological' to the 'scientific' method of observation of social reality is linked with his assumption that the capitalist process of production itself abolishes the traditional legitimations of domination, in so far as uprooted and pauperized men themselves are at last forced to 'contemplate their mutual relations with sober eyes'. For Marx, 'sober' means empirico-scientific, without any premises other than those which are 'open to confirmation in a purely empirical fashion'.[14] With the confrontation of ideology and science he returns to a certain extent from the shadowland of idealistic dialectics to the firm ground of the empiricist-materialistic tradition, whose enthusiasm for 'immediacy', especially that of Feuerbach's philosophy with its 'starting-point in the positive, the sensuously definite',[15] has left definite traces in this opposition. Nevertheless the influence of Feuerbach, whom Marx had already criticized in *The German Ideology* in regard to a return to insights of idealistic philosophy, has affected only the externals of Marx's thought; its essential content is already determined by the criticism of Feuerbach's materialism and of the whole materialistic tradition. The decisive indication of this is to be found in the second of the *Theses on Feuerbach*: 'The question whether human thinking can arrive at objective truth is not a theoretical but a *practical* question. Man has to prove the truth, that is, the reality and power, the "this-sidedness" of his thinking, in practice.'[16] However, for Marx the paradigm for a theoretical truth that proves itself in practice (that is, 'through the mediation of industry') was that of natural science.[17] This shows clearly the sole standpoint from which Marx was able to carry out a purely functional conjunction of ideologies and forms of domination: the standpoint of empirical science – the only one to have shown its practical truth in contrast to the destruction of ideological illusion. It is now evident how closely interwoven are Marx's interpretation of history, his modification of the concept of ideology and his pragmatic concept of theory, and how, from this reciprocal dependence of various aspects of his theory, the misconception that the end of ideology was identical with the transition from ideology to 'positive science' could arise. 'Where speculation ceases, there in real life, real, positive science begins – the representation of the practical activity, of the practical process of human development.'[18]

[14] *The German Ideology*, p. 20.

[15] Cf. *Economic and Philosophical Manuscripts*, *MA*, vol. 1, p. 639, pp. 603 ff.

[16] *MEW*, vol. 3, p. 5.

[17] Cf. *Economic and Philosophical Manuscripts*, p. 603.

[18] *MEW*, vol. 3, p. 27.

5
Marx's New Science

LOUIS ALTHUSSER

I

In 1845, Marx broke radically with every theory that based history and politics on an essence of man. This unique rupture contained three indissociable elements.

(1) The formation of a theory of history and politics based on radically new concepts: the concepts of social formation, productive forces, relations of production, superstructure, ideologies, determination in the last instance by the economy, specific determination of the other levels, etc.
(2) A radical critique of the *theoretical* pretensions of every philosophical humanism.
(3) The definition of humanism as an *ideology*.

This new conception is completely rigorous as well, but it is a new rigour: the essence criticized (2) is defined as an ideology (3), a category belonging to the new theory of society and history (1).

This rupture with every *philosophical* anthropology or humanism is no secondary detail; it is Marx's scientific discovery.

It means that Marx rejected the problematic of the earlier philosophy and adopted a new problematic in one and the same act. The earlier idealist ('bourgeois') philosophy depended in all its domains and arguments (its 'theory of knowledge', its conception of history, its political economy, its

The first excerpt is taken from Louis Althusser, *For Marx* (Harmondsworth: Allen Lane, The Penguin Press, 1969) pp. 227–36.

The second excerpt is from Louis Althusser, *Reading Capital* (London: New Left Books, 1970) pp. 177–81. Both excerpts are reprinted by permission of New Left Books.

ethics, its aesthetics, etc.) on a problematic of *human nature* (or the essence of man). For centuries, this problematic had been transparency itself, and no one had thought of questioning it even in its internal modifications.

This problematic was neither vague nor loose; on the contrary, it was constituted by a coherent system of precise concepts tightly articulated together. When Marx confronted it, it implied the two complementary postulates he defined in the Sixth Thesis on Feuerbach:

(1) that there is a universal essence of man;
(2) that this essence is the attribute of '*each single individual*' who is its real subject.

These two postulates are complementary and indissociable. But their existence and their unity presuppose a whole empiricist–idealist world outlook. If the essence of man is to be a universal attribute, it is essential that *concrete subjects* exist as absolute givens; this implies an *empiricism of the subject*. If these empirical individuals are to be men, it is essential that each carries in himself the whole human essence, if not in fact, at least in principle; this implies an *idealism of the essence*. So empiricism of the subject implies idealism of the essence and vice versa. This relation can be inverted into its 'opposite' – empiricism of the concept/idealism of the subject. But the inversion respects the basic structure of the problematic, which remains fixed.

In this type-structure it is possible to recognize not only the principle of theories of society (from Hobbes to Rousseau), of political economy (from Petty to Ricardo), of ethics (from Descartes to Kant), but also the very principle of the (pre-Marxist) idealist and materialist 'theory of knowledge' (from Locke to Feuerbach, via Kant). The content of the human essence or of the empirical subjects may vary (as can be seen from Descartes to Feuerbach); the subject may change from empiricism to idealism (as can be seen from Locke to Kant): the terms presented and their relations only vary within the invariant type-structure which constitutes this very problematic: *an empiricism of the subject always corresponds to an idealism of the essence* (*or an empiricism of the essence to an idealism of the subject*).

By rejecting the essence of man as his theoretical basis, Marx rejected the whole of this organic system of postulates. He drove the philosophical categories of the *subject*, of *empiricism*, of the *ideal essence*, etc., from all the domains in which they had been supreme. Not only from political economy (rejection of the myth of *homo oeconomicus*, that is, of the individual with definite faculties and needs as the *subject* of the classical economy); not just from history (rejection of social atomism and ethico-political idealism); not just from ethics (rejection of the Kantian ethical idea); but also from philosophy itself: for Marx's materialism excludes the empiricism of the subject (and its inverse: the transcendental subject) and the idealism of the concept (and its inverse: the empiricism of the concept).

This total theoretical revolution was only empowered to reject the old concepts because it replaced them by new concepts. In fact Marx established a new problematic, a new systematic way of asking questions of the world, new principles and a new method. This discovery is immediately contained in the theory of historical materialism, in which Marx did not only propose a new theory of the history of societies, but at the same time implicitly, but necessarily, a new 'philosophy', infinite in its implications. Thus, when Marx replaced the old couple individuals/human essence in the theory of history by new concepts (forces of production, relations of production, etc.), he was, in fact, simultaneously proposing a new conception of 'philosophy'. He replaced the old postulates (empiricism/idealism of the subject, empiricism/idealism of the essence) which were the basis not only for idealism but also for pre-Marxist materialism, by a historico-dialectical materialism of *praxis*: that is, by a theory of the different specific *levels* of *human practice* (economic practice, political practice, ideological practice, scientific practice) in their characteristic articulations, based on the specific articulations of the unity of human society. In a word, Marx substituted for the 'ideological' and universal concept of Feuerbachian 'practice' a concrete conception of the specific differences that enables us to situate each particular practice in the specific differences of the social structure.

So, to understand what was radically new in Marx's contribution, we must become aware not only of the novelty of the concepts of historical materialism, but also of the depth of the theoretical revolution they imply and inaugurate. On this condition it is possible to define humanism's status, and reject its *theoretical* pretensions while recognizing its practical function as an ideology.

Strictly in respect to theory, therefore, one can and must speak openly of *Marx's theoretical anti-humanism*, and see in this *theoretical anti-humanism* the absolute (negative) precondition of the (positive) knowledge of the human world itself, and of its practical transformation. It is impossible to *know* anything about men except on the absolute precondition that the philosophical (theoretical) myth of man is reduced to ashes. So any thought that appeals to Marx for any kind of restoration of a theoretical anthropology or humanism is no more than ashes, *theoretically*. But in practice it could pile up a monument of pre-Marxist ideology that would weigh down on real history and threaten to lead it into blind alleys.

For the corollary of theoretical Marxist anti-humanism is the recognition and knowledge of humanism itself: as an *ideology*. Marx never fell into the idealist illusion of believing that the knowledge of an object might ultimately replace the object or dissipate its existence. Cartesians, knowing that the sun was two thousand leagues away, were astonished that this distance only looked like two hundred paces: they could not even find enough of God to fill in this gap. Marx never believed that a knowledge of the nature of *money* (a social relation) could destroy its *appearance*, its form of existence – a thing, for this appearance was its very being, as necessary as the existing mode of production.[1] Marx never believed that an ideology might be dissipated by a knowledge of it: for the knowledge of this ideology, as the knowledge of its conditions of possibility, of its structure, of its specific logic and of its practical role,

[1] The whole, fashionable, theory of 'reification' depends on a projection of the theory of alienation found in the early texts, particularly the *1844 Manuscripts*, on to the theory of 'fetishism' in *Capital*. In the *1844 Manuscripts*, the objectification of the human essence is claimed as the indispensable preliminary to the reappropriation of the human essence by man. Throughout the process of objectification, man only exists in the form of an objectivity in which he meets his own essence in the appearance of a foreign, non-human, essence. This 'objectification' is not called 'reification' even though it is called

within a given society, is simultaneously knowledge of the conditions of its necessity. So Marx's theoretical *anti-humanism* does not suppress anything in the historical *existence* of humanism. In the real world philosophies of man are found after Marx as often as before, and today even some Marxists are tempted to develop the themes of a new theoretical humanism. Furthermore, Marx's theoretical anti-humanism, by relating it to its conditions of existence, recognizes a necessity for humanism as an *ideology*, a conditional necessity. The recognition of this necessity is not purely speculative. On it alone can Marxism base a policy in relation to the existing ideological forms, of every kind: religion, ethics, art, philosophy, law – and in the very front rank, humanism. When (eventually) a Marxist policy of humanist ideology, that is, a political attitude to humanism, is achieved – a policy which may be either a rejection or a critique, or a use, or a support, or a development, or a humanist renewal of contemporary forms of ideology in the *ethico-political* domain – this policy will only have been possible on the absolute condition that it is based on Marxist philosophy, and a precondition for this is theoretical *anti-humanism*.

So everything depends on the knowledge of the nature of humanism as an ideology.

There can be no question of attempting a profound definition of ideology here. It will suffice to know very schematically that an ideology is a system (with its own logic and

inhuman. Inhumanity is not represented *par excellence* by the model of a 'thing': but sometimes by the model of animality (or even of pre-animality – the man who no longer even has simple animal relations with nature), sometimes by the model of the omnipotence and fascination of transcendence (God, the State) and of money, which is, of course, a 'thing'. In *Capital* the only social relation that is presented in the form of a *thing* (this piece of metal) is *money*. But the conception of money as a *thing* (that is, the confusion of value with use-value in money) does not correspond to the reality of this 'thing': it is not the brutality of a simple 'thing' that man is faced with when he is in direct relation with money; it is a *power* (or a *lack* of it) over things and men. An ideology of reification that sees 'things' everywhere in human relations confuses in this category 'thing' (a category more foreign to Marx cannot be imagined) every social relation, conceived according to the model of a money-thing ideology.

rigour) of representations (images, myths, ideas or concepts, depending on the case) endowed with a historical existence and role within a given society. Without embarking on the problem of the relations between a science and its (ideological) past, we can say that ideology, as a system of representations, is distinguished from science in that in it the practico-social function is more important than the theoretical function (function as knowledge).

What is the nature of this social function? To understand it we must refer to the Marxist theory of history. The 'subjects' of history are given human societies. They present themselves as totalities whose unity is constituted by a certain specific type of *complexity*, which introduces instances, that, following Engels, we can, very schematically, reduce to three: the economy, politics and ideology. So in every society we can posit, in forms which are sometimes very paradoxical, the existence of an economic activity as the base, a political organization and 'ideological' forms (religion, ethics, philosophy, etc.) *So ideology is as such an organic part of every social totality*. It is as if human societies could not survive without these *specific formations*, these systems of representations (at various levels), their ideologies. Human societies secrete ideology as the very element and atmosphere indispensable to their historical respiration and life. Only an ideological world outlook could have imagined societies *without ideology* and accepted the utopian idea of a world in which ideology (not just one of its historical forms) would disappear without trace, to be replaced by *science*. For example, this utopia is the principle behind the idea that ethics, which is in its essence ideology, could be replaced by science or become scientific through and through; or that religion could be destroyed by science which would in some way take its place; that *art* could merge with knowledge or become 'everyday life', etc.

And I am not going to steer clear of the crucial question: *historical materialism cannot conceive that even a communist society could ever do without ideology*, be it ethics, art or 'world outlook'. Obviously it is possible to foresee important modifications in its ideological forms and their relations and even the disappearance of certain existing forms or a shift of their functions to neighbouring forms; it is also possible (on the premise of already acquired experience) to foresee the development of new ideological forms (e.g. the ideologies of 'the scientific world outlook' and 'communist humanism') but in the present state of Marxist theory strictly conceived, it is not conceivable that communism, a new mode of production implying determinate forces of production and relations of production, could do without a social organization of production, and corresponding ideological forms.

So ideology is not an aberration or a contingent excrescence of History: it is a structure essential to the historical life of societies. Further, only the existence and the recognition of its necessity enable us to act on ideology and transform ideology into an instrument of deliberate action on history.

It is customary to suggest that ideology belongs to the region of 'consciousness'. We must not be misled by this appellation, which is still contaminated by the idealist problematic that preceded Marx. In truth, ideology has very little to do with 'consciousness', even supposing this term to have an unambiguous meaning. It is profoundly *unconscious*, even when it presents itself in a reflected form (as in pre-Marxist 'philosophy'). Ideology is indeed a system of representations, but in the majority of cases these representations have nothing to do with 'consciousness': they are usually images and occasionally concepts, but it is above all as *structures* that they impose on the vast majority of men, not via their 'consciousness'. They are perceived–accepted–suffered cultural objects and they act functionally on men via a process that escapes them. Men 'live' their ideologies as the Cartesian 'saw' or did not see – if he was not looking at it – the moon two hundred paces away: *not at all as a form of consciousness, but as an object of their 'world'* – as their '*world*' itself. But what do we mean, then, when we say that ideology is a matter of men's 'consciousness'? First, that ideology is distinct from other social instances, but also that men *live* their actions, usually referred to freedom and 'consciousness' by the classical tradition, in ideology, *by and through ideology*; in short, that the 'lived' relation between men and the world, including History (in political action or inaction), passes through ideology, or better, *is ideology itself.* This is the sense in which Marx said that it is in ideology (as the locus of political struggle) that men *become conscious* of their place in the world and in history, it is within this ideological unconsciousness that men succeed in altering the 'lived' relation between them and the world and acquiring that new form of specific unconsciousness called 'consciousness'.

So ideology is a matter of the *lived* relation between men and their world. This relation, that only appears as '*conscious*' on condition that it is *unconscious*, in the same way only seems to be simple on condition that it is complex, that it is not a simple relation but a relation between relations, a second-degree relation. In ideology men do indeed express, not the relation between them and their conditions of existence, but *the way* they live the relation between them and their conditions of existence: this presupposes both a real relation and an '*imaginary*', '*lived*' relation. Ideology, then, is the expression of the relation between men and their 'world', that is, the (overdetermined) unity of the real relation and the imaginary relation between them and their real conditions of existence. In ideology the real relation is inevitably invested in the imaginary relation, a relation that *expresses* a *will* (conservative, conformist, reformist or revolutionary), a hope or a nostalgia, rather than describing a reality.

It is in this overdetermination of the real by the imaginary and of the imaginary by the real that ideology is *active* in principle, that it reinforces or modifies the relation between men and their conditions of existence, in the imaginary relation itself. It follows that this action can never be purely *instrumental*; the men who would use an ideology purely as a means of action, as a tool, find that they have been caught by it, implicated by it, just when they are using it and believe themselves to be absolute masters of it.

This is perfectly clear in the case of a *class society*. The ruling ideology is then the ideology of the ruling *class*. But the ruling class does not maintain with the ruling ideology, which is its own ideology, an external and lucid relation of pure utility and cunning. When, during the eighteenth century, the 'rising class', the bourgeoisie, developed a humanist ideology of equality, freedom and reason, it gave its own demands the form of universality, since it hoped thereby to enrol at its side, by their education to this end, the very men it would liberate only for their exploitation. This is the Rousseauan myth of the origins of inequality: the rich holding forth to the poor in 'the most deliberate discourse' ever conceived, so as to persaude them to live their slavery as their freedom. In reality, the bourgeoisie has to believe in its own myth before it can convince others, and not only so as to convince others, since what it lives in its ideology is *the very relation* between it and its real conditions of existence which allows it simultaneously to act on itself (provide itself with a legal and ethical consciousness, and the legal and ethical conditions of economic liberalism) and on others (those it exploits and is going to exploit in the future: the 'free labourers') so as to take up, occupy and maintain its historical role as a ruling class. Thus, in a very exact sense, the bourgeoisie *lives* in the ideology of *freedom* the relation between it and its conditions of existence: that is, *its* real relation (the law of a liberal capitalist economy) *but invested in an imaginary relation* (all men are free, including the free labourers). Its ideology consists of this play on the word *freedom*, which betrays the bourgeois wish to mystify those ('free men'!) it exploits, blackmailing them with freedom so as to keep them in harness, as much as the bourgeoisie's need to *live* its own class rule as the freedom of those it is exploiting. Just as a people that exploits another cannot be free, so a class that *uses* an ideology is its captive too. So when we speak of the class function of an ideology it must be understood that the ruling ideology is indeed the ideology of the ruling class and that the former serves the latter not only in its rule over the exploited class, *but in its own constitution of itself as the ruling class*, by making it accept the lived relation between itself and the world as real and justified.

But, we must go further and ask what becomes of *ideology* in a society in which classes have disappeared. What we have just said allows us to answer this question. If the whole social function of ideology could be summed up cynically as a myth (such as Plato's 'beautiful lies' or the techniques of modern advertising) fabricated and manipulated from the outside by the ruling class to fool those it is exploiting, then ideology would disappear with classes. But as we have seen that even in the case of a class society ideology is active on the ruling class itself and contributes to its moulding, to the modification of its attitudes to adapt it to its real conditions of existence (for example, legal freedom) – it is clear that *ideology (as a system of mass repre-*

sentations) is indispensable in any society if men are to be formed, transformed and equipped to respond to the demands of their conditions of existence. If, as Marx said, history is a perpetual transformation of men's conditions of existence, and if this is equally true of a socialist society, then men must be ceaselessly transformed so as to adapt them to these conditions; if this 'adaptation' cannot be left to spontaneity but must be constantly assumed, dominated and controlled, it is in ideology that this demand is expressed, that this distance is measured, that this contradiction is lived and that its resolution is 'activated'. It is in ideology that the classless society *lives* the inadequacy/adequacy of the relation between it and the world, it is in it and by it that it transforms men's 'consciousness', that is, their attitudes and behaviour so as to raise them to the level of their tasks and the conditions of their existence.

In a class society ideology is the relay whereby, and the element in which, the relation between men and their conditions of existence is settled to the profit of the ruling class. In a classless society ideology is the relay whereby, and the element in which, the relation between men and their conditions of existence is lived to the profit of all men.

II

In the text I have just quoted [on the feudal mode of production, in *Capital*, vol. III, ch. 47, section ii] we have seen Marx prove that a certain form of combination of the elements present necessarily implied a certain form of domination and servitude indispensable to the survival of this combination, i.e. a certain *political* configuration (*Gestaltung*) of society. We can see precisely where the necessity and form of the political 'formation' is founded: at the level of the *Verbindungen* which constitute the modes of liaison between the agents of production and the means of production, at the level of the relations of property, possession, disposition, etc.[2] These types of connec-

[2] One important specification. The term 'property' used by Marx can lead to the belief that the relations of production are *identical* with legal relations. But law is not the relations of production. The latter belong to the infrastructure, the former to the superstructure.

tion, according to the diversification or non-diversification of the agents of production into direct labourers and masters, make the existence of a political organization intended to impose and maintain the defined types of connections by means of material force (that of the State) and of moral power (that of ideologies) either *necessary* (class societies) or *superfluous* (classless societies). This shows that certain relations of production presuppose the existence of a legal-political and ideological *superstructure* as a condition of their peculiar existence, and why this superstructure is necessarily *specific* (since it is a function of the specific relations of production that call for it). It also shows that certain other relations of production do not call for a political superstructure, but only for an ideological superstructure (classless societies). Finally, it shows that the nature of the relations of production considered not only calls or does not call for a certain form of superstructure, but also establishes the *degree of effectivity* delegated to a certain level of the social totality. Irrespective of all these consequences, we can draw one conclusion at any rate where the relations of production are concerned: they relate to the superstructural forms they call for as so many conditions of their own existence. The relations of production cannot therefore be thought in their concept while abstracting from their specific superstructural conditions of existence. To take only one example, it is quite clear that the analysis of the buying and selling of labour power in which capitalist relations of production *exist* (the separation between the owners of the means of production on the one hand and the wage-workers on the other), directly presupposes, for an understanding of its object, a consideration of the *formal legal relations* which establish the buyer (the capitalist) as much as the seller (the wage-labourer) as legal subjects – as well as a whole political and ideological superstructure which maintains and contains the economic agents in the distribution of roles, which makes a minority of exploiters the owners of the means of production, and the majority of the population producers of surplus-value. The whole superstructure of the society considered is thus implicit and present in a specific way in the relations of production, i.e. in the fixed structure of the distribution of means of production and economic functions between determinate categories of production agents. Or in other words, if the structure of the relations of production defines the economic as such, a definition of the concept of the relations of production in a determinate mode of production is necessarily reached via the definition of the concept of the totality of the distinct levels of society and their peculiar type of articulation (i.e. effectivity).

In no sense is this a formal demand; it is the absolute theoretical condition governing the definition of the *economic* itself. It is enough to refer to the innumerable problems raised by this definition where modes of production other than the capitalist one are concerned to realize the decisive importance of this recourse: Marx often says that what is hidden in capitalist society is clearly visible in feudal society or in the primitive community, but precisely in the latter societies we can clearly see that *the economic is not directly and clearly visible*! – just as in these same societies we *can also clearly see* that the degree of effectivity of the different levels of the social structure *is not clearly visible*! Anthropologists and ethnologists 'know' what to confine themselves to when, seeking the economic, they come upon kinship relations, religious institutions, etc.; specialists in medieval history 'know' what to confine themselves to when, seeking for the dominant determination of history in the 'economy', they find it in politics or religion.[3] In all these cases, there is no *immediate* grasp of the economic, there is no raw economic 'given', any more than there is any immediately 'given' effectivity in any of the levels. In all these cases, the identification of the economic is achieved by *the construction of its concept*, which presupposes a definition of the specific existence and articulation of the different levels of the structure of the whole, as they are necessarily implied by the structure of the mode of production considered. To construct the concept of the economic is to define it rigorously as a level, instance or region of the structure of a mode of production: it is therefore to define its peculiar *site*, its *extension*, and its *limits* within that structure; if we like to return to the old Platonic image, it is to 'divide up' the region of the economic correctly in the whole, according to its peculiar

[3] Cf. Godelier's article 'Objet et méthode de l'anthropologie économique' (*L'Homme*, October 1965, and in *Rationalisté et irrationalisté en économie*, Paris 1966).

'articulation', *without mistaking this articulation*. The 'division' of the 'given', or empiricist division, always mistakes the articulation, precisely because it projects on to the 'real' the arbitrary articulations and divisions of its underlying ideology. There is no correct division and therefore no correct articulation, except on condition of possessing and therefore constructing its concept. In other words, in primitive societies it is not possible to regard any *fact*, any *practice* apparently unrelated to the 'economy' (such as the practices which are produced by kinship rites or religious rites, or by the relations between groups in 'potlatch' competition), *as rigorously economic*, without first having constructed the concept of the differentiation of the structure of the social whole into these different practices or levels, without having *discovered* their peculiar meaning in the structure of the whole, without having identified in the disconcerting diversity of these practices the *region* of economic practice, its configuration and its modalities. It is probable that the majority of the difficulties of contemporary ethnology and anthropology arise from their approaching the 'facts', the 'givens' of (descriptive) ethnography, without taking the theoretical precaution of constructing the concept of their object: this omission commits them to projecting on to reality the categories which define the economic for them in practice, i.e. the categories of the economics of contemporary society, which, to make matters worse, are often themselves empiricist. This is enough to multiply aporia. If we follow Marx here, too, this detour via primitive societies, etc., will only have been necessary in order to see clearly in them what our own society hides from us: i.e., in order to *see clearly* in them that the economic is *never clearly visible*, does not coincide with the 'given' in them any more than in any other reality (political, ideological, etc.). This is all the more 'obvious' for the capitalist mode of production in that we know that the latter is the mode of production in which *fetishism* affects the economic region *par excellence*. Despite the massive 'obviousness' of the economic 'given' in the capitalist mode of production, and precisely because of the 'massive' character of this fetishised 'obviousness', the only way to the essence of the economic is to construct its concept, i.e. to reveal the *site* occupied in the structure of the whole by the region of the economic, therefore to reveal the articulation of this region with other regions (legal-political and ideological superstructure), and the degree of *presence* (or effectivity) of the other regions in the economic region itself. Here, too, this requirement can be faced directly as a positive theoretical requirement: it can also be omitted, and it then reveals itself in peculiar effects, either theoretical (contradictions and thresholds in the explanation) or practical (e.g. difficulties in planning techniques, whether socialist or capitalist). That, very schematically, is the first conclusion we can draw from Marx's determination of the economic by the *relations of production*.

The second conclusion is not less important. If the relations of production now appear to us as a regional *structure*, itself *inscribed* in the structure of the social totality, we are interested in this because of its *structural* nature. Here both the mirage of a theoretical anthropology and the mirage of a homogeneous space of *given* economic phenomena dissolve simultaneously. Not only is the economic a structured region occupying its peculiar place in the global structure of the social whole, but even in its own site, in its (relative) regional autonomy, it functions as a regional *structure* and as such determines its elements. Here once again we find the results of the other papers in this book: i.e. the fact that the structure of the relations of production determines the *places* and *functions* occupied and adopted by the agents of production, who are never anything more than the occupants of these places, in so far as they are the 'supports' (*Träger*) of these functions. The true 'subjects' (in the sense of constitutive subjects of the process) are therefore not these occupants or functionaries, are not, despite all appearances, the 'obviousnesses' of the 'given' of naïve anthropology, 'concrete individuals', 'real men' – but *the definition and distribution of these places and functions. The true 'subjects' are these definers and distributors: the relations of production* (and political and ideological social relations). But since these are 'relations', they cannot be thought within the category *subject*. And if by chance anyone proposes to reduce these relations of production to relations between men, i.e. '*human relations*', he is violating Marx's thought, for so long as we apply a truly critical reading to some of his rare ambiguous formulations, Marx shows in the greatest depth that the *relations* of production (and political and ideological social relations) are irreducible to any anthropological inter-subjectivity – since they only combine agents and objects in a specific structure of the distribution of relations, places and functions, occupied and 'supported' by objects and agents of production.

It is clear once again, then, how the *concept* of his object distinguishes Marx radically from his predecessors and why criticisms of him have run wide of the mark. To think the concept of production is to think the concept of the unity of its conditions: the mode of production. To think the mode of production is to think not only the material conditions but also the social conditions of production. In each case, it is to produce the concept which governs the definition of the economically 'operational' concepts (I use the word 'operational' deliberately, since it is often used by economists) out of the concept of their object. We know which concept in the capitalist mode of production expressed the fact of capitalist relations of production in economic reality itself: *the concept of surplus value*. The unity of the material and social conditions of capitalist production is expressed by the direct relationship between variable capital and the production of surplus-value. The fact that surplus-value is not a measurable reality arises from the fact that it is not a thing, but the concept of a relationship, the concept of an existing social structure of production, of an existence visible and measurable *only in its 'effects'*, in the sense we shall soon define. The fact that it only exists in its effects does not mean that it can be grasped completely in any one of its determinate effects: for that it would have to be *completely present* in that effect, whereas it is only present there, as a structure, in its *determinate* absence. It is only present in the totality, in the total movement of its effects, in what Marx calls the 'developed totality of its form of existence', for reasons bound up with its very nature. It is a relation of production between the agents of the production process and the means of production, i.e. the very structure that dominates the process in the totality of its development and of its existence. The *object* of production, the land, minerals, coal, cotton, the *instruments of production*, tools, machines, etc., are '*things*' or visible, assignable, measurable realities: they are not *structures*. The relations of production are structures – and the ordinary economist may scrutinize economic 'facts' (prices, exchanges, wages, profits, rents, etc., – all those 'measurable' facts) as much as he likes; he will no more 'see' any *structure* at that level than the pre-Newtonian 'physicist' could 'see' the law of attraction in falling bodies, or the pre-Lavoisierian chemist could 'see' oxygen in 'dephlogisticated' air. Naturally, just as bodies were 'seen' to fall before Newton, the 'exploitation' of the majority of men by a minority was 'seen' before Marx. But the concept of the economic 'forms' of that exploitation, the concept of the economic existence of the relations of production, of the domination and determination of the whole sphere of political economy by that *structure* did not then have any theoretical existence. Even if Smith and Ricardo did 'produce', in the 'fact' of rent and profit, the 'fact' of surplus value, they remained in the dark, not realizing what they had 'produced', since they could not think it in its concept, nor draw from it its theoretical consequences. They were a hundred miles away from being able to *think* it, since neither they nor the culture of their time had ever imagined that a 'fact' might be the existence of a *relation* of 'combination', a relation of complexity, consubstantial with the entire mode of production, dominating its present, its crisis, its future, determining as the law of its structure the entire economic reality, down to the visible detail of the empirical phenomena – while remaining *invisible* even in their blinding obviousness.

6

Structuralism and Marxism

MAURICE GODELIER

We can now see the epistemological conditions of a scientific analysis of the various means of production and the relations between economics and society gradually being defined and restored. An analysis of this kind is only possible when real structures are taken into account, remembering not to confuse, as empiricism does, the real with the visible; we also need a materialist approach without reducing the various structures and examples of social reality to the epiphenomena of man's material relations with his environment. If anthropology must be structural and materialist in order to be thoroughly scientific, should it not be inspired by the works of Claude Lévi-Strauss as much if not more than those of Marx? Though Lévi-Strauss devotes little space to the study of economics, it is vital to make a very close analysis of the main points of his methods of structural analysis and his study of both the relations between economics and society and society in relation to history, in order to evaluate the theoretical significance and limits of his materialist structuralism and to understand the difference between the thought of Lévi-Strauss and Marx.

There are two methodological principles, recognized by functionalism, structuralism and Marxism alike, which are basic to the scientific study of social facts. The first stipulates that analyses of social relations must not be analysed in isolation, but considered in their reciprocal relationships – as entities forming 'systems'. The second stipulates that these systems must be analysed in their internal logic prior to analysing their genesis and evolution. In a way these two principles mean that modern scientific thought has to confront

Excerpt from Maurice Godelier, *Perspectives in Marxist Anthropology*. Translated by Robert Brain. (Cambridge: Cambridge University Press, 1977) pp. 44–51. Reprinted by permission of Cambridge University Press.

nineteenth-century evolutionism, historicism and diffusionism, in so far as these doctrines – in spite of differing concepts as to the evolution of societies – were often content with a superficial analysis of the real functioning of customs and institutions within the societies studied, and the bulk of their efforts were devoted to unearthing their origins and retracing their history through earlier stages of this purely conjectural evolution of mankind. But, apart from this agreement, which only concerns the abstract formulation of these two principles and not the concrete facts of putting them into practice, there is a total opposition between functionalism, as against structuralism, and Marxism when it comes to understanding the term 'social structure'. For Radcliffe-Brown and Nadel, a social structure is the 'order, the arrangement' of man's apparent relationships, an arrangement derived from the reciprocal complementarity of these relationships.[1] For functionalists, therefore, 'structure' is one 'aspect' of the real; they maintain that this reality exists outside the human mind. For Leach, on the other hand, structure is an ideal order which the mind brings to things converting the multiform flux of the real to simplified representations which allow reality to be grasped; it has pragmatic value and permits action and social practice.[2]

For Lévi-Strauss, structures are part of reality, are reality in fact, and here he is in agreement with Radcliffe-Brown and in opposition to the idealist empiricism of Leach. However, for Lévi-Strauss, as well as for Marx, structures are not directly

[1] Radcliffe-Brown, in D. Forde and A. R. Radcliffe-Brown (eds.), *African Systems of Kinship and Marriage*, p. 82. 'The components of the social structure are human beings', the social structure itself being 'an arrangement of persons in relationships institutionally defined and regulated.' F. Nadel, *The Theory of Social Structure*, 'Preliminaries'.

[2] E. Leach: *Political Systems of Highland Burma*, pp. 4–5, Introduction: 'I hold that social structure in practical situations (as contrasted with the sociologist's abstract model) consists of a set of ideas about the distribution of power between persons and groups of persons.' Then turning away from the model of informants to that of the anthropologist, Leach, somewhat like Radcliffe-Brown, states: 'We may discuss social structure simply in terms of the principles of organisation that unite the component parts of the system.' And in conclusion, as distinct from Radcliffe-Brown: 'The structures which the anthropologist describes are models which exist only as logical constructions in his own mind.'

visible or observable realities, but levels of reality which exist beyond man's visible relations and whose functioning constitutes the deeper logic of a social system – the underlying order by which the apparent order must be explained. This is the meaning of Lévi-Strauss's famous formula, which Leach and some structuralists have insisted on interpreting in an idealist and formalist sense. They prefer the first to the second phrase: 'The term "social structure" has nothing to do with empirical reality but with models which are built up after it. . . . social relations consist of the raw materials out of which the models making up the social structure are built.'

In replying to Maybury-Lewis, Lévi-Strauss had already insisted on the fact that:

> Ultimate proof of the molecular structure is provided by the electron microscope which enables us to see the *actual* molecules. This feat does not mean that in the future the molecule will become more visible to the naked eye. Similarly, it is pointless to expect that structural analysis will change the *perception* of concrete social relations. It will only explain them better.

And in his introduction to *From Honey to Ashes*, he again asserts in categorical terms:

> I have thus completed my demonstration of the fact that, whereas in the public mind there is frequently confusion between structuralism, idealism and formalism, structuralism has only to be confronted with true manifestations of idealism and formalism for its own deterministic and realistic inspiration to become clearly manifest.

In order to analyse structures whose reality, he claims, lies outside the human mind beyond the superficial aspect of social relations, Lévi-Strauss puts forward three methodological principles. He considers that:

(*a*) all structure is a determined ensemble of relations all connected according to internal laws of change which have yet to be discovered;
(*b*) all structure combines specific elements, which are its proper components and that for this reason it is useless to insist

on 'reducing' one structure to another or 'deducing' one structure from another;
(*c*) among different structures belonging to the same system, there is a relationship of compatibility whose laws must be discovered, but this compatibility should not be regarded as the effect of essential selection mechanisms for the success of a biological process of environmental adaptation.

It is obvious that Marx was working along the same lines when, after showing that economic categories of wages, profit and income are defined and dealt with in daily life by agents of the capitalist mode of production, he declares that these things express the visible relations between owners of labour, owners of capital and owners of land; they have a pragmatic value in this sense, as Leach would say, since they permit the organization and direction of these visible relations without having any scientific value; they conceal the fundamental fact that profit and income for one person is the unpaid labour of others:

> The *final pattern* of economic relations as seen *on the surface*, in their real existence and consequently in the conceptions by which the bearers and agents of these relations *seek to understand* them, is very much different from, and indeed quite the reverse of, their *inner but concealed essential pattern* and the *conception corresponding* to it.[3]

It must also be remembered that Marx's theoretical greatness was in demonstrating that industrial and commercial profits, financial interest and income from land – which seem to come from totally different sources and actions – are so many *distinct* yet *changed* forms of surplus value. They are forms of distribution among the different social groups which form the capitalist class, distinct forms of the global process of capitalist exploi-

[3] Karl Marx, *A Contribution to the Critique of Political Economy*, p. 20. '. . . these relations of production correspond to a given stage in the development of the material forces of production. The totality of these relations of production constitutes the economic structure of society – the real foundation, on which legal and political superstructures arise and to which definite forms of social consciousness correspond.' And in *Capital*, vol. I, p. 82: 'Don Quixote long ago paid the penalty for wrongly imagining that knight-errantry was equally compatible with all the economic forms of society.'

tation of wage-earning producers.

We know in fact that Marx was the first to formulate a hypothesis about the presence of essential relations of correspondence and structural compatibility between the forces of production and relations of production, as also between the mode of production and superstructures, without any intention of reducing the former to being merely epiphenomena of the latter. Does Lévi-Strauss's structuralism merge into Marx's historical materialism? It would seem so. But in order to answer this question, it is essential to get nearer to what Lévi-Strauss understands by history and to understand his ideas on causality in economics, as well as seeing how he has applied them in theoretical practice.

For Claude Lévi-Strauss, it is 'tedious as well as useless, in this connection, to amass arguments to prove that all societies are in history and change: that this is so is patent.'[4] History is not only 'histoire "froide"', where 'societies which create the minimum of disorder . . . tend to remain indefinitely in their initial state.'[5] It is also made from 'non-recurrent chains of events whose effects accumulate to produce economic and social upheavals'.[6] To explain these changes, Claude Lévi-Strauss accepts 'the incontestable primacy of infrastructures' as 'a law of order'.[7]

> I do not at all mean to suggest that ideological transformations give rise to social ones. Only the reverse is in fact true. Men's conception of the relations between nature and culture is a function of modifications of their own social relations . . . We are merely studying the shadows on the wall of the Cave.[8]

And Lévi-Strauss himself claims that, with his studies on myths and the 'savage mind', he wants 'to contribute' to a theory of superstructures hinted at by Marx.[9] We can only note that these theoretical principles are contradicted in *From Honey to Ashes*, where he discourses on the fundamental historical

[4] C. Lévi-Strauss, *The Savage Mind*, p. 234.
[5] C. Lévi-Strauss, *Conversations with G. Charbonnier*, p. 33.
[6] C. Lévi-Strauss, *The Savage Mind*, p. 235.
[7] Ibid., p. 130.
[8] Ibid., p. 117.
[9] C. Lévi-Strauss, *La Pensée sauvage*, 1962, p. 178.

turmoil in ancient Greek society, 'when mythology gave way to philosophy and the latter emerged as the necessary precondition of scientific thought'. Here we see 'one historical occurrence, which can have no meaning beyond its actual happening at that place and in that time'.[10] History, however, subject to a law of order by which the whole of society is organized, remains deprived of all necessity and the origins of western philosophy and science are explained away as simple accidents. 'I am not rejecting history. On the contrary, structural analysis accords history a paramount place, the place that rightfully belongs to that irreducible contingency without which necessity would be inconceivable.'[11] And Claude Lévi-Strauss quoted Tylor's phrase of 1871 for his epigraph to *Elementary Structures of Kinship*: 'The tendency of modern inquiry is more and more towards the conclusion that if law is anywhere, it is everywhere.' With this he finally finds himself in agreement with empiricism which sees in history a mere succession of accidental events.

> To return to ethnology, it was one of us – E. R. Leach – who remarked somewhere that 'the evolutionists never discussed in detail – still less observed – what actually happened when a society in Stage A changed into a society at Stage B; it was merely argued that all Stage B societies must somehow have evolved out of Stage A societies.'[12]

Now we have come back to the same standpoint as the functionalist empiricist.[13] 'The historian has changes, the anthropologist structures,' and this is because the changes, 'the processes are not analytical objects, but the particular way in

[10] C. Lévi-Strauss, *From Honey to Ashes*, p. 473.

[11] Ibid., p. 474.

[12] C. Lévi-Strauss, 'Les limites de la notion de structure en ethnologie', *Sens et usage au terme structure*, ed. Roger Bastide, p. 45. The passage from Leach quoted by Lévi-Strauss comes from *Political Systems of Highland Burma*, p. 283.

[13] The same as Leach, who states clearly: 'The generation of British anthropologists of which I am one has proudly proclaimed its belief in the irrelevance of history for the understanding of social organisation . . . We functionalist anthropologists are not really 'antihistorical' by principle; it is simply that we do not know how to fit historical materials into our framework of concepts.' E. Leach, *Political Systems of Highland Burma*, p. 282.

which temporality is experienced by a subject:'[14] a thesis in radical opposition to the thesis of the law of order in social structure and their changes, which Lévi-Strauss took from Marx.

How does he arrive at this point? How can he obliterate, *annul* in his *practice*, those theoretical principles to which he refers, but which evidently remain largely inoperative? Here we are not going to make an internal analysis of Lévi-Strauss's work and we make no claims to estimate their scientific value. But let us admit straight away that his work has made an impact in two domains, those of kinship theory and ideological theory, and that all progress now has to be made with the help of his successes as well as his failures. Fundamental questions such as the incest prohibition, exogamy and endogamy, cross-cousin marriage, dual organizations which were formerly treated separately and inadequately have all been linked together and explained as deriving from the basic fact of marriage as an exchange, the exchange of women; and that kinship relations are primarily relations between groups rather than relations between individuals. In distinguishing two possible mechanisms of exchange, restricted exchange and generalized exchange, Lévi-Strauss discovered an *order* in a vast ensemble of kinship systems which before seemed to have little in common and which were part of societies which had had no historical contact. And this order is an order of transformation. A huge Mendelian tableau of 'types' of kinship systems was gradually constructed. This tableau does not cover the 'complex' kinship structures, which only define a limited circle of kin, leaving other mechanisms, such as economics or psychology, the process of determining the interconnection.[15]

Nevertheless, structural analysis, while not denying history, cannot go hand in hand with it, since it has separated the analysis of 'types' of kinship relations from the analysis of their 'functions'. These functions are neither ignored nor denied, but they are never explored for what they are. And so the question of any *real articulation* between kinship relations and other social

[14] C. Lévi-Strauss, 'Les limites de la notion de structure en ethnologie', p. 44.

[15] C. Lévi-Strauss, *Les Structures élémentaires de la parenté*, PUF, 1949, p. ix.

structures which characterize historically determined, concrete societies is never analysed: Lévi-Strauss confines himself to extracting from concrete facts a 'formal system' of kinship relations, a system which he then studies in its internal logic and compares with other types, either similar or different, but belonging, even in their differences, to the same group of transformations.

In this connection, it could be said that Lévi-Strauss, unlike the functionalists, never studies real societies and does not try to account for their diversity or internal complexity. Of course, it is not that he is unaware of these problems, but he has never treated them systematically. Thus, concerning Murdock's correlation of patrilineal institutions and 'highest levels of culture', Lévi-Strauss declares:

> It is true that in societies where political power takes precedence over other forms of organization, the duality which would result from the masculinity of political authority and the matrilineal character of descent could not subsist. Consequently, societies attaining this level of political organization tend to generalize the paternal right.[16]

In spite of the woolly notion 'stage of political organization', Lévi-Strauss is here confronting the fact of the emergence, historically, of societies within which kinship relations are no longer playing a dominant role, and instead politico-ideological relations are beginning to take over. Why and under what circumstances did it become so? Why are patrilineal rights more compatible with this new type of social structure? Lévi-Strauss does not answer these questions, nor does he even explain under what circumstances such societies appear – societies in which kinship systems and marriage have little or nothing to say about the kind of person one may marry. Allusion is made to the fact that in these societies, wealth, money, bridewealth and social hierarchy play a determining role in the choice of marriage partners; but how is this so, and where does history come into it? Not that history, for a Marxist,

[16] *Elementary Structures of Kinship*, p. 116. Lévi-Strauss refers to G. P. Murdock's text, 'Correlation of Matrilineal and Patrilineal Institutions', *Studies in The Science of Society*, presented to A. G. Keller, New Haven, 1937.

is a category which explains; on the contrary, it is a category that has to be explained. Historical materialism is not another 'model' of history, nor another 'philosophy' of history. It is primarily a theory of society, a hypothesis about the articulation of its inner levels and about the specific hierarchical causality of each of these levels. And when it is able to discover the types and mechanisms of this causality and articulation, Marxism will show its ability to be a true instrument of historical science.[17]

To have more understanding on this point, we have to go beyond a structural analysis of kinship forms and the uncovering of formal codes and a grammar of Amerindian myths. These structural analyses may be indispensable, but they are not sufficient in themselves. Lévi-Strauss recognizes this himself when he criticizes with justification the principle of looking solely at the accidental events of history and at the diffusion of exogenous causes, for the *raisons d'être* of a kinship system:

> 'A *functional* system, e.g. a kinship system, can never be interpreted in an integral fashion by diffusionist hypotheses. The system is bound up with the *total structure* of the society employing it and consequently its nature depends more on the *intrinsic* characteristics of such a society than on cultural contacts and migrations.'[18]

In order to go beyond a structural analysis of the types of social relations or modes of thought, we must practise this kind of morphological analysis in such a way as to discover the intrinsic connection between *form, function, mode of articulation and*

[17] Karl Marx, Letter to the Editor of *Otechestvenniye Zapisky*, late 1877, addressed to Chukovsky in reply to Mikhailovsky, one of the Narodnik socialist party leaders: 'But that is too little for my critic. He feels obliged to transform my sketch of the origins of capitalism in Western Europe into a historical-philosophical theory of a universal movement necessarily imposed upon all peoples, no matter what the historical circumstances in which they are placed, and which will lead, in the last resort, to an economic system in which the greatly increased productivity of social labour will make possible the harmonious development of man. But I must protest. He does me too much honour, and at the same time discredits me.' *Marx-Engels Correspondence*, Lawrence & Wishart, 1956.

[18] C. Lévi-Strauss, *Elementary Structures of Kinship*, p. 390. [Godelier's italics. Tr.]

conditions for the appearance and transformation of these social relations and the ways of thinking in specific societies studied by historians and anthropologists. In our opinion, it is only by a resolute involvement along these lines that we may hope to make any progress in a scientific analysis of a field usually neglected or maltreated by materialists, and where idealism, whether it derives from functionalism or structuralism, for this very reason has a privileged role. In the same way this is how we shall make progress in the field of ideology and, as a result, as far as symbolic forms of social relations and practice are concerned.

Elsewhere,[19] we have shown how Lévi-Strauss has made enormous advances in a theory of ideologies, which he has tried to develop along Marxist lines; using Amerindian myths, he revealed in precise detail that all those elements of ecological, economic and social reality are transposed into the myths, showing that they are the thoughts of men living in specific social and material relations. At the same time, he also reveals that, at the core of this mode of social thought, there is present and functioning a formal logic of analogy, i.e. the activity of human thought which reasons about the world and organizes the content of experience in nature and society into symbolic forms of metaphor and metonym. In fact, Lévi-Strauss, even should he take exception to the interpretation, has brought together under his unique phrase 'la pensée sauvage' a dual content; one refers to nature, that is to say to formal capacities of the mind whereby reasoning is done by analogy, and by equivalence, more generally, to 'pensée à l'état sauvage', 'a direct expression of the structure of the mind (and behind the mind, probably, of the brain)'.[20] The other element refers to 'la pensée des sauvages', to the way men think while they are actually hunting, fishing, or gathering honey, growing cassava or maize and living in bands or tribes. But what is neglected and missing from this gigantic theoretical exercise is an analysis of the articulation of form and content, of thought in

[19] Maurice Godelier, 'Mythe et histoire, réflexions sur les fondements de la pensée sauvage', *Les Annales*, special issue, 'Histoire et structure', August 1971, pp. 541–68.

[20] C. Lévi-Strauss, *Totemism*, p. 163.

its 'savage' state and the thought of 'savages', the social functioning of these representations and the symbolic practices which accompany them, the transformation of these functions and their content, the circumstances of their transformation. Finally, that which exists as a *void* in thought, which is like keeping an object of thought outside thought itself, is an analysis of forms and fundamentals in the 'fetishization' of social relations, an analysis which few Marxists have attempted; and on which depends not only a scientific explanation of political and religious elements in general, but also and foremost an explanation of the circumstances and stages of development of rank, caste or class societies, and even an explanation for the disappearance from history of former classless societies. It is precisely in order to achieve this complex task, a task which presupposes a combination of multiple theoretical practices, that Marx's hypothesis on the determination of types of society, and their evolution and modes of thought by the conditions of production and *reproduction* in material life, must be used as the central hypothesis: 'The history of religion itself, without its material basis, lacks criteria. Indeed, by analysis, it is easier to discover the content, the terrestrial nucleus of religion's mist-enveloped conceptions than, conversely, it is to reveal how the actual conditions of life gradually assume an ethereal form.'[21] We hope we have shown, despite appearances and contradictory statements, that it is to this central hypothesis that functionalism and structuralism must necessarily lead, as soon as they start penetrating more deeply into the logic of the societies under analysis.[22]

[21] Karl Marx, *Le Capital*, vol. I, sect. 4, ch. 15, Ed. Sociales, vol. 2, p. 50. (trans. from French).

[22] One cannot but admire the offhand way in which Edmund Leach, having shown that the analysis of property relations is 'of the utmost importance' for his general argument, writes in *Political Systems* . . . (op. cit., p. 141): 'In the *last* analysis the power relations in *any* society must be *based* upon the control of real goods and the primary sources of production, but this Marxist generalization does not carry us very far.' (!) [Godelier's italics. Tr.]

7
Marx's Political Economy

MEGHNAD DESAI

. . . the previous chapters have concerned themselves with clarifying, explaining and sometimes developing Marx's economic theory. Not surprisingly, the dominant theme is of a competitive capitalism, accumulating and revolutionizing technology without interruption. In this stylized model of nineteenth-century competitive capitalism, the state hardly gets a mention either for its economic or its social and political role. By the same token, the workers enter into a wage contract where wage is fixed prior to and independent of the type of work they perform. Trade union organization, rise of social democratic parties (in the early sense of the word), impact of social reform legislation and the growth of political democracy are all post-Marxian historical phenomena as far as the stylized model is concerned.[1]

In this chapter we shall look at all various problems involved in using the Marxian economic theory to understand contemporary capitalism.[2] This not only raises all the familiar problems of proceeding from an abstract stylized model to a

Excerpt from Meghnad Desai, *Marxian Economics* (Oxford: Basil Blackwell, 1979) pp. 199–213. Reprinted by permission of Basil Blackwell.

[1] This is not to say that trade unions did not exist in the nineteenth century but that their emergence as an important and recognized party in the wage bargain is a post-1914 phenomenon. Similarly, it is not usually appreciated that universal adult suffrage is an achievement of the twentieth century, since the abolition of property qualification, of sex discrimination and of racial discrimination in voting rights (for example in the USA) are very recent accomplishments.

[2] This is not to say that we cannot understand pre-capitalist societies or post-capitalist societies such as the Soviet Union, China or Cuba from a Marxian perspective. Of the many attempts to do this, I shall cite but one. See M. Ellman (1975). He has used Marxian schemes imaginatively to analyze the source of surplus value to finance the Soviet First Five Year Plan.

concrete historical situation, but much more, it raises the problem of the extent to which Marx's model should be updated or revised. Once it is updated or revised, the next task is how to make the transition from the theoretical model to contemporary reality.[3] . . . We now know that Marx addressed himself to questions that Hegel had taken up and offered an outline of an alternative solution as early as 1845–6. By 1846 Marx had arrived at the concept of the proletariat (contrasting with Hegel's notion of Bureaucracy) as the universal class. He had come to look upon private property as a fetter rather than a precondition of free development of human potential. He had also seen beyond Hegel's notion of the German State as the epitome of human development to communism as the ideal.[4]

In this context, we must remember that Marx, like Hegel, accepted the separation of Man (*homme*) and citizen (*citoyen*), the division between State and Civil Society as a fact. This was the Rousseau problem. Hegel thought the French Revolution had failed to bridge the gap, while Marx thought that it had only confirmed the gap. Civil society, the domain of contract and private property, of *economic relations*, was seen to be drifting away from political society and the state and to be developing autonomously. This separation of the economic and the political was caused by the breakdown of extra-economic coercion in economic life that was part of feudalism. The emergence of free labour, as we saw in Chapter II, was a central event in the development of capitalism.

This separation of the economic and the political, of the state from the civil society, was thus a starting-point of Marx's thought. The question of whether such separation was histori-

[3] While the theory-data transition has to be done in all subjects, Marxists discussing these problems have usually made a muddle of it. Marx himself did not keep different levels of abstraction separate. One person to emphasize these separate levels and to attempt to keep them separate is the Japanese scholar Prof. Uno, whose work is relatively little known. See, however, T. Sekine Uno-Riron (1975). An English translation of Prof. Uno's major work is to be published quite soon by Harvester Press.

[4] Some of what follows on Marx, Hegel and the state is a potted version of Joseph O'Malley's excellent introduction to Marx's *Critique of Hegel's Philosophy of Right* (1970). The interpretation of Adam Smith's work is, however, my own.

cally a fact in the early nineteenth century even in an advanced capitalist country such as England is an open question. Adam Smith had, however, shown convincingly that the civil society *could* develop without political interference and perhaps *ought* to do so. From this it was a small step to take as a starting-point for theoretical analysis that indeed the civil society *did* develop independently of the political.

Starting as a political philosopher and developing his arguments as a critique of Hegel's political philosophy, Marx concentrated his efforts increasingly on the understanding of the economic mechanism of the civil society. One can date this shift in his efforts after the failure of the 1848 revolution in France and the restoration of a Bonaparte. The twenty years between 1851 and 1871 were taken up with economic researches. (After 1871 and the collapse of the Paris Commune Marx took up study of the societies on the 'periphery' of the capitalist mode. He studied anthropology and developed an interest in Russia.) Throughout this period, the separation of state and civil society was maintained in his analysis.

This separation is the starting-point of many of the problems we have in updating Marx's analysis. An attitude of absolute reverence to every word he wrote (even when in contradiction with other words he wrote) does not help. But aside from that, the analytical problems are enormous. There is, to begin with, the problem that value categories are not directly perceived. A three-fold account in terms of value, price and quantities, or equivalently of the commodity, money and physical circuits of capital, has to be given. Any crude matching of price, wage and profit data to value measures only makes analysis difficult. This is so even for the competitive capitalist model that is developed independently of political institutions. But if one had to take historical data from the nineteenth century and interpret them in terms of Marxian categories, there is the further problem that, as a historical description, the separation of civil and political society is not accurate. The major role the state played in economic development of Germany, Japan, Italy and Russia in late nineteenth century has been well documented. In France, the state has always played a major role. Only in England, and even there only after 1845 (after the passage of Free Trade legislation and Banking Acts), could one pretend that the state was absent from the civil society. Even in England the state played an active role in maintaining the overseas Empire.

One would need a major theoretical effort at synthesizing the state with Marx's model of competitive capitalism. The role of the state in sponsoring social welfare legislation, due either to the push given by the anti-bourgeois aristocracy, as in Britain, or as a result of calculation, as in the case of Bismarck, is already evident in the nineteenth century. Do we consider this as an attempt to socialize the cost of reproduction of labour power or as a palliative for the reserve army of unemployed? Such a question cannot be answered until one can redefine concepts such as the value of labour power in an abstract model which allows for the role of the state in reproduction of social relations. If the value of labour power is defined in the context of a two-class model with wage bargain as between the individual labourer and the capitalist, then all outside influences will seem arbitrary.

This is also reflected in the crude theory that the state is only an agent of ruling-class interests – a committee for the bourgeoisie. Recent works by Marxian political theorists have emphasized the autonomy of the state, its relative independence of the ruling classes.[5] In a two-class model of the civil society where at the beginning the state has been ruled out, one can introduce the state only by arbitrarily relating it to one class or another. Both at the level of abstract analysis and for understanding historical events this is a wrong approach.

Modern approaches to developing Marxian theory are also compounded by another difficulty. This is that following Hilferding and Lenin, it is said that capitalism entered a monopoly phase in the twentieth century. This monopoly phase is to be understood as being in addition to the class monopoly of ownership of means of production. This monopoly phase was described in terms of increase in size and concentration of industries, of the linkage between them provided by finance capital by Hilferding. Lenin used this concept (in conjunction with Bukharin's theory) to understand rivalry among imperialist powers in the First World War as motivated

[5] Miliband (1977) among others.

by struggle between national capitals for markets. Thus, in the monopoly phase increasing concentration of capital made it possible for Marxists to speak of national capital and to see the state as an agent of national capital in external relations.

Thus a somewhat simple dichotomy emerged. In the competitive phase, the state played a passive role in Marxian models. In the monopoly phase, the state is interlinked with capitalist society. This simple dichotomy has been a serious obstacle to development of Marxian economic theory. First because, as we said above, the separation of the state and the economy in the competitive phase is a simplification which is analytically unsatisfactory and historically inaccurate. On the other hand, it leads to an implicit belief that the competitive phase is the original or natural phase of capitalism. This is reflected in teleological labels such as the highest phase of capitalism, the last phase or the old age (*le troisième age* in Mandel's words) of capitalism reserved for recent periods. But historically capitalism emerged with mercantilism, where the state played an active role in mobilization of economic surplus from trade and empire. The monopoly phase with active role of the state precedes the competitive phase of capitalism historically.

But we have to deal with the analytical problem most of all. The separation of the state and the civil society in one age and the emergence of monopoly capitalism with state involvement are not subsequent stages in the hierarchy of models. We have an analytical model of competitive capitalism, in isolation from the state, in Marx's work, although it has many missing elements. The next step would be an analytical model of monopoly capital or a fusing of competitive model with the state. But we lack any analytical model of monopoly capitalism. We do not know, in other words, how for example the value-price transformation differs in monopoly capitalism from competitive capitalism. We do not know whether the wage relationship is reproduced differently or how accumulation and realization problems interact.

When discussing monopoly capitalism, one often takes the full competitive model and only adds monopoly as a complicating model (indeed as much neoclassical economic theory does). This is done frequently in measuring rates of exploitation from wage data. Or we get a combination of Marxian labels with mainstream economic analysis. Thus the theory of monopolistic competition of Chamberlin is often taken up along with Kalecki's theory as the Marxian theory of monopoly capital. The connection between value and price is severed and profits are linked not to surplus value but to high mark-up above costs maintained by market power. Such is the theory of Baran and Sweezy in their *Monopoly Capital*, which we have already discussed on an earlier occasion.[6]

Mandel in his *Late Capitalism* has put forward a sketch of how monopoly capitalism works. His work covers a broad panorama of developments during the last hundred years but here we shall concentrate on monopoly capitalism. Mandel begins with the idea that the equalization of profit rates across industries is only a long-run tendency. Actual economic movement takes place through uneven development and difference in level of profit rates. This is the dynamic disequilibrium path even in the competitive phase. There may be movements of capital in search of high profits tending to even out differences but this is not actually accomplished. But in monopoly capital, there is not even a theoretical tendency for profit rates to equalize. Although monopolies are never absolute and are subject to forces of competition, there is a constant reproduction of unequal profit rates.

Through accumulation and technical progress, monopoly seeks to make super profits, higher-than-average profits. This may come about through differences in organic composition of capital between enterprises in the monopoly sector and out of it, by forcing down the price of labour and of constant capital purchased from outside and by constant improvements in productivity. Mandel argues, 'In all these cases we are dealing with surplus-profits which do *not* enter the process of equalization in the short term, and so do not lead simply to a growth in the average rate of profit.'

These surplus-profits do not, therefore, go into the pool of profits which are then distributed so as to equalize the rate of profit as in Marx's solution of the value-price transformation. To some extent, surplus-profits of the monopoly sector are due

[6] Desai, *Marxian Economic Theory*, 1974.

to a diversion of surplus value of the non-monopolized sector. Recall that price-value transformation breaks the link between surplus value produced by an individual firm/industry and its profits. Mandel is extending this idea to model the transfer of surplus value from a non-monopoly sector to a monopoly sector.

Thus one can think of an economy in two sectors – monopolized and competitive. They may produce different commodities but not necessarily so. Mandel's model can then be formulated as saying that there is one profit rate prevailing in the competitive sector and that the monopoly sector has either one or many rates which are all higher than the competitive rate. Monopolies sustain (reproduce) the differential profit rate by using barriers to entry, among other weapons. But they face limits to their ability to prevent the equalization of profit rates. Thus, while barriers may be placed against small capitals from within an industry or a country, large capitals from other industries or countries will enter into competition if the differential gets very large. Thus monopoly power is never absolute but always relative. Also it does not always reside in the same firm. A monopolistic firm one day may find itself thrown on the scrap heap of competition by the superior technology of another firm.

Mandel's attempts to provide a numerical scheme to illustrate his thesis (pp. 532–4) are somewhat vitiated by the fact that he adopts both the erroneous price-value transformation method of *Capital* vol. III as well as an arbitrary accumulation behaviour reminiscent of the Scheme for Extended Reproduction of *Capital* vol. II. Thus accumulation rates are assumed without any market logic and input values are not, but output values are transformed into prices. This aside, Mandel tries to state a law of monopoly capital as follows: 'The higher the monopoly profit over the average profit, and the larger the monopolized sector, the faster must the monopoly profit drop to the level of the average social profit operative at the start, or decline together with it' (p. 535).

The only evidence Mandel offers in support of his law is a numerical example, which, as we said above, has many arbitrary features. Still, Mandel's assertion should form the subject of further investigation. Mandel's statements on monopoly capital form part of a wider historical and descriptive investigation. Thus he contrasts phases of long expansion with an undertone of optimism with phases that have an undertone of contraction. These phases are not so regular as to be called cycles and have more than purely economic causes underlying them. Thus the long expansionary phase from 1940–5 till the end of the 1960s could be traced to the weakened position of the working class at the end of the Depression, which led to a reduction in real wage growth, a boost of technological discoveries in the war that brought about the third technological revolution, and to an expansion of the market on an international scale. But in these developments, the state played a large role, guaranteeing the tempo of military investments, especially in research and development, easing the realization problem by fiscal policy and rescuing the loss-making enterprises by subsidy or nationalization.

The growth of state expenditure, viewed benevolently through the quarter-century following the Second World War, is now everywhere being viewed with alarm. Recent experiences of inflation and recession in all the developed capitalist countries have led to divisions among economists and disturbed the confident note of the 1960s. It seemed then that full employment and a more or less steady growth was a permanent feature, with inflation and balance-of-payments disequilibria only niggling worries. The seventies began with the collapse of the Bretton Woods system and witnessed increasing intervention in wage bargains and price setting by governments, the increasing sense of an ecological threat to the maintenance of existing life styles, the massive transfer of economic surplus to the OPEC countries and a period of high unemployment that has now lasted nearly five years.

Increased state expenditure has been linked to inflation by Marxist writers much as the monetarists have done, though their reasoning differs.

Marxist economists have emphasized the constraints put by the total mass of surplus value on total realizable profits. They have often emphasized that fiscal expansion can ease the realization problem but not increase the mass of surplus value. This remains a debatable point. As we said above, the concepts are taken from a purely capitalist model and transposed to the mixed economy. Thus the state's ability to raise surplus value depends on whether one considers public-sector employees productive or unproductive. The purest definition of productive labour that we mentioned in the first part does not permit any government employee (except perhaps in nationalized manufacturing enterprises) to be labelled as productive. Much debate has been generated on this point but this is an instance in which citing chapter and verse from Marx is no help. One needs to understand what role the notion of productive labour plays in the model of pure capitalism and then seek to define similar concepts for the mixed model. Thus in the pure model exchange value of labour power coincides with the wage costs borne by the employer and the income received (and consumed) by the worker. But in an era of social security taxes, deductions for pensions, social and health care and insurance provided from public funds with free or subsidised educational and vocational facilities, there is a wedge between these two sides. What the employer pays, the worker does not receive, at least immediately. What the worker consumes, what reproduces him, is often not paid for by his income. The worker and the employer pay taxes to finance the 'social wage', but just as surplus-value and profits do not coincide for the firm, the payments and receipts do not coincide for the individual worker and often not even for the class. In such a context, it is hard to distinguish who is employed from revenue and who from capital. The complex of taxes and subsidies puts an additional layer of complication to the task of unravelling the price relationships in terms of value categories. What is more, we lack the appropriate value categories to handle the state-economy interaction even in an abstract model.

Much progress is, however, being made on the conceptual and the empirical fronts in this respect. Many economists are coming to grips with the task of unscrambling national income accounts in terms of value categories. On the theoretical side, we should mention James O'Connor's book *The Fiscal Crisis of the State*, which has many points of similarity with Mandel's *Late Capitalism*. O'Connor divides the economy into three sectors – the monopoly sector, the competitive sector and the state sector. The monopoly sector is technologically progressive, with high wages and high relative rate of surplus value where trade unions play an active role in bargaining and where cost-plus pricing is the rule. The technologically progressive nature of the monopoly sector means that even in expansionary phases it expands its employment by small amounts. On average, it sheds labour instead of absorbing it. This labour, along with many less skilled and underprivileged workers (women, immigrants, blacks, youth) form the labour force in the competitive sector. Here the technology is not very progressive and absolute rate of surplus value is the source of profit. Output expands by expanding employment. In this sector unions have to struggle for recognition. It includes the reserve army of unemployed – those who are 'hired last and fired first'. The cost of maintaining the reserve army – unemployment compensation, social security, poverty programmes and so on – is borne by the state sector. The state sector also bears the costs of research and development and the more risky undertakings – costs that are now socialized, though the benefits they generate accrue to the monopoly sector in the form of additional profits that are privately appropriated. The private appropriation of profits and the socialization of costs – costs of maintaining the labour force as well as of education and of research and development – represents for O'Connor the major contradiction that leads to increasing fiscal burden.

The monopoly sector needs the competitive sector as a supplier of reserve labour as well as of raw material and component inputs. The pricing system transfers surplus value from the competitive sector to the monopoly sector. The monopoly sector also needs the state, and its attitudes towards state activity are 'progressive' or benevolent. This is because of the willingness of the state to bear the social costs – social wage and research and development. But the unwillingness of either of the two private sectors to bear the costs in terms of taxation leads to continuous deficits. The state has to accommodate the political demands of surplus labour and of capital and herein lies the nub of the fiscal problem.

Mandel and O'Connor reject any crude theory of the state. They recognize that the state has relative autonomy and that its form does not correspond exactly to the production relationships. O'Connor sees the state as performing the twin tasks of accumulation and legitimation. In its accumulation task, the state's expenditure represents social capital. In this, *social constant capital* represents expenditure that will increase labour productivity and consequently the rate of profit. *Social variable capital* concerns the expenditures that lower the (private) reproduction costs of labour and hence raise the rate of profit. On the other hand, *social expenses* are projects required to maintain social harmony – to fulfil the legitimation function.

Obviously each item of expenditure may partake of one or more such features. But the crucial part of O'Connor's thesis has to do with limitations on the growth of employment in the monopoly sector and of productivity in the competitive sector which puts restrictions on the state's capacity to balance its budget. The state has to spend money on social expenses because of the slow growth of employment due to the failure of the monopoly sector to generate full employment. This is in turn due to limitations on the growth of market demand.

The monopoly sector generates surplus labour, that is, productivity grows faster than total demand and employment falls in the long run. The monopoly sector wages are determined by bilateral bargaining and follow productivity and price-level increases. But this is a high-wage island, entry to which is restricted. Prices in the monopoly sector are on a mark-up basis. But given stagnant or declining employment, and rising prices for its own products, the monopoly sector finds a limited market for its products among its wage-earners. The competitive sector is a sea of lower-wage, less than fully employed workers. Prices have fallen with productivity increases and profits are being constantly squeezed, while wages are determined by market forces of demand and supply in this sector. But, on the whole, the competitive sector does not represent a growing market for the monopoly sector. The terms of trade are going against the competitive sector; hence, its real purchasing power in terms of monopoly-sector products is shrinking. Thus the monopoly sector is producing surplus products to be disposed of either by state expenditure providing a market or by exports. Wages in the state sector are linked to the monopoly-sector wages but productivity does not grow here. This is one of the causes of the fiscal crisis.

O'Connor's book relates much more to US experience than to European experience, but it represents, along with Mandel's work, some common strands of thinking. Thus they both present a picture of differential profit rates in the monopoly as against the competitive sector. They both explore the dependence of the monopoly sector on the competitive sector as well as the dependence of the monopoly sector on the state sector. But both their theories are dependent on limitations of growth of market of the monopoly sector. This has not been satisfactorily demonstrated in their work.

As we said above, Marxists and monetarists have often sounded alike in their attack on Keynesian remedies and on the growth of state expenditure. The monetarists theorize about the natural rate of unemployment as an insuperable barrier that stands in the way of attempts by governments to reduce unemployment and they are sceptical of wage-price controls as counter-inflationary measures. The orthodox Keynesian answer has been to locate inflation in the wage-price spiral caused by trade union militancy and the tendency for wage increases to be passed on to price increases. Both these approaches appear in their Marxist guise in the form of limitations of market due to slow growth of employment and wages or of the mass of social labour. The wage explosion thesis is turned into an attack on capital by workers, as an example of the political determination of wages in the modern society.

The demand for higher state expenditure has traditionally come from working-class organizations. Full employment policies were adopted not merely as a cunning trick by big capital but after considerable struggle on the part of social democratic parties. It was the mobilization of population for the war effort which led in a number of countries, especially in the UK and USA, to the strengthening of this demand. Capitalist societies were now living in a democratic world, as they had not in the nineteenth century. The promises of the First World War – 'a land fit for heroes' – were not fulfilled, and massive deflation following the full employment and inflationary experience of 1916–21 led to unemployment and a long depression in the UK. The US Depression came later, but was none the less a massive blow to living standards. A repetition of such experience in the context of democratic politics, especially after 1945, was unthinkable. Even today, we think of high unemployment not as 10 per cent or 25 per cent but as 5 per cent. While Keynes provided the theory and the policy rules to guide in this task, it was not a demand granted from above but won from below.

This is not just a historical accident. The state has relative autonomy, and this autonomy is strengthened by widely spread franchise and the exercise of political democracy. In societies where either of these conditions are not fulfilled – in the nineteenth-century or in contemporary 'socialist' countries – the state does become 'the committee of the ruling class'. Indeed, it is because the state is perceived as potentially autonomous – an institution which by political action can be made to realize its potential for autonomy – that over the last century trade unions and social democratic parties have concentrated on the demands that the state play a more active role. Thus in securing health care, unemployment benefits, a guaranteed wage, trade union rights, safety at work and so on through government action, the struggle over the past century has quite rightly succeeded. No doubt the capitalist can take advantage of these arrangements and manipulate them for profit, but that is no sign that capital, even big capital, *demanded* full employment and state intervention. The struggle to make these gains more beneficial to the lower-paid will continue, but this does not mean that the gains are illusory.

Even inflation must be seen in a class perspective. During the 1950s and 1960s inflation was viewed benevolently, as it aided personal and corporate wealth accumulation. But over the period, the share of wages in income was also rising. In the UK, at any rate, serious complaints about inflation began when it started to hurt middle- and higher-income groups. The wage-control policies began to narrow differentials (this again being a necessary price for a political incomes policy in a democratic society).

Thus in judging inflation one has to ask who it benefits and who it hurts. An inflation that eliminates the rentier is different from an inflation that hits the poor and unemployed. Similarly, in countering the growing budget deficit, one has to look for what expenditure cuts will mean in terms of their distributive impact on different classes. In the last three years or so, a 'Social Contract' has been accepted without widespread resistance in the UK because inflation has been seen as hurting workers. The idea that 'inflation hurts everybody' and especially the workers, has been conveyed by governments, and it is not entirely false consciousness that has led many to accept this idea.

This shift in attitudes towards state expenditure and inflation can be understood only through detailed analytical and statistical study of the various roles played by the state in the modern economy. Ian Gough (1975) has made one such attempt. He begins with a critique of O'Connor while basically accepting the social capital/social expenses division. He rejects functional theories of the state that assign to it the task of ensuring profitability or legitimation. He rightly criticizes the appellation of unproductive labour for all state expenditure. Such a characterization can be made only if the state is viewed as an appendage to the civil society. Such a view gives no role for the class struggle. This is not to say that the state is completely autonomous or neutral, but that it is potentially so. Without the political background of adult franchise and democracy, as we said above, the state cannot be seen as autonomous.

Gough also points out that the growth in state expenditure was financed without a secular increase in borrowing in the 1950s and 1960s. It is only in the 1970s that the fiscal crisis has been serious, and one must not project recent events backward and forward through time. In the trend of expenditure, armaments have had a declining share and social services – the social wage – an increasing one. There has also been a growth in state aid to private industry and in legal and coercive apparatus. Gough also distinguishes between spending and transfers and counters the commonly held notion that the state takes resources away from the private ('productive') sector.

Gough quite rightly places the growth of state expenditure in a historical and international perspective. Though he does not point this out, some of the state aid to private industry in Europe came as a result of rivalry with American multinationals. It was to protect national capital, often publicly owned, against inroads by the larger, more efficient multinationals. On social expenses, Gough points out that 'the strength of working class pressure can roughly be gauged by the *comprehensiveness* and the *level* of the social benefits' (p. 75).

Any effort to understand contemporary capitalism in a Marxist framework is bound to be fraught with problems. We have concentrated on the need to develop analytical models that can encompass the state and the economy both in the classical competitive and the modern monopolistic competitive forms. But even the model of pure capitalism that Marx left behind was an unfinished one. The uncompleted nature of Marx's work has dictated a number of tasks of clarification and filling in the missing pieces. Thus an integration of money, commodity and physical circuits to provide a theory of crisis and cycles within the assumptions of *Capital* is still an open challenge.[7] We then need to re-examine the separation of state and civil society that Marx took as a starting-point, though his plan of work clearly indicates that he intended to return to the state in future volumes of *Capital*. Then we need to look at the models of 'monopoly capital' that have been put forward and subject them to the same scrutiny that the well-worn parts of Marx's work, such as the Transformation Problem, have undergone. At the same time the task of relating the models to historical data will always remain. There is no shortage of issues to consider.

[7] See the work of Palloix (1977) for use of the three circuits of capital framework.

8

Towards a Sociological Analysis of Property Relations

ANDRAS HEGEDUS

> There is a continual movement of growth in productive forces, of destruction in social relations, of formation in ideas; the only immutable thing is the abstraction of movement – *mors immortalis*.
>
> Marx, *The Poverty of Philosophy*

One of the most characteristic features of the marxist theory of society has been to prove the outstanding importance of the dominant property[1] relations in the life of concrete social and economic formations, and to deduce from these essential relations the existence of historical forces such as classes and class struggles. Marx explained how differing socio-economic formations develop and succeed each other primarily through the changes in property relations which result from these social struggles, and from the development of the forces of production; and he defined the periods of social progress mainly on the basis of the changes that occur in this respect. Therefore, if we wish to analyse the socialist societies of our time on a marxist basis, our main point of departure must be the property relations which have developed in them. And first of all we have to ask whether the problem of property (in the marxist sense) exists in these countries as a vital existential problem for a particular class or stratum, just as the abolition of feudal property relations was an existential problem for the bourgeois classes, or just as in nineteenth-century Europe it was the

Excerpt from Andras Hegedus, *Socialism and Bureaucracy* (London: Allison & Busby, 1976) pp. 93–105. Reprinted by permission of Allison & Busby.

[1] Throughout this essay the words 'property' and 'ownership', 'proprietor' and 'owner' are synonymous, whereas 'possession' is one of the *functions* of 'ownership'.

fundamental interest of the working class to transform bourgeois property relations.

It is especially difficult to examine questions of this kind in the social sciences, because every conclusion which the researcher reaches on the basis of his examination of the facts may collide with certain ideological tenets and even with political interests. But they are the problems which most demand a scientific analysis of social relations, in the interests of both practice and the progress of scientific thought; and they demand that we go beyond the unquestioning adoption of positions.

PROPERTY RELATIONS AS THE 'ORGANIZING PRINCIPLE' OF SOCIAL RELATIONS

According to Marx, property relations are always embedded in society as a whole; that is to say, they do not consist solely in the ownership of objects, but are a kind of central point in the complex system of relationships between different classes and strata. Marx demonstrated that ownership of the means of production is the essential social relationship upon which all the complex interrelations among people are built. As early as *Moralising Critique and Critical Morals*, he wrote that bourgeois private property was 'the sum total of the bourgeois relations of production'. In Oskar Lange's words, this meant that 'the ownership of the means of production . . . is the foundation, or we might say the "organizing principle" which determined both the relations of production and the relations of distribution.'[2] In Marx's approach, the notion of property relations as essential social relations is one of the points of departure for any deep-going social analysis; it must be understood that they are embedded in social relations (mainly productive ones) as a whole. Marx wrote in *The Poverty of Philosophy*: 'To define bourgeois property thus is simply to give an exposition of all the social relations of bourgeois production. To try to give a definition of property as an independent relation, a category apart, an abstract and eternal idea, can be

[2] See Oskar Lange, *Political Economy*.

nothing but an illusion of metaphysics or of jurisprudence.'

This quotation gives rise to two seemingly topical questions. How can one describe socialist property, in socialism, without taking into account all the essential social relations which are dominant in these societies? Why should the attempt to do so be anything but 'an illusion of metaphysics and jurisprudence'?

If we want to know what are the essential social relations of socialist property relations, and whether a basic property problem exists in the socialist countries, then we must first survey all those social consequences in which these property relations are manifested, and in which they assume a concrete form. What I am therefore seeking are the phenomena through which property relations as essential social relations 'materialize' into decisions and social action, in the same way that the immanent, essential attribute of the commodity, its value, expresses itself in the price. I term the exercise of property relations in this sense 'ownership-exercise',[3] and I include the following legal and practical capacities within the scope of this concept; (*a*) the capacity to direct people's activities as the executors of productive labour, i.e. the exercise of *power* and the directing of people; (*b*) the capacity for disposition over the means of production and the structure of production, i.e. the directing of objects; (*c*) the capacity to use, appropriate or at least distribute the surplus product; (*d*) the capacity to alienate and transfer by hereditary means the objects of property, the means of production or financial capital. And if it is not the owner in the juridical sense who practises these capacities, then the question of control over the practice of these rights arises.

In the course of history these capacities to decide and to act, which can be included in the concept of 'ownership-exercise', have not always belonged to the *juridical* owner; either through some legal provision or simply through social custom, the owner may not in fact practise some of the capacities which come under the concept of ownership-exercise – he may have assigned them to others, or they may have been assigned to others compulsorily by society. In various ways, and to a greater or lesser extent, a type of restricted ownership-exercise

[3] This term translates a neologism in the Hungarian, *tulojdonlás*. It must be read throughout this essay in the light of Hegedus's definition here. [Tr.]

has arisen, separate from the juridical owner, mainly in respect of capacities (*a*), (*b*) and (*c*), though not of (*d*). I shall call this restricted type of ownership-exercise 'possession' or 'possessing', in accordance with Marx's terminology.

The essential difference between property and possession is often obliterated, both in everyday parlance and in scientific thinking. Marx spoke about the serf under feudalism being a direct producer who was not a proprietor but only a possessor, and whose surplus labour belonged to the land owner. But Oskar Lange, for example, took property to be a type of possession which is socially recognized and protected, and in fact he put the emphasis on possession:

> The fundamental relationship among men is brought about on the basis of possession of the means of production. What we are dealing with here is not chance possession, but possession recognized by the members of society, which is guarded by the socially recognized rules of human coexistence and perhaps by the sanctions meted out against the contravention of these rules, i.e. by custom and by law. This kind of possession is called property.[4]

But in history, property on the one hand, and possession as restricted ownership-exercise on the other, have often been separated in the way that I have explained. I therefore consider it justified to consider possession to be the manifestation of property relations as an essential relation, in which various forms and degrees of separation from the juridical proprietor may develop.

Unless we are to remain content with the abstractions of jurisprudence or ideology, we must first of all survey those consequences of socialist property relations which manifest themselves in ownership-exercise or possession. The analysis of these consequences is the most important aspect of the sociological examination of property relations, although it must be remembered that just as the price of goods is not exactly identical with their value, ownership-exercise and possession are also mere expressions of property relations as the essential relations of the whole society.

[4] Ibid.

PROPERTY AND POWER

When the notions of property and power are placed alongside each other, they revive debates which are centuries old. Without trying to give any exact definition, I mean by 'power' the legal and practical capacity, supplied by the division of labour, of individual persons or groups to influence the behaviour of other persons with consequences for the latter's livelihood, and to determine their own behaviour themselves. Thus essentially, though with some amplification, I adopt Max Weber's definition, according to which power is 'the chance for one or several persons to assert their own will, within some social relation, against the resistance of other participants'. It will be noted that this indicates a narrower interpretation of power as far as the concept of ownership-exercise is concerned; I exclude the power of objects or reified relations over man, or to use Marx's words, that 'inhuman power which rules over the capitalist too'.

The source of power is property; the source of property is power. The two viewpoints are sharply opposed to each other, and they are the expression of ideologies that have become political and material forces. Marx was faced with the problem that one of the most important outward forms of property relations as essential relations was the development of power relations. The answer which he gave to the question of the relationship between property and power, in his polemic with Heinzen, is still of importance for the sociological analysis of property relations. According to Marx, property relations have primacy over power:

> How the 'acquisition of money' changes into the 'acquisition of power' or 'property' into 'political domination', how between two kinds of power, instead of there being a firm difference (which Mr Heinzen sanctions as a *dogma*), there are on the contrary connections which go as far as being a union, of this Mr Heinzen may quickly convince himself if he takes a look at how the serfs *bought* their freedom, how the communes *bought* their municipal rights, how the bourgeois on the one hand wheedled the money out of the pockets of the feudal lords through trade and industry and changed their landed property into fleeting bills of exchange, and how on the other hand they

> helped the absolute monarchy to victory over the great feudal lords who had been thus undermined, and how they *bought* their titles from them.[5]

In Marx's analysis of *capitalist* society, the supreme problematic was indeed the process through which the 'acquisition of money' turned into the acquisition of power, since the structure of capitalist society arose chiefly as a result of this process. But this in no way implies that the 'acquisition of power' is then *free* from the 'acquisition of money' (in this respect, it is relevant to recall the historical process through which the hierarchic order of the European feudal societies came into being). The mistake of the 'official' marxism of the European social democratic parties consisted precisely in giving primacy to the property relations over the power relations in all circumstances, irrespective of the historical situation, on the assumption that the latter could always be 'bought' by the proprietor. But this kind of mechanical view is far removed from Marx's attitude to history. Marx gave primacy to the property relations in the ontological sense, and above all in the historical emergence of capitalist property: 'the political rule of the bourgeois class is a consequence of those modern production relations which are proclaimed as inevitable and eternal laws by the bourgeois economists.'[6] It must not be forgotten, either, that in the polemic between Marx and Heinzen, power still appeared primarily as political or (in other words) administrative power, which in the form of the state was apparently entirely separate from the property relations. Marx obviously considered it his main task to demonstrate the dependence of the bourgeois 'state', this apparently supreme power, on the property relations. He did not consider it worth debating whether property and power were identical or not: he called them a tautology, 'which is already contained in the words themselves', but continually emphasized that even in its narrower sense, property was the direct or indirect source of power.

[5] See Marx, 'Moralizing Critique and Critical Morals' [Articles published in the *Deutsche Brüsseler Zeitung*, October/November 1847. Ed.]

[6] Ibid.

In the modern capitalist societies, the separation of property from power is not limited to politics but extends to almost every sphere of social and private life, and has become to a large extent a characteristic of economic administration too. In modern capitalism, the proprietor does not only acquire power through the state, which through various mechanisms is separate from him, but he also gives power to others in his own internal sphere, i.e. in the management of the enterprise. One of the phenomena which is most deserving of the attention of marxist analysis is this (partial) separation of property from power in the economic sphere; this is a conspicuous feature in the recent development of Western societies, and it marks them off not only from feudalism but also from classical capitalism. The intrusion of political power into the economic sphere (the state sector) means a certain separation between the essential owner, the capitalist state, and the institutions practising power (which belong to the category of ownership-exercise). And even if this does not change the dominant nature of bourgeois private property, it has brought about a very important modification in the property relations as essential relations, understood in Marx's terms, i.e. not divorced from the social relations but interpreted as an 'organizing principle'.

PROPERTY AND POWER OVER OBJECTS

Disposition over the objective relations of the production process forms an integral part of the exercise of property rights (or what I have termed 'ownership-exercise'), and indicates first of all the determination of the structure of production (what shall be produced), the object of labour (what it shall be produced from), and the means of labour (how it shall be produced).

In pre-capitalist times the owner, or whoever personified him, was often faced with difficulties in his right of ownership-exercise, and was forced to transfer to others not only his power over people but also his power over objects. Typical cases of this were the 'bureaucratic' empires of antiquity and China, where the ruler, personifying the ownership of the state, transferred these rights to a hierarchically ordered state administration. European feudalism provided a basically different solution to this problem: the *seigneur* and the landlord retained their power over their vassals and serfs, but transferred to them almost entirely the right of disposition over objects. It was precisely this kind of feudalism which made it possible for bourgeois private property to emerge, and thereby provided the opportunity for a dynamism of development that was unprecedented in history.

The principal moment in the development of bourgeois private property, besides this disposition over objects, was the achievement of power by the bourgeoisie over itself, which relatively quickly became power over others. It is no accident that the main protagonist in this process was precisely the serf who disposed of these objects. But with the development of bourgeois private property, the right to dispose of objects to others began to be transferred too; the first instance of this was the development of the joint stock company. Although every shareholder in the joint stock company actually disposes of his shares as his property, is entitled to appropriate the surplus value and may sell his shares at any time, the greater part of the ownership capacities nevertheless belongs to enterprise management: the majority of shareholders are unable to participate in ownership-exercise, and often they do not even have real control over the enterprise management which acts in their name. However, the real managers of capitalist enterprises lead the masses of shareholders to believe that they are capable of exercising real control over the managers; this is a special domain in the management of capitalist enterprises, the domain of 'expert manipulation'. (American literature on management sociology provides innumerable examples of this: see, for example, Reinhard Bendix's *Work and Authority in Industry*, 1956.) The separation between the person of the proprietor and actual disposition over the relations of production also extends to the larger forms of private family property, and in this way the management apparatuses which have developed in the capitalist societies are able to exercise power (in the organization of production) and possession (in the objective relations of production) at the same time. In modern capitalism, this has been added to by the increased importance of state property; this gives to certain state organs the kinds of jurisdiction which the administrations of capitalist enterprises have.

PROPERTY AND DISPOSITION OVER THE SURPLUS PRODUCT

There is a close historical link between property, on the one hand, and disposition over the surplus product (the legal and practical capacity to appropriate it) on the other; this is one of the keys to the understanding of the property relations which exist in the current socialist societies. Ever since the possibility of producing a surplus product has existed, social struggles have in the last resort never been fought only for power or for disposition over the objective factors of production, but for the distribution of the surplus product; and the concrete property relations, power structures and various modes of ownership-exercise and possession have developed in this unceasing struggle.

In the course of history, disposition over the surplus product has not always belonged in the final analysis to the proprietor himself, because he has been forced to share this power of disposition either with authorities greater than himself (*seigneur*, monarch, etc.) or with those to whom he has transferred (in the sense mentioned above) his power of ownership over persons or over the objective factors of production. This means, of course, that not only is the actual right of disposition over the surplus product divided, but the surplus product itself is divided too. From this it also follows that the 'division' is a permanent source of conflict between the groups taking part in ownership-exercise.

In classical capitalism, the capitalist himself by and large exercised the right to dispose of the surplus product, just as he held the power of disposition over persons and over the objective factors of production. But this independence was considerably clipped by developments in the last century. On the one hand the capitalist state has taken an increasingly active part in distributing the surplus value (either by siphoning it off or by direct intervention); and on the other hand, the managements of the capitalist enterprises have also been demanding to have a hand in it. (As many Western sociological studies can testify, managements are chiefly interested in the increase of reserve funds and investments, while the capitalists, especially the shareholders, are mainly interested in maximizing dividends.)

THE INHERITANCE OF PROPERTY, ITS ALIENATION, AND CONTROL OVER POSSESSION

One of the most important elements in ownership-exercise is the inheritance and alienation of property, in which the property relations as essential social relations often attain their most pregnant form of expression. That is why I did not include this element in the notion of restricted possession which I applied to the other three capacities of ownership-exercise. The proprietor may transfer his personal power, the right of disposition over the objective conditions of production and the surplus product, or at least part of the latter; but if he renounces the right to alienate his property, he ceases to be a proprietor. On many occasions in history, however, these *sui generis* rights of the proprietor *as* proprietor have been restricted, in most cases in the name of some 'collective' proprietor above him.

The proprietor's control over the possessor must be included among his *sui generis* rights. When we examine the exercise of any kind of power based on property relations and the various forms of ownership-exercise and possession, we must always ask whether there exists some kind of real control over those who dispose of power and exercise possession in the name of the proprietor. And if the answer is yes, we must examine how far this control extends, who or which groups exercise it, and what are the historical roots of their right and capacity to control.

THE EVOLUTION OF THE FORCES OF PRODUCTION AND PROPERTY RELATIONS

The multi-faceted theory of property relations which can be found in Marx's works has been deprived of its concrete nature by the schematism which has become dominant in marxist theory. It has been turned into the system of interconnections of some mystical power, which appears to rule over society as the laws of nature do over the material world. What has been obscured? The supreme importance of social struggle, in which the property relations assume their concrete form, and through which considerably differing types of ownership-exercise and possession develop, even at one and the same level of productive forces. Instead of supplying concrete historical analysis, the simplified conception of marxism has given rise to interpretations stating that the evolution of productive forces changes the property relations by the force of a law of nature, as it were. The necessary result of this view is overemphasis on the importance of the economic sphere, an overemphasis which a great number of marxists have long fought against, and notably Engels, Lukács and Gramsci. Berlinguer[7] draws attention to Togliatti's remarks about Gramsci, that 'he never considered the economic structure to be a mysterious, hidden force from which the various situations developed automatically.' Lenin himself was opposed to the 'official' view on almost every principal question of the strategy and structure of revolutionary social democracy. Although the October revolution was not only victorious over the bourgeoisie but also rendered palpably obsolete the ossification of marxism into a dogma, many of the tenets of this dogmatic marxism nevertheless lived on in the country where socialism had become victorious; it was now difficult not only to analyse the new phenomena in capitalism, but also to carry out any realistic self-analysis of the new socialist societies. We cannot yet give a satisfactory answer to the question of how and by what means, and under the influence of what social forces, schematism had become one of the main planks of official science in the USSR by the end of the twenties, reaching the textbooks themselves during the thirties. It is impossible to ignore its influence on the stalinist theory of socialism, and especially on the tenets referring to property relations. The latter, especially where they touched on the new property re-

[7] Enrico Berlinguer, at the Tenth Congress of the Italian Communist Party, 1962.

lations, were considered irrevocable; their effect on ownership-exercise and possession made any realistic analysis extremely difficult, because the official viewpoint was protected by the severest clauses of the penal code against any attempt at confrontation, however justifiable this confrontation might be.

While this view of socialist property relations was ossified into a dogma for decades, the abolition of private property not only occurred in an increasing number of new countries but also took on increasingly varied forms. In such circumstances it has become a task of primary importance, not only for the social sciences but also for social practice, to examine the newly developed property relations without deliberately overlooking the power structures that have sprung up, the actual possibilities of possession, and the consequent power of disposition over the surplus product.

In this study, I am looking for an answer to these questions only in respect of the present conditions in the *European* socialist countries, and not of an analysis *in general* of every society that has abolished private property. I stress this because, in my view, all the historical conditions are now ripe for overcoming once and for all the idea that property relations, the forms of ownership-exercise and possession and of state organizations, must necessarily be *identical* in every respect in all societies which have abolished private ownership of the means of production, and that every deviation from this pattern is some sort of negative phenomenon. In our era we must also overcome the notion, which was dominant for a time and which in itself was already a way of correcting the 'cult of personality' conception, that some variations which are a result of national characteristics can be recognized, but only within the scope of social laws that are considered to be generally and inevitably valid. In spite of the progressive role that this notion has played in the past, it allows no room for the possibility that different solutions may occur as the result of complex processes of social struggle, and thus that one alternative or another, all differing significantly from each other but all surpassing bourgeois private property to the same extent, may be equally victorious. At the moment, however, when this happens in practice, it is considered by the defenders of the first alternative to be a violation of socialist principles.

THE NEW PROPERTY RELATIONS AS THE NEGATION OF BOURGEOIS PRIVATE PROPERTY

What we know of the property relations which have developed in the socialist societies of Europe consists first of all in a negation: there is no private property, or to put it more precisely, a new property relationship has been created by the abolition of bourgeois private ownership of the means of production, and by various methods such as nationalization, mass collectivization, etc. What this negation actually means can only be decided through a concrete analysis of reality; this is the only way we can find out how far and in what respects the new has in fact surpassed the old. History has seen many kinds of forces which are negative in their *effects*; however important the negation of the prevailing 'establishment' may be at any given time, we certainly cannot identify it automatically with progress or with the quest for power. The question can only be answered if we first take account of the role which bourgeois private property has played in history.

The emergence of bourgeois private ownership of the means of production undoubtedly released powerful forces on to the historical scene, and it was mainly for this reason that mankind's progress began to accelerate at an unprecedented rate. Protestant 'ethics' simply gave the ideological 'green light' to the development of this form of ownership. I believe this needs stressing, because the dogmatic and simplified version of marxism often emphasizes only the negative consequences of bourgeois private property: its anti-humanism, and its inability to function with optimum efficiency. This is dangerous not only because it gives a false view of the (past or present) world which maintains private property, but also because it impairs the realistic analysis of those property relations which prevail in socialism, and hampers any attempt to judge whether what has happened is more than a simple negation and whether it may be considered (and if so, in what sense) to actually surpass the previous conditions.

The importance of bourgeois private property in the development of the productive forces can best be measured by using the historical example which comes from comparing the Asiatic mode of production with post-Renaissance European development. In those countries where, as a result of various historical circumstances, the Asiatic mode of production became the prevailing form, the development of the more advanced forms of private property was blocked (the reasons for this have been analysed sufficiently in the existing literature); it was mainly for this reason that the development of the productive forces was interrupted for a period of centuries. The development of bourgeois private property in Europe, however, brought with it not only an economic dynamism which had been inconceivable in the preceding historical periods, but also social movements which expected the 'common weal' to emerge from the abolition of private property and were ready to fight for this at whatever cost. From the eighteenth century onwards, Europe has been the scene of repeated social endeavours to replace private property with social forms of property, whether by means of specific social struggles or of utopian reforms. But however valuable these experiments have been for the history of mankind, in some way or other and after some period of time they have proved to be unviable. The same fate befell both Fourier's communistic communities and the noble ideas of the Paris Commune.

The overcoming of bourgeois private property has become a reality in our century, but it is far from being a historical necessity which occurs automatically. The progress of the productive forces and likewise of social relations has reached a level where it has become possible to dispense with and replace all the positive aspects which bourgeois property brought with it (and chiefly those to do with the dynamics of development), and to set in motion the kind of driving forces which were unable to evolve in the framework of private property. The relatively advanced level of the forces of production and of social relations in the twentieth century has enabled the previously anarchic and utopian socialist attempts at abolishing and surpassing bourgeois private property to develop into a force spanning the globe, which has now led to the development of new forms of government in many countries.

It follows from this that several kinds of state system may be built in accordance with the property relations which develop after the abolition of private property. Property relations never do determine the form of government unequivocally; this is valid not only for those societies built on private ownership of the means of production but also for the societies which surpass them. This is not because there are no extremely close links between the specific mode of ownership-exercise (the property relations as the outward form of the essential relations) and the state system. Rather, it is because after the abolition of private property, in systems of social economic management which differ according to the objective conditions of the society's existence and according to social struggles (i.e. the people who themselves make history), extremely varied forms have developed and will develop, both of ownership-exercise and of the state system.

This reveals itself in capitalism, too, although bourgeois private property is undoubtedly the dominant form which determines everything else. On the one hand there is a great variety of power structures and systems of siphoning off surplus value. On the other hand, it is also a fact that forms of ownership have developed or survived which differ essentially from each other in their mode of ownership-exercise (co-operative, institutional, state property, etc.); that is to say, here too we may distinguish to a considerable extent between different types of ownership-exercise and possession. When Marx, in his analysis of classical capitalism, foresaw the possibility of abolishing private property and emphasized the historical inevitability of this change, he also sensed that an evolution was taking place within capitalist property relations too; for example, he looked at the development of joint stock companies and at the emergence of various kinds of co-operative in this light. However, history has taken a course which differs considerably from Marx's prognosis. In the more advanced countries, capitalism has been able to adapt itself to the development of the productive forces better than Marx had assumed. Meanwhile the conditions for socialist revolution became ripe in the less advanced countries too, and because of the consistent struggle of the revolutionary forces and the historical circumstances, the overcoming of private property occurred here first.

9
The Materialist Conception of History

RUDOLF HILFERDING

Marx called his conception of history the 'materialist' conception of history. That unfortunate designation has been responsible, in no small degree, for repeated misunderstandings and sterile polemics. But the use of this term is understandable. While transcending Hegel's philosophy Marx remained under the influence of this philosophy, and in 'negating' it he believed that he was still employing its dialectical method. He therefore opposed his 'materialist' conception to idealist speculation, whereas in reality, as Marx himself insists again and again, it is a matter of the opposition between scientific inquiry and philosophical speculation. The object of this inquiry makes Marx's conception of history a *sociological* conception of history. What that means requires closer analysis.

In his Preface to *A Contribution to the Critique of Political Economy*, Marx writes:

> I was led by my studies [of Hegel's system] to the conclusion that legal relations as well as forms of State could neither be understood by themselves, nor explained by the so-called general progress of the human mind, but that they are rooted in the material conditions of life. In the social production which men carry on they enter into definite relations that are indispensable and independent of their will; these relations of production correspond to a definite stage of development of their material powers of production. The totality of these relations of production constitutes the economic structure of society – the real foundation, on which legal and political superstructures

Excerpt from Rudolf Hilferding, *Das historische Problem*. Translated by Tom Bottomore. Published by permission of Dr Peter Milford. The German text of this work, left unfinished at Hilferding's death in 1941, was first published, with an introduction by Benedikt Kautsky, in *Zeitschrift für Politik* (new series) vol. I, no. 4, December 1954, pp. 293–324.

> arise and to which definite forms of social consciousness correspond. The mode of production of material life determines the general character of the social, political, and spiritual processes of life. It is not the consciousness of men that determines their being, but, on the contrary, their social being determines their consciousness. At a certain stage of their development, the material forces of production in society come in conflict with the existing relations of production, or – what is but a legal expression for the same thing – with the property relations within which they had been at work before. From forms of development of the forces of production these relations turn into their fetters. Then occurs a period of social revolution. With the change of the economic foundation the entire immense superstructure is more or less rapidly transformed. In considering such transformations, the distinction should always be made between the material transformation of the economic conditions of production which can be determined with the precision of natural science, and the legal, political, religious, aesthetic or philosophical – in short, ideological – forms in which men become conscious of this conflict and fight it out. Just as our opinion of an individual is not based on what he thinks of himself, so can we not judge of such a period of transformation by its own consciousness; on the contrary, this consciousness must rather be explained from the contradictions of material life, from the existing conflict between the social forces of production and the relations of production.

In the first place, it should be emphasized again that this conception of history (erroneously called 'materialist') does not involve the ontological, metaphysical or epistemological problem of the relation between mind and matter, but only the question of a method which will enable us to attain a scientific knowledge of the historical process.

The relation of historical science to philosophy is exactly the same in principle as that of the physical sciences, biology, or economics. It is the business of epistemology to draw conclusions from the current results of scientific inquiry, and to examine, let us say, what modifications the modern theory of relativity may entail for categories such as time, space and causality, or what philosophical world view – if metaphysical need cannot dispense with one – accords with the findings of social science. But if theology and philosophical speculation at one time laid down certain items of knowledge as being unalterable by scientific research and sought to impose their own methods of cognition as the only admissible ones, the relationship has now been *reversed*. Science forms, quite independently, its own methods of research, and its results constitute the data of epistemology. On the other side, the Marxian conception of history does not imply a commitment to a particular epistemology or philosophical system any more than does, say, biology. What is irreconcilable with science of any kind is *dogma* established by speculation. But the question as to which elaboration of the findings of science in a theory of knowledge is the right one, conforming most closely with the results and the methods of research of science itself, is a separate question which has to be resolved by epistemology.

It is quite comprehensible, therefore, that a Marxist, like a natural scientist, when he adopts a particular position with regard to epistemological problems, cannot do so as a Marxist – since he would then simply propound dogmatic epistemological conclusions of his own – but must do so as an epistemologist. This explains why Marxism as such cannot postulate a specific philosophical view, and why Marxists who concern themselves with these problems are in fact as little able to derive philosophical conclusions, in an *a priori* fashion, on the basis of their specific scientific perspective, as are other scientists. It is impossible to assign Marxism to any particular philosophical system.

The basic concept in Marx's conception of history is the *relation to production*. This is not a matter of a particular relation between an individual and a certain quantity of productive forces, or of the behaviour of an individual in the application of his tools and the use of the land, but the relation of people to each other, that is, the relationships of beings who are *socialized* because they produce, and by the manner in which they produce. The production relation is not, therefore, a mechanical, natural state of affairs, but a social condition 'entered' into by thinking, willing and acting human beings, or to put it more precisely perhaps, a condition in which they find themselves at any given time. Far from the 'forces of production' in their physical, natural state producing in some mystical way the corresponding forms of thought and volition, it is the social cooperation of human beings which turns wood, stones and land – in short, the products of nature – into *productive forces*, to the extent that this social cooperation allows at any given time.

It is the real human being, the thinking, willing and acting man, with his needs and interests, who constitutes the precondition for production relations. That is why the young Marx initially wanted to call his new conception, formulated in opposition to Hegel, naturalist or humanist. For the common element in philosophy after Hegel, which sought to develop his system in a more enlightened way while still working within its framework, was the attempt to substitute for the development of the world spirit the development of real human beings. What distinguishes Marx's thought from the humanism of Feuerbach and others, however, is that he replaces the abstract human being, with his ascribed qualities, by the real, historical human being, who has emerged in specific social conditions, and investigates the law-governed character of these social conditions. Concepts such as 'naturalist' and 'humanist' would have been too narrow, whereas 'materialist', suitably redefined, might have expressed some kind of synthesis of these two concepts.

The production relation, therefore, is the relation of human beings to each other and to the existing forces of production. As such, it is always a property relationship as well, which is only 'a legal expression for the same thing', that is, a legal relationship. The law may be extremely primitive, still uncodified, existing only as a conventional or customary law, but without law there can be no social or production relations. 'Productive forces', then, do not create law or ideas of law in the sense in which, according to a certain kind of materialism based upon natural science (although this is more of a bogy than a theory), specific combinations or oscillations of matter manifest themselves as ideas. On the contrary, natural objects only become productive forces in a relation of production into which human beings enter, under existing, given natural conditions which they continually alter through their social behaviour. A production relation is always, therefore, at the same time a legal relation, and every economic structure has inherent in it a specific property, hence legal, relation.

A legal system, however, is always a power relation, i.e. a

political relation, as well. Law presupposes the power to make it effective. Such power may be rudimentary and limited, traditional and based upon the natural tie of consanguinity, and exercised by one or several of the elders of the clan, but it goes hand in hand with the production relation and is one of its essential elements. It is the force which consciously regulates the production relation – the state power – and its scope and exercise are themselves rooted in the nature of the existing relations of production.[1]

The state is the conscious organization of society, endowed with executive power. By its very nature, therefore, it is a power organization. Its existence poses two problems.

Some social processes are directly subordinated to the commands of the state and are consciously regulated. Others remain outside the sphere of direct state regulation and function on the basis of their own laws, exempt from state control and in that sense autonomous; as for example, the economy, and also the whole of intellectual life in a liberal state (ideally conceived), even though this autonomy can only be exercised within the legal limits established and protected by the state. In every society the question arises concerning, first, the autonomous laws governing the spheres which are not controlled by the state, then the structure and interests of the state power itself, and finally the interdependence and interrelations of these two spheres. These are questions which arise, in principle, in every form of production relation, even the simplest. The struggle between the sphere free of state control and the state power may be of two kinds: it may be a struggle by

[1] Friedrich Engels, on the basis of his studies of prehistory, restricted the concept of the state to organized political power in class societies. Important as the distinction between class and classless society is, it is not easy to see why the supreme organized political power necessarily present in every society should not be called a state, unless one wants to preserve the historically unjustified conception of a production relation unregulated by law and functioning without an executive organ of society. Nevertheless Engels' conception remained for a long time authoritative in the socialist vocabulary, particularly in Germany. It seemed beside the point to speak of a 'socialist state' or a 'people's state', since after the abolition of classes the 'state' would also disappear. It was customary to speak of a socialist society or community and to take a certain pride in being accused by opponents of hostility to the state.

the most powerful and pre-eminent group in the autonomous sector to influence or dominate the state, or a struggle against the state in order to maintain or extend the sphere which is free from state control by limiting the power of the state.

Second, the state develops into a separate power organization with its own organs. As a power organization it acquires a certain *independence* vis-à-vis society, or various sectors of society, and has its own interests: the maintenance and expansion of its power both at home and abroad, the furtherance of those developmental tendencies in the autonomous sphere which conform with its own interests, and the curbing of other tendencies. At the same time, however, the state is subject to the *influences* which emanate from the autonomous sphere of society. The state power is thus an independent factor with its own significance and capacity for action, but on the other hand also a product of society, the forces of which continually strive to determine its conduct. However, it is a mistake to overlook the distinctive importance of the state and to treat it simply as the executive organ of a social group. The interests of the state power should not simply be identified with the interests of a social group, at least not wholly or in every social situation. To a greater or lesser extent, and with varying degrees of effectiveness, the state power is an independent factor in historical development.

The struggles of social groups and classes are in part struggles among themselves, which take place in that sphere which is not controlled by the state and not consciously regulated by society (for example, struggles between workers' and employers' organizations over the division of the labour product, in conditions where freedom of association is legally established); in part, struggles by classes for a *share in the state power*. The power interests of the state are directly affected by the latter struggles, and it intervenes as an important independent factor whenever these interests so require. These interests of the state may indeed coincide with those of social groups, but this need not happen in every case, nor need its interests coincide completely. The result of such struggles, particularly when they have led to a strengthening of state power, can in turn change or modify the interests of those social groups themselves which appeared to dominate the state before the struggles erupted. Such a situation is most likely to occur when there is a certain equilibrium of class forces.

The 'production relation', therefore, is by no means a simple and natural affair. It is neither a mass of natural objects which can serve in production for the satisfaction of human needs, nor the relation of human beings to these objects. For this would remain a purely technical relation, which at the extreme might be conceived abstractly as the relationship of an isolated individual, but which could only develop in historical reality within society. The production relation is always the sum total of the interrelations among human beings, into which they enter, and in which they are placed, in order to be able to produce and so satisfy their needs, maintain and improve their lives. These are the interrelations of human beings socialized for and through production in a definite and specific way. The production relation, the economic structure, is not therefore something given by nature, but a social phenomenon, and as such it is always a legal and political relationship as well, the nature of which is determined by the needs of production. . . .

Marx never elaborated his conception of history in a systematic form. His emancipation from philosophy led at the same time to the rejection of any system such as that of Hegel, in which not only was all previous knowledge summated, but the essence of future development could also be outlined. Marx's conception of history was intended as a *method of inquiry*, and as with every scientific method its value can only be judged, in the last resort, by applying it. The application of his method, as we have seen, has two aspects: an objective analysis of the production relation, and an account of how the state of affairs discovered by this means affects historically relevant action.

The objective analysis which Marx employed is to be found in *Capital*, and the social psychological consequences for capitalist society are then drawn out. The development of the forces of production, imposed by the capitalist laws of competition, concentration and accumulation, breaks through the capitalist laws of ownership, which cease to be a means of increasing the forces of production and become instead a fetter upon their growth. Social antagonisms become ever more acute. The classes which have emerged in the capitalist production relation enter into increasingly bitter conflict. The wage-earning class recognizes that its cultural and material emancipation requires that capitalism be overcome. As a result of the capitalist laws of motion themselves, its numbers and importance in the process of production grow, and along with this its class *consciousness*, the consciousness of its historical task. The working class develops its own political, legal and moral conceptions in opposition to the dominant ideas of bourgeois society. The conflict between these opposed ideas, which has grown out of the social situation and the divergence of interests, leads finally to a social revolution, in the course of a struggle for political power which is indispensable for the transformation of the social order.

Marx was unable to finish the chapter on classes which was to have completed *Capital* and provided a political and historical summing up. He refers to the three great classes of capitalist society: the landowners whose income derives from rent, the capitalists whose income comes from profit, and the wage workers whose income is derived from the wages of labour. But it is also evident from all Marx's formulations that he sees the basis of classes in the immediate process of production, distinguishes between them according to the principal forms of income, determined directly by the process of production, and attributes to them a specific class-consciousness determined by their position in the process of production.

This raises some crucial problems. In addition to the basic classes which are engaged in the production process and have their interests determined by it, the nature of the production relation gives rise to *other social groups*, whose function may be indispensable to the system of production and whose action can have a crucial importance. The most significant element is the state power, with all its different organs, which is indispensable to any production relation. Marx indicated again and again the great importance of 'force' in the origin and transformation of production relations, and his political goal – the conquest of political power by the working class – shows what immense significance he assigned to it. But he does not attribute any autonomy to this power. The state is conceived as the organization of the ruling classes, the nature of its policies being determined by their interests.

Now there are certainly some historical periods to which, in large measure, this conception applies. Such would be the case particularly when a class, with its particular interests, overshadows all other social groups; for instance during the first stage of assuming political power and establishing in a new form, or restructuring, the relations of production, and during the time when its rule is still little contested. During the classical period of English liberalism, for example, the interests of the bourgeoisie, and in particular those of industrial capital, in fact largely determined the policy of the English state. But that does not alter the fact that every state organization also has its *own interests*, the maintenance and promotion of its own power, which are not identical, and need not always coincide, with those of the ruling class. They are interests which may, under certain circumstances, be asserted very vigorously, since the state is a social organization armed with coercive power, and by virtue of its extensive apparatus – the army, the bureaucracy, the judiciary, teachers and professors, and perhaps, the church – is able to exert a great and direct social influence. The possibility of the state asserting its interests independently at any particular time depends upon specific political circumstances; it will be all the greater, the more it is the case, in a given stage of development, that classes or social groups neutralize each other in their endeavours, and in their exercise of the power which they can bring to bear upon the political leadership – in short, the more there prevails that 'equilibrium of class forces' of which Engels spoke.

The growing independence of the state power, its effort to realize its own specific interests in society, is most likely to be successfully achieved when it is a matter of maintaining or *strengthening its own existence*. The struggle against feudalism in order to establish the absolute monarchy, and therewith the modern state, was a struggle of the state power against the ruling class. This struggle was supported by the *bourgeoisie* – or more accurately, by a section of it – which was still a subordinate class. Naturally, a certain degree of economic development – which also meant bourgeois and urban development – had to be achieved, the productive forces of society and hence the growth of wealth outside the feudal sphere had to reach a certain level, before the goal of centralizing the state became possible and could thus be envisaged. Bourgeois wealth had to be in a position to supply the means for creating and maintaining standing armies and a modern bureaucracy, and for developing transport and communications. Only through the development of this economic base did the creation of the modern state become possible. But it was created by state power and its interests. It was supported by that section of the nascent bourgeoisie – by industrial, and to some extent by commercial, capital – which had a strong and conscious interest in the establishment of a centralized unitary state, the abolition of guild restrictions and internal tariff barriers, etc., whereas the bourgeoisie of the guilds, and the peasantry which was still dominated by feudal lords, remained passive. But the initiator and sponsor of this political development, which was crucial for the transformation of the existing production relation and for the establishment of modern capitalism, was the independent power of the state, which made it possible for economic development to get under way.

The creation of the *modern state*, and along with it the political and legal preconditions indispensable to capitalist development, was thus made possible by the development of the production relation. But it was not the product either of the bourgeoisie or of its class struggle. It would be economic mysticism to maintain that it was the bourgeoisie alone which created the modern state, however much it subsequently made the state 'its own' in the course of its struggles. That this policy of the state served the interests of the bourgeoisie does not prove that it grew out of those interests – *post hoc* is not *propter hoc* – even though they paralleled and were linked with the really decisive interests: namely, those of the state. At this stage bourgeois ideologists – philosophers, teachers of law, and cameralists – supported absolutism, and the mercantilist system in its early form is an expression of the bond between the most progressive section of the bourgeoisie and the interest of the state. The formulation of the new ideas was important and even indispensable for the systematic implementation of state policy and for the sublimation of the state's interests into the general interest. But the historical *causa movens* was the power interest of the state organization.

The growing independence of the state's own interest

emerges particularly strongly in external political crises, when what is involved is either the defence of the state's existence or the extension of its power. The state power then appears directly as the general interest of all social groups, and the conflicts among them diminish in face of the common danger, giving way to mutual cooperation.

Finally, the manner in which the state power is exercised is also affected by the structural combination of its various organs, and by its social recruitment. The latter is itself influenced by the historical process in which the modern state emerged. Where, as in Prussia, this ends with a compromise between the monarchy and the aristocracy, the leading positions in the army and the administration remain the preserve of the aristocracy, which is thus able to retain some of its political power, though in a changed form. In Western Europe, on the other hand, the dominance of the bourgeoisie in the army and the administration was accomplished much more fully. Just as the pattern of recruitment varies greatly between different countries, so also does the position of the bureaucracy, and its degree of independence from political influences. In Prussia, the bureaucracy carried on a stubborn fight to defend its position, even against the government, and achieved complete success with the enactment of a statute which protected careers against any outside intervention, and in particular made dismissal dependent upon review by a commission constituted by the bureaucracy itself, so that it became practically impossible to get rid of an official. In Imperial Germany the government was dominated by the bureaucratic and military elites; the bureaucracy was not controlled by political power, but on the contrary largely determined the exercise of political power. In Western Europe, on the other hand, the bureaucracy had far less independence in relation to political bodies, and notably to the parliaments, which governed directly and effectively.

The increasing independence of the state power is by no means adequately expressed in present-day systems of government. It is much more easily embodied in an absolute monarchy than in a liberal or democratic regime. But whatever the regime, it depends upon the relation of classes to the state power and to each other. The significance of the struggle for parliamentary government was precisely to subject the state power to the influence of society – that is to say, to a political will which is the product of the existing class struggle – and so to restrict its independence as much as possible, or at the extreme to abolish such independence. As a result of the 'equilibrium of class forces', but also as a consequence of the growing autonomy of the state power during the war, the state eventually became more independent than ever before.

The manner in which the bourgeoisie confronted the state, and the extent to which it could make the state an instrument of its interests, varied substantially in different countries and led to considerable differences in the relationship between the state and classes. In Germany the state power was far more independent, and hence the assertion of pure power interests was much stronger than in Western Europe. This differentiation in the relationship with class also affects the position of the bureaucracy. In England a high degree of political neutrality is expected from members of the civil service; the civil servant cannot be a candidate in elections without first resigning from the service. The German bureaucracy expresses at almost every level a hierarchical, authoritarian ideology, and represents a closed status group, immune to any outside influence; if an official is elected he retains his office and his career prospects. In France the bureaucracy is extensively politicized, and this is even more the case in the United States, where until recently a career civil service scarcely existed. Modern developments, involving the assumption of new responsibilities, especially in the economic and social field, have enhanced the qualitative as well the quantitative importance of the state apparatus.

Since Marx did not provide an explicit analysis of the concept of class, nor an account of the development of classes, there is no basis for a polemic. But it seems clear at least that the structure of groups in a society may be far more complicated than is suggested by the division into classes, if this is limited to the basic classes. The differentiation of the principal classes according to type of income is correct from an economic point of view, but is inadequate in social terms. This is evident in the case of landowners, for both peasants and large landowners would be included in the class, despite the very great tension between these groups under certain circumstances. The same is true, though perhaps to a lesser extent, of the other two classes; the highly paid engineer and the factory worker are both wage labourers in economic terms, but they may differ greatly in social position. The economic, qualitative equality of a type of income may well lead to entirely different social positions according to the size of that income.

In addition to the three types of income arising directly from production there are derived incomes; incomes which are transferred to others by those who receive rent, profit or wages. According to Marx these include the income (profit) from commercial and interest-bearing capital, and also the wages of workers and employees in commerce and the banks. It is clear that the distinction between original and derived income is economically important, but it may not be crucial, by itself, in determining the orientation of social interests. There are, furthermore, those social groups which have been described rather superficially as 'pre-capitalist classes', namely peasants and artisans.

An analysis limited to the basic classes runs the risk, when it is carried over into the social field, of neglecting, in the first place, the conflicts of interest which arise within a class and may have great political and historical significance, such as those between commercial, bank, and industrial capital, between peasants and large landowners, between workers in old handicraft establishments and those of modern factories, as happened in England at the time of the industrial revolution. Second, it may fail to consider as independent forces such social groups as the various agencies of the state, or the intellectuals, and simply subsume their interests under those of one or other of the basic classes. Third, it may ignore those social groups which are located between the basic classes, such as the peasants and the middle strata, which are themselves further differentiated. An analysis which differentiates along economic lines tends only too readily to subsume all the interests which are active in society under the interests of the basic economic classes; it thus fails to meet the requirements of historical analysis, and perhaps also of political analysis. For this reason it is more appropriate to speak of 'social groups'; and Marx himself, in such historical writings as *The Class Struggles in France* and *The Eighteenth Brumaire*, provided a model of this kind of analysis.

10

Social Classes and the State

NICOS POULANTZAS

I

What are social classes in Marxist theory?

They are groupings of social agents, defined principally but not exclusively by their place in the production process, i.e. in the economic sphere. The economic place of the social agents has a principal role in determining social classes. But from that we cannot conclude that this economic place is sufficient to determine social classes. Marxism states that the economic does indeed have the determinant role in the mode of production or a social formation; but the political and the ideological (the superstructure) also have a very important role. In fact, whenever Marx, Engels, Lenin and Mao analyse social classes, far from limiting themselves to economic criteria alone, they make explicit reference to political and ideological criteria.

For Marxism, social classes involve in one and the same process both class contradictions and class struggle; social classes do not firstly exist as such, and only then enter into a class struggle. Social classes conincide with class practices, i.e. the class struggle, and are only defined in their mutual opposition.

The class determination, while it coincides with the practices struggle. Social classes coincide with class practices, i.e. the relations, designates certain objective places occupied by the social agents in the social division of labour: places which are independent of the will of these agents.

It may thus be said that a social class is defined by its place in the ensemble of social practices, i.e. by its place in the social

Excerpt from Nicos Poulantzas, *Classes in Contemporary Capitalism* (London: New Left Books, 1975) pp. 14–27. Reprinted by permission of New Left Books.

division of labour as a whole. This includes political and ideological relations. Social class, in this sense, is a concept which denotes the effects of the structure within the social division of labour (social relations and social practices). This place thus corresponds to what I shall refer to as the structural determination of class, i.e. to the existence within class practices of determination by the structure – by the relations of production, and by the places of political and ideological domination/subordination. Classes exist only in the class struggle.

This structural determination of classes, which thus exists only as the class struggle, must however be distinguished from class position in each specific conjuncture – the focal point of the always unique historic individuality of a social formation, in other words the concrete situation of the class struggle. In stressing the importance of political and ideological relations in determining social classes, and the fact that social classes only exist in the form of class struggle and practices, class determination must not be reduced, in a voluntarist fashion, to class position. The importance of this lies in those cases in which a distance arises between the structural determination of classes and the class positions in the conjuncture. . . .

(*a*) A social class, or a fraction or stratum of a class, may take up a class position that does not correspond to its interests, which are defined by the class determination that fixes the horizon of the class's struggle. The typical example of this is the labour aristocracy, which in certain conjunctures takes up class positions that are in fact bourgeois. This does not mean, however, that it becomes, in such cases, a part of the bourgeoisie; it remains, from the fact of its structural class determination, part of the working class, and constitutes, as Lenin put it, a 'stratum' of the latter. In other words, its class determination is not reducible to its class position.

If we now take the inverse case, certain classes or fractions and strata of classes other than the working class, and the petty bourgeoisie in particular, may in specific conjunctures take up proletarian class positions, or positions aligned with that of the working class. This does not then mean that they become part of the working class. To give a simple example: production technicians often have proletarian class positions, frequently taking the side of the working class in strikes, for instance. But this does not mean that they have then become part of the working class, since their structural class determination is not reducible to their class position. Moreover, it is precisely by virtue of its class determination that this grouping sometimes takes the side of the working class, and sometimes the side of the bourgeoisie (bourgeois class positions). Technicians no more form part of the bourgeoisie each time that they take up bourgeois class positions than they form part of the proletariat when they take up the positions of the latter. To reduce the structural determination of class to class position would be tantamount to abandoning the objective determination of the places of social classes for a 'relational' ideology of 'social movements'.

(*b*) It must be emphasized that ideological and political relations, i.e. the places of political and ideological domination and subordination, are themselves part of the structural determination of class: there is no question of objective place being the result only of economic place within the relations of production, while political and ideological elements belong simply to class positions. We are not faced, as an old error would have it, on the one hand with an economic 'structure' that alone defines class places, and on the other hand with a class struggle extending to the political and ideological domain. This error today often takes the form of a distinction between '(economic) class situation' on the one hand, and politico-ideological class position on the other. From the start structural class determination involves economic, political and ideological class struggle, and these struggles are all expressed in the form of class positions in the conjuncture.

This also means that the analyses presented here have nothing in common with the Hegelian schema with its class-in-itself (economic class situation, uniquely objective determination of class by the process of production) and class-for-itself (class endowed with its own 'class consciousness' and an autonomous political organization = class struggle), which in the Marxist tradition is associated with Lukács. This in turn implies:

(*a*) That every objective class place in the productive process is necessarily characterized by effects on the structural determination of this class in all aspects, i.e. also by a specific place of this class in the political and ideological relations of the social division of labour. For example, to say that there is a working class in economic relations necessarily implies a specific place for this class in ideological and political relations, even if in certain countries and certain historical periods this class does not have its own 'class consciousness' or an autonomous political organization. This means that in such cases, even if it is heavily contaminated by bourgeois ideology, its economic existence is still expressed in certain specific material politico-ideological practices which burst through its bourgeois 'discourse': this is what Lenin designated, if very descriptively, as class instinct. To understand this, of course, it is necessary to break with a whole conception of ideology as a 'system of ideas' or a coherent 'discourse', and to understand it as an ensemble of material practices. This gives the lie to all those ideologies arguing the 'integration' of the working class, and ultimately it means only one thing: there is no need for there to be 'class consciousness' or autonomous political organizations for the class struggle to take place, and to take place in every domain of social reality.

(*b*) 'Class consciousness' and autonomous political organization, i.e. as far as the working class is concerned, a revolutionary proletarian ideology and an autonomous party of class struggle, refer to the terrain of class positions and the conjuncture, and constitute the conditions for the intervention of classes as social forces.

The principal aspect of an analysis of social classes is that of their places in the class struggle; it is not that of the agents that compose them. Social classes are not empirical groups of individuals, social groups, that are 'composed' by simple addition; the relations of these agents among themselves are thus not interpersonal relations. The class membership of the various agents depends on the class places that they occupy: it is moreover distinct from the class origin, the social origin, of the agents. The importance of these questions will become clear when we discuss the problem of the reproduction of social classes and their agents. Let us just signal here:

(*a*) in the relation between social classes and their agents, the pertinent question that needs to be posed is not that of the class to which this or that particular individual belongs (since what really matters are social groupings), nor that of the statistical and rigidly empirical boundaries of 'social groups' (since what really matters are the classes in the class struggle);

(*b*) the major factor in this respect is not that of 'social inequalities' between groups or individuals: these social inequalities are only the effect, on the agents, of the social classes, i.e. of the objective places they occupy, which can only disappear with the abolition of the division of society into classes. In a word, class society is not a matter of some inequality of 'opportunity' between 'individuals', a notion which implies that there is opportunity and that this depends wholly (or almost so) on the individuals, in the sense that the most capable and best individuals can always rise above their 'social milieu'.

In the determination of social classes, the principal role is played by place in the economic relations. What then does Marxist theory mean by 'economic'?

The economic sphere (or space) is determined by the *process* of production, and the place of the agents, their distribution into social classes, is determined by the *relations* of production.

Of course, the economic includes not only production, but also the whole cycle of production-consumption-distribution, the 'moments' of this appearing, in their unity, as those of the production process. In the capitalist mode of production, what is involved is the overall reproduction cycle of social capital: productive capital, commodity capital, money capital. In this unity, however, it is production which plays the determinant role. The distinction between the classes at this level is not, for example, a distinction based on relative sizes of income (a distinction between 'rich' and 'poor'), as was believed by a long pre-Marxist tradition and as is still believed today by a whole series of sociologists. The undoubted distinction between relative levels of income is itself only a consequence of the relations of production.

What then is the production process, and what are the relations of production which constitute it? In the production process, we find first of all the labour process: this refers to man's relation to nature in general. But the labour process always appears in a historically determined social form. It exists only in its unity with certain relations of production.

In a society divided into classes, the relations of production consist of a double relationship which encompasses men's relations to nature in material production. The two relationships are, first, the relationship between the agents of production and the object and means of labour (the productive forces); second, and through this, relations between men and other men, class relations.

These two relationships thus involve:

(*a*) the relationship between the non-worker (the owner) and the object and means of labour;
(*b*) the relationship between the immediate producer (the direct worker) and the object and means of labour.

The relationships have two aspects to them:

(*a*) economic ownership: by this is meant real economic control of the means of production, i.e. the power to assign the means of production to given uses and so to dispose of the products obtained;
(*b*) possession; by this is meant the capacity to put the means of production into operation.

In every society divided into classes, the first relationship (owners/means of production) always goes together with the first aspect: it is the owners who have real control of the means of production and thus exploit the direct producers by extorting surplus labour from them in various forms.

But this ownership is to be understood as real economic ownership, control of the means of production, to be distinguished from legal ownership, which is sanctioned by law and belongs to the superstructure. The law, of course, generally ratifies economic ownership, but it is possible for the forms of legal ownership not to coincide with real economic ownership. In this case, it is the latter which is determinant in defining the places of social classes, that is to say, the place of the dominant and exploiting class.

The second relationship – that between the direct producers

(the workers) and the means and object of labour, defines the exploited class in the relations of production. It can take various forms, according to the various modes of production in which it occurs.

In pre-capitalist modes of production, the direct producers (the workers) were not entirely 'separated' from the object and means of labour. In the case of the feudal mode of production, for instance, even though the lord had both legal and economic ownership of the land, the serf had possession of his parcel of land, which was protected by custom. He could not be purely and simply dispossessed by the lord; this was only achieved, as in England for example, by way of the whole bloody process of enclosures in the transition from feudalism to capitalism, what Marx referred to as the primitive accumulation of capital. In such modes of production, exploitation is predominantly by direct extraction of surplus labour, in the form of *corvée* payable in labour or in kind. In other words, economic ownership and possession are distinct in that they do not both depend on the same relationship between owners and means of production.

In the capitalist mode of production, by contrast, the direct producers (the working class) are completely dispossessed of their means of labour, of which the capitalists have the actual possession; Marx called this the phenomenon of the 'naked worker'. The worker possesses nothing but his labour-power, which he sells. It is this decisive modification of the place of the direct producers in the relations of production which makes labour itself into a commodity, and this determines the generalization of the commodity form, rather than the other way round: the fact that labour is a commodity is not the effect of a prior generalization of the celebrated 'commodity relations'. The extraction of surplus-value is thus achieved in this case not directly, but by way of the labour incorporated into commodities, in other words by the creation and monopolization of surplus-value.

This entails the following:

The relations of production must be understood both as an articulation of the various relationships which constitute them, and in their union with the labour process: it is this which defines the dominant relation of exploitation characterizing a mode of production, and which determines the class that is exploited within this dominant relation. The property relationship should not be used alone, to denote negatively all those who do not dispose of economic ownership, i.e. all non-owners, as the class exploited within this dominant relation. The class exploited within this dominant relation (the basic exploited class: the working class in the capitalist mode of production) is that which performs the productive labour of that mode of production. Therefore in the capitalist mode of production, all non-owners are not thereby workers.

The production process, on the other hand, is defined not by technological factors, but by the relationships between agents and the means of labour, and hence between the agents themselves, in other words by the unity of the labour process, the productive forces and the relations of production. The labour process and the productive forces, including technology, do not exist in themselves, but always in their constitutive connection with the relations of production. Hence one cannot speak, in societies divided into classes, of 'productive labour' as such, in a neutral sense. In a society divided into classes, that labour is productive which corresponds to the relations of production of the mode in question, i.e. that which gives rise to the specific and dominant form of exploitation. Production, in these societies, means at the same time, and as one and the same process, class division, exploitation, and class struggle.

It follows that it is not wages that define the working class economically: wages are a form of distribution of the social product, corresponding to market relations and the forms of 'contract' governing the purchase and sale of labour-power. Although every worker is a wage-earner, every wage-earner is certainly not a worker, for not every wage-earner is engaged in productive labour. If social classes are not defined at the economic level by a gradation of incomes (rich/poor), they are still less defined by the location of their agents in the hierarchy of wages and salaries. This location certainly has its value as an important index of class determination, but it is only the effect of the latter, just as are all those things that are generally referred to as social inequalities: the distribution of income, taxation, etc. No more than other social inequalities is the wage differential a unilinear scale, a continuous and homogenous staircase, with or without landings, on which individuals or groups are located, certain groups at a 'higher' level, others at a 'lower' one: wage differentials are, rather, the *effect* of class barriers.

This being said, it is still necessary to emphasize that these class barriers and their extended reproduction have the effect of imposing specific and concentrated social inequalities on certain groupings of agents, according to the various classes in which they are distributed: in particular, on young people and on old people, not to enter here into the case of women, which is of a different order and, besides, more complex. This is because, in the case of women, what is involved is not simply certain overdetermined effects on them of the division of society into classes, but, more precisely, a specific articulation, within the social division of labour, of the class division and the sexual division.

The production process is thus composed of the unity of the labour process and the relations of production. But within this unity, it is not the labour process, including technology and the technical process, that plays the dominant role; the relations of production always dominate the labour process and the productive forces, stamping them with their own pattern and appearance. It is precisely this domination of the forces of production by the relations of production which gives their articulation the form of a *process* of production and reproduction.

This dominant role of the relations of production over the productive forces and the labour process is what gives rise to the constitutive role of political and ideological relations in the structural determination of social classes. The relations of production and the relationships which comprise them (economic ownership/possession) are expressed in the form of powers which derive from them, in other words class powers; these powers are constitutively tied to the political and ideological relations which sanction and legitimize them. These relations are not simply added on to relations of production that are 'already there', but are themselves present, in the form specific to each mode of production, in the constitution of the relations of production. The process of production and exploitation is at the same time a process of reproduction of the relations of political and ideological domination and subordination.

This implies, finally, that in the places of the social classes within the relations of production themselves, it is the social division of labour, in the form that this is given by the specific presence of political and ideological relations actually within the production process, which dominates the technical division of labour; we shall see the full consequences of this particularly in the question of the 'management and supervision' of the labour process, but also in that of the class determination of engineers and production technicians. Let us simply note here that it is by taking account of these basic Marxist propositions that we shall be able to grasp the decisive role of the division between manual labour and mental labour in the determination of social classes.

This is the right point to recall the basic distinction between mode of production and social formation: I shall restrict myself here to a few summary remarks, for this distinction has a theoretical importance which I shall have ample occasion to return to in the following essays.

In speaking of a mode of production, an abstract and formal object, one is still keeping to a general and abstract level, even though the concept mode of production itself already embraces relations of production, political relations and ideological relations: for example, the slave, feudal, capitalist modes of production, etc. These modes of production, however, only exist and reproduce themselves within social formations that are historically determinate: France, Germany, Britain, etc., at such and such a moment of the historic process. These social formations are always unique, because they are concrete and singular real objects.

Now a social formation comprises several modes – and also forms – of production, in a specific articulation. For example, European capitalist societies at the start of the twentieth century were composed of (i) elements of the feudal mode of production, (ii) the form of simple commodity production and manufacture (the form of the transition from feudalism to capitalism) and (iii) the capitalist mode of production in its competitive and monopoly forms. Yet these societies were certainly capitalist societies, in so far as the capitalist mode of production was dominant in them. In fact, in every social formation, we find the dominance of one mode of production, which produces complex effects of dissolution and conservation on the other modes of production and which gives these societies their overall character (feudal, capitalist, etc.). The one exception is the case of societies in transition, which are, on the contrary, characterized by an equilibrium between the various modes and forms of production.

To return to social classes. If we confine ourselves to modes of production alone, we find that each of them involves two classes present in their full economic, political and ideological determination – the exploiting class, which is politically and ideologically dominant, and the exploited class, which is politically and ideologically dominated: masters and slaves in the slave mode of production, lords and serfs in the feudal mode of production, bourgeois and workers in the capitalist mode of production. But a concrete society (a social formation) involves more than two classes, in so far as it is composed of various modes and forms of production. No social formation involves only two classes, but the two fundamental classes of any social formation are those of the dominant mode of production in that formation.

Social formations, however, are not the simple concretization or extension of modes and forms of production existing in their 'pure' form; they are not produced by the latter being simply 'stacked together' in space. The social formations in which the class struggle is enacted are the actual sites of the existence and reproduction of the modes and forms of production. A mode of production does not reproduce itself, or even exist, in the pure state, and still less can it be historically periodized as such. It is the class struggle in the social formations which is the motor of history; the process of history has these formations as its locus of existence.

This has considerable implications for the analysis of social classes. The classes of a social formation cannot be 'deduced', in their concrete struggle, from an abstract analysis of the modes and forms of production which are present in it, for this is not how they are found in the social formation. On the one hand, their very existence is affected by the concrete struggle that takes place within the social formation, and it is here in particular that we find the phenomenon of the polarization of other classes and class fractions around the two basic classes. In capitalist societies these are the bourgeoisie and the proletariat, which has decisive and very complex effects on these other classes, as well as on the two basic classes themselves. On the other hand, the classes of one social formation only exist in the context of the relations of this formation with other social formations, hence of the class relations of this formation with those of other formations. Here we have touched on the problem of imperialism and the imperialistic chain; imperialism, which precisely is the extended reproduction of capitalism, has its locus of existence in social formations, and not in the capitalist mode of production as such.

The Marxist theory of social classes further distinguishes *fractions* and *strata* of a class, according to the various classes, on the basis of differentiations in the economic sphere, and of the role, a quite particular one in these cases, of political and ideological relations. The theory also distinguishes social *categories*, defined principally by their place in the political and ideological relations: these include the state bureaucracy, defined by its relation to the state apparatuses, and the intellectuals, defined by their role in elaborating and deploying ideology. These differentiations, for which reference to political and ideological relations is always indispensable, are of great importance; these fractions, strata and categories may often, in suitable concrete conjunctures, assume the rule of relatively autonomous social forces.

It is none the less the case that we are not confronted here with 'social groups' external to, alongside, or above classes. The fractions are class fractions: the commercial bourgeoisie for example is a fraction of the bourgeoisie; similarly, the labour aristocracy is a fraction of the working class. Even social categories have a class membership, their agents generally belonging to several different social classes.

This is one of the particular and basic points of difference between the Marxist theory and the various ideologies of social stratification that dominate present-day sociology. According to these, social classes – whose existence all contemporary sociologists admit – would only be one form of classification, a partial and regional one (bearing in particular on the economic level alone) within a more general stratification. This stratification would give rise, in political and ideological relations, to social groups parallel and external to classes, on which they were superimposed. Max Weber already showed the way in this, and the various currents of political 'elite theory' need only be mentioned here.

The articulation of the structural determination of classes and of class positions within a social formation, the locus of existence of conjunctures, requires particular concepts. I shall call these *concepts of strategy*, embracing in particular such phenomena as class polarization and class alliance. Among these, on the side of the dominant classes, is the concept of the 'power bloc', designating a specific alliance of dominant classes and fractions; also, on the side of the dominated classes, the concept of the 'people', designating a specific alliance of these classes and fractions. These concepts are not of the same status as those with which we have dealt up till now: whether a class, fraction or stratum forms part of the power bloc, or part of the people, will depend on the social formation, its stages, phases and conjunctures. But this also indicates that the classes, fractions and strata that form part of these alliances do not for all that lose their class determination and dissolve into an undifferentiated type of merger or alliance. Just to take one example: when the national bourgeoisie forms part of the people, it still remains a bourgeoisie (leading to contradictions among the people); these classes and fractions do not dissolve into one another, as a certain idealist usage of the term 'popular masses', or even the term 'wage-earning class', might suggest.

II

We can now pose the question of the apparatuses, in particular the branches and apparatuses of the state, and the question of their relation to social classes. Here I shall confine myself to indicating certain of the roles played by the state apparatuses in the existence and reproduction of social classes.

The principal role of the state apparatuses is to maintain the unity and cohesion of a social formation by concentrating and sanctioning class domination, and in this way reproducing social relations, i.e. class relations. Political and ideological relations are materialized and embodied, as material practices, in the state apparatuses. These apparatuses include, on the one hand, the repressive state apparatus in the strict sense and its branches: army, police, prisons, judiciary, civil service; on the other hand, the ideological state apparatuses: the educational apparatus, the religious apparatus (the churches), the information apparatus (radio, television, press), the cultural apparatus (cinema, theatre, publishing), the trade-union apparatus of class collaboration and the bourgeois and petty-bourgeois political parties, etc., as well as in a certain respect, at least in the capitalist mode of production, the family. But as well as the state apparatuses, there is also the economic apparatus in the most strict sense of the term, the 'business' or the 'factory' which, as the centre of appropriation of nature, materializes and embodies the economic relations in their articulation with politico-ideological relations.

Given that the determination of classes involves political and ideological relations, and that the latter only exist in so far as they are materialized in the apparatuses, the analysis of social classes (class struggle) can only be undertaken in terms of their relationship with the apparatuses, and with the state apparatuses in particular. Social classes and their reproduction only exist by way of the relationship linking them to the state and economic apparatuses; these apparatuses are not simply 'added on' to the class struggle as appendices, but play a constitutive role in it. In particular, whenever we go on to analyse politico-ideological relations, from the division between manual and mental labour to the bureaucratization of certain work processes and the despotism of the factory, we shall be concretely examining the apparatuses.

It remains none the less true that it is the class struggle that plays the primary and basic role in the complex relationship between class struggles and apparatuses, and this is a decisive point to note, given the errors of numerous present-day arguments on these questions. The apparatuses are never anything other than the materialization and condensation of class relations; in a sense, they 'presuppose' them, so long as it is understood that what is involved here is not a relation of chronological causality (the chicken or the egg). Now according to a constant of bourgeois ideology in the 'social sciences', which might be loosely referred to as the 'institutionalist-functionalist' current, it is apparatuses and institutions that determine social groups (classes), with class relations arising from the situation of agents in institutional relationships. This current exhibits in specific forms the couple idealism/empiricism, in the specific form of humanism/economism, both of which are characteristic of bourgeois ideology. This was already notably so with Max Weber; for him it was relations of 'power' which resulted in class relations, these 'power' relations having as their specific field and original locus of constitution relations within institutions or associations of the 'authoritarian' type (*Herrschaftsverbände*). This ideological lineage (and rooting a bit further back, one always comes across Hegel) has considerable repercussions, even in the most concrete questions, and permeates the whole of academic sociology in the currently dominant form of 'organization theory'. It is not restricted to the state apparatuses, but takes in the economic apparatus itself (the problem of the 'enterprise').

We can thus define both the relationship and the distinction between state power and state apparatuses. State apparatuses do not possess a 'power' of their own, but materialize and concentrate class relations, relations which are precisely what is embraced by the concept 'power'. The state is not an 'entity' with an intrinsic instrumental essence, but it is itself a relation, more precisely the condensation of a class relation. This implies that:

(*a*) the various functions (economic, political, ideological) that the state apparatuses fulfil in the reproduction of social relations are not 'neutral' functions *sui generis*, initially existing as such and later being simply 'diverted' or 'misappropriated' by the ruling classes; these functions depend on the state power inscribed in the very structure of its apparatuses, in other words on the classes and class fractions which occupy the terrain of political domination;

(*b*) this political domination is itself bound up with the existence and functioning of the state apparatuses.

It follows that a radical transformation of social relations cannot be limited to a change in state power, but has to 'revolutionize' the state apparatuses themselves. In the process of socialist revolution, the working class cannot confine itself to taking the place of the bourgeoisie at the level of state power, but it has also radically to transform (to 'smash') the apparatuses of the bourgeois state and replace them by proletarian state apparatuses.

Here again, however, it is state power, directly articulated with the class struggle, that determines the role and the functioning of the state apparatuses.

(*a*) This is expressed, from the point of view of the revolutionization of the state apparatuses, by the fact that the working class and the popular massses cannot 'smash' the state apparatuses except by seizing state power.

(*b*) It is also expressed in the overall concrete functioning of the state apparatuses in every social formation. If the state apparatuses are not reducible to state power, it is none the less true that it is the particular configuration of the terrain of class domination, of state power (power bloc, hegemonic and governing classes or fractions, etc., as well as class alliances and supporting classes) which determines, in the last instance, both the role of this or that apparatus or branch of the state in the reproduction of social relations, the articulation of economic, political and ideological functions within this apparatus or branch, and the concrete arrangement of the various apparatuses and branches. In other words, the role that this or that apparatus or branch of the state (education, army, parties, etc.) plays in the cohesion of the social formation, the representation of class interests and the reproduction of social relations, is not a function of its intrinsic nature, but depends on the state power.

More generally, any analysis of a social formation must take into direct consideration both the relations of class struggle, the power relations, and the state apparatuses which materialize, concentrate and reflect these relations. Nevertheless, in the relationship between the class struggle and the apparatuses, it is the class struggle which is fundamental. It is not the 'institutional' forms and their modification which result in 'social movements', as for example current ideology about a 'blocked society' would have it, but rather the class struggle which determines the forms and modifications of the apparatuses.

These last points will stand out more clearly if one considers things from the point of view of the extended reproduction of social classes. In fact, social classes only exist in the context of the class struggle, with its historical and dynamic dimension.

Classes, fractions, strata and categories can only be discerned, or even defined, by taking into consideration the historic perspective of the class struggle, and this directly raises the question of their reproduction.

A mode of production can only exist in social formations if it reproduces itself. In the last analysis, this reproduction is nothing other than the extended reproduction of its social relations: it is the class struggle that is the motor of history. Thus Marx says that, in the end, what capitalism produces is simply the bourgeoisie and the proletariat; capitalism simply produces its own reproduction.

Thus the site of the reproduction process is not, as a superficial reading of the second volume of *Capital* might suggest, the 'economic space' alone, and the process does not consist of a self-regulating automatism by which social capital is accumulated. Reproduction, being understood as the extended reproduction of social classes, immediately means reproduction of the political and ideological relations of class determination.

11

Ideology

JÜRGEN HABERMAS

By the middle of the nineteenth century the capitalist mode of production had developed so fully in England and France that Marx was able to identify the locus of the institutional framework of society in the relations of production and at the same time criticize the legitimating basis constituted by the exchange of equivalents. He carried out the critique of bourgeois ideology in the form of *political economy*. His labour theory of value destroyed the semblance of freedom, by means of which the legal institution of the free labour contract had made unrecognizable the relationship of social force that underlay the wage-labour relationship. Marcuse's criticism of Weber is that the latter, disregarding this Marxian insight, upholds an abstract concept of rationalization, which not merely fails to express the specific class content of the adaptation of the institutional framework to the developing systems of purposive-rational action, but conceals it. Marcuse knows that the Marxian analysis can no longer be applied as it stands to advanced capitalist society, with which Weber was already confronted. But he wants to show through the example of Weber that the evolution of modern society in the framework of state-regulated capitalism cannot be conceptualized if liberal capitalism has not been analysed adequately.

Since the last quarter of the nineteenth century two developmental tendencies have become noticeable in the most advanced capitalist countries: an increase in state intervention in order to secure the system's stability, and a growing interdependence of research and technology, which has turned the sciences into the leading productive force. Both tendencies have

Excerpt from Jürgen Habermas, *Toward a Rational Society* (Boston: Beacon Press, 1970) pp. 100–14.

destroyed the particular constellation of institutional framework and sub-systems of purposive-rational action which characterized liberal capitalism, thereby eliminating the conditions relevant for the application of political economy in the version correctly formulated by Marx for liberal capitalism. I believe that Marcuse's basic thesis, according to which technology and science today also take on the function of legitimating political power, is the key to analyzing the changed constellation.

The permanent regulation of the economic process by means of state intervention arose as a defence mechanism against the dysfunctional tendencies which threaten the system, that capitalism generates when left to itself. Capitalism's actual development manifestly contradicted the capitalist idea of a bourgeois society, emancipated from domination, in which power is neutralized. The root ideology of just exchange, which Marx unmasked in theory, collapsed in practice. The form of capital utilization through private ownership could only be maintained by the governmental corrective of a social and economic policy that stabilized the business cycle. The institutional framework of society was repoliticized. It no longer coincides immediately with the relations of production, i.e. with an order of private law that secures capitalist economic activity and the corresponding general guarantees of order provided by the bourgeois state. But this means a change in the relation of the economy to the political system: politics is no longer *only* a phenomenon of the superstructure. If society no longer 'autonomously' perpetuates itself through self-regulation as a sphere preceding and lying at the basis of the state – and its ability to do so was the really novel feature of the capitalist mode of production – then society and the state are no longer in the relationship that Marxian theory had defined as that of base and superstructure. Then, however, a critical theory of society can no longer be constructed in the exclusive form of a critique of political economy. A point of view that methodically isolates the economic laws of motion of society can claim to grasp the overall structure of social life in its essential categories only as long as politics depends on the economic base. It becomes inapplicable when the 'base' has to be comprehended as in itself a function of governmental activity and political conflicts. According to Marx, the critique of political economy was the theory of bourgeois society only as *critique of ideology*. If, however, the ideology of just exchange disintegrates, then the power structure can no longer be criticized *immediately* at the level of the relations of production.

With the collapse of this ideology, political power requires a new legitimation. Now since the power indirectly exercised over the exchange process is itself operating under political control and state regulation, legitimation can no longer be derived from the unpolitical order constituted by the relations of production. To this extent the requirement for direct legitimation, which exists in precapitalist societies, reappears. On the other hand, the resuscitation of immediate political domination (in the traditional form of legitimation on the basis of cosmological world views) has become impossible. For traditions have already been disempowered. Moreover, in industrially developed societies the results of bourgeois emancipation from immediate political domination (civil and political rights and the mechanism of general elections) can be fully ignored only in periods of reaction. Formally democratic government in systems of state-regulated capitalism is subject to a need for legitimation which cannot be met by a return to a pre-bourgeois form. Hence the ideology of free exchange is replaced by a substitute programme. The latter is oriented not to the social results of the institution of the market but to those of government action designed to compensate for the dysfunctions of free exchange. This policy combines the element of the bourgeois ideology of achievement (which, however, displaces assignment of status according to the standard of individual achievement from the market to the school system) with a guaranteed minimum level of welfare, which offers secure employment and a stable income. This substitute programme obliges the political system to maintain stabilizing conditions for an economy that guards against risks to growth and guarantees social security and the chance for individual upward mobility. What is needed to this end is latitude for manipulation by state interventions that, at the cost of limiting the institutions of private law, secure the private form of capital utilization *and bind the masses' loyalty to this form*.

In so far as government action is directed toward the

economic system's stability and growth, politics now takes on a peculiarly negative character. For it is oriented toward the elimination of dysfunctions and the avoidance of risks that threaten the system: not, in other words, toward the *realization of practical goals* but toward the *solution of technical problems*. Claus Offe pointed this out in his paper at the 1968 Frankfurt Sociological Conference:

> In this structure of the relation of economy and the state, 'politics' degenerates into action that follows numerous and continually emerging 'avoidance imperatives': the mass of differentiated social-scientific information that flows into the political system allows both the early identification of risk zones and the treatment of actual dangers. What is new about this structure is . . . that the risks to stability built into the mechanism of private capital utilization in highly organized markets, risks that can be manipulated, prescribe preventive actions and measures that *must* be accepted as long as they are to accord with the existing legitimation resources (i.e., substitute programme).[1]

Offe perceives that through these preventive action-orientations, government activity is restricted to administratively soluble technical problems, so that practical questions evaporate, so to speak. *Practical substance is eliminated.*

Old-style politics was forced, merely through its traditional form of legitimation, to define itself in relation to practical goals: the 'good life' was interpreted in a context defined by interaction relations. The same still held for the ideology of bourgeois society. The substitute programme prevailing today, in contrast, is aimed exclusively at the functioning of a manipulated system. It eliminates practical questions and therewith precludes discussion about the adoption of standards; the latter could emerge only from a democratic decision-making process. The solution of technical problems is not dependent on public discussion. Rather, public discussions could render prob-

[1] Claus Offe, 'Politische Herrschaft und Klassenstrukturen', in Gisela Kress and Dieter Senghaas (eds.), *Politikwissenschaft*. The quotation in the text is from the original manuscript, which differs in formulation from the published text.

lematic the framework within which the tasks of government action present themselves as technical ones. Therefore the new politics of state interventionism requires a depoliticization of the mass of the population. To the extent that practical questions are eliminated, the public realm also loses its political function. At the same time, the institutional framework of society is still distinct from the systems of purposive-rational action themselves. Its organization continues to be a problem of *practice* linked to communication, not one of *technology*, no matter how scientifically guided. Hence, the bracketing out of practice associated with the new kind of politics is not automatic. The substitute programme, which legitimates power today, leaves unfilled a vital need for legitimation: how will the depoliticization of the masses be made plausible to them? Marcuse would be able to answer: by having technology and science *also* take on the role of an ideology.

Since the end of the nineteenth century the other developmental tendency characteristic of advanced capitalism has become increasingly momentous: the scientization of technology. The institutional pressure to augment the productivity of labour through the introduction of new technology has always existed under capitalism. But innovations depended on sporadic inventions, which, while economically motivated, were still fortuitous in character. This changed as technical development entered into a feedback relation with the progress of the modern sciences. With the advent of large-scale industrial research, science, technology, and industrial utilization were fused into a system. Since then, industrial research has been linked up with research under government contract, which primarily promotes scientific and technical progress in the military sector. From there information flows back into the sectors of civilian production. Thus technology and science become a leading productive force, rendering inoperative the conditions for Marx's labour theory of value. It is no longer meaningful to calculate the amount of capital investment in research and development on the basis of the value of unskilled (simple) labour power, when scientific-technical progress has become an independent source of surplus value, in relation to which the only source of surplus value considered by Marx, namely the labour power of the immediate producers, plays an ever smaller role.[2]

As long as the productive forces were visibly linked to the rational decisions and instrumental action of men engaged in social production, they could be understood as the potential for a growing power of technical control and not be confused with the institutional framework in which they are embedded. However, with the institutionalization of scientific-technical progress, the potential of the productive forces has assumed a form owing to which men lose consciousness of the dualism of work and interaction.

It is true that social interests still determine the direction, functions, and pace of technical progress. But these interests define the social system so much as a whole that they coincide with the interest in maintaining the system. *As such* the private form of capital utilization and a distribution mechanism for social rewards that guarantees the loyalty of the masses are removed from discussion. The quasi-autonomous progress of science and technology then appears as an independent variable on which the most important single system variable, namely economic growth, depends. Thus arises a perspective in which the development of the social system *seems* to be determined by the logic of scientific-technical progress. The immanent law of this progress seems to produce objective exigencies, which must be obeyed by any politics oriented toward functional needs. But when this semblance has taken root effectively, then propaganda can refer to the role of technology and science in order to explain and legitimate why in modern societies the process of democratic decision-making about practical problems loses its function and 'must' be replaced by plebiscitary decisions about alternative sets of leaders of administrative personnel. This technocracy thesis has been worked out in several versions on the intellectual level.[3] What seems to me more important is that it can also

[2] The most recent explication of this is Eugen Löbl, *Geistige Arbeit – die wahre Quelle des Reichtums*, translated from the Czech by Leopold Grünwald.

[3] See Helmut Schelsky, *Der Mensch in der wissenschaftlichen Zivilisation*; Jacques Ellul, *The Technological Society*; and Arnold Gehlen, 'Über kulturelle Kristallisationen', in *Studien zur Anthropologie und Soziologie*, and 'Über

become a background ideology that penetrates into the consciousness of the depoliticized mass of the population, where it can take on legitimating power.[4] It is a singular achievement of this ideology to detach society's self-understanding from the frame of reference of communicative action and from the concepts of symbolic interaction and replace it with a scientific model. Accordingly the culturally defined self-understanding of a social life-world is replaced by the self-reification of men under categories of purposive-rational action and adaptive behaviour.

The model according to which the planned reconstruction of society is to proceed is taken from systems analysis. It is possible in principle to comprehend and analyze individual enterprises and organizations, even political or economic subsystems and social systems as a whole, according to the pattern of self-regulated systems. It makes a difference, of course, whether we use a cybernetic frame of reference for analytic purposes or *organize* a given social system in accordance with this pattern as a man-machine system. But the transferral of the analytic model to the level of social organization is implied by the very approach taken by systems analysis. Carrying out this intention of an instinct-like self-stabilization of social systems yields the peculiar perspective that the structure of one of the two types of action, namely the behavioural system of purposive-rational action, not only predominates over the institutional framework but gradually absorbs communicative action as such. If, with Arnold Gehlen, one were to see the inner logic of technical development as the step-by-step disconnection of the behavioural system of purposive-rational action from the human organism and its transferral to machines, then the technocratic intention could be understood as the last stage of this development. For the first time man can not only, as *homo faber*, completely objectify himself and confront the achievements that have taken on independent life in his products; he

kulturelle Evolution', in *Die Philosophie und die Frage nach dem Fortschritt*, M. Hahn and F. Wiedmann (eds.).

[4] To my knowledge there are no empirical studies concerned specifically with the propagation of this background ideology. We are dependent on extrapolations from the findings of other investigations.

can in addition, as *homo fabricatus*, be integrated into his technical apparatus if the structure of purposive-rational action can be successfully reproduced on the level of social systems. According to this idea the institutional framework of society – which previously was rooted in a different type of action – would now, in a fundamental reversal, be *absorbed* by the subsystems of purposive-rational action, which were embedded in it.

Of course this technocratic intention has not been realized anywhere even in its beginnings. But it serves as an ideology for the new politics, which is adapted to technical problems and brackets out practical questions. Furthermore it does correspond to certain developmental tendencies that could lead to a creeping erosion of what we have called the institutional framework. The manifest domination of the authoritarian state gives way to the manipulative compulsions of technical-operational administration. The moral realization of a normative order is a function of communicative action oriented to shared cultural meaning and presupposing the internalization of values. It is increasingly supplanted by conditioned behaviour, while large organizations as such are increasingly patterned after the structure of purposive-rational action. The industrially most advanced societies seem to approximate the model of behavioural control steered by external stimuli rather than guided by norms. Indirect control through fabricated stimuli has increased, especially in areas of putative subjective freedom (such as electoral, consumer, and leisure behaviour). Socio-psychologically, the era is typified less by the authoritarian personality than by the destructuring of the superego. The increase in *adaptive behaviour* is, however, only the obverse of the dissolution of the sphere of linguistically mediated interaction by the structure of purposive-rational action. This is paralleled subjectively by the disappearance of the difference between purposive-rational action and interaction from the consciousness not only of the sciences of man, but of men themselves. The concealment of this difference proves the ideological power of the technocratic consciousness.

In consequence of the two tendencies that have been discussed, capitalist society has changed to the point where two key categories of Marxian theory, namely class struggle and ideology, can no longer be employed as they stand.

It was on the basis of the capitalist mode of production that the struggle of social classes as such was first constituted, thereby creating an objective situation from which the class structure of traditional society, with its immediately political constitution, could be *recognized* in retrospect. State-regulated capitalism, which emerged from a reaction against the dangers to the system produced by open class antagonism, suspends class conflict. The system of advanced capitalism is so defined by a policy of securing the loyalty of the wage-earning masses through rewards, that is, by avoiding conflict, that the conflict still built into the structure of society in virtue of the private mode of capital utilization is the very area of conflict which has the greatest probability of remaining latent. It recedes behind others, which, while conditioned by the mode of production, can no longer assume the form of class conflicts. In the paper cited, Claus Offe has analysed this paradoxical state of affairs, showing that open conflicts about social interests break out with greater probability the less their frustration has dangerous consequences for the system. The needs with the greatest conflict potential are those on the periphery of the area of state intervention. They are far from the central conflict being kept in a state of latency, and therefore they are not seen as having priority among dangers to be warded off. Conflicts are set off by these needs to the extent that disproportionately scattered state interventions produce backward areas of development and corresponding disparity tensions:

> The disparity between areas of life grows above all in view of the differential state of development obtaining between the actually institutionalized and the possible level of technical and social progress. The disproportion between the most modern apparatuses for industrial and military purposes and the stagnating organization of the transport, health, and educational systems is just as well known an example of this disparity between areas of life as is the contradiction between rational planning and regulation in taxation and finance policy and the unplanned, haphazard development of cities and regions. Such contradictions can no longer be designated accurately as antagonisms between classes, yet they can still be interpreted as results of the

> still dominant process of the private utilization of capital and of a specifically capitalist power structure. In this process the prevailing interests are those which, without being clearly localizable, are in a position, on the basis of the established mechanism of the capitalist economy, to react to disturbances of the conditions of their stability by producing risks relevant to the system as a whole.[5]

The interests bearing on the maintenance of the mode of production can no longer be 'clearly localized' in the social system as class interests. For the power structure, aimed as it is at avoiding dangers to the system, precisely excludes 'domination' (as immediate political or economically mediated social force) exercised in such a manner that one class subject *confronts* another as an identifiable group.

This means not that class antagonisms have been abolished but that they have become *latent*. Class distinctions persist in the form of sub-cultural traditions and corresponding differences not only in the standard of living and life-style but also in political attitude. The social structure also makes it probable that the class of wage earners will be hit harder than other groups by social disparities. And finally, the generalized interest in perpetuating the system is still anchored today, on the level of immediate life chances, in a structure of privilege. The concept of an interest that has become *completely* independent of living subjects would cancel itself out. But with the deflection of dangers to the system in state-regulated capitalism, the political system has incorporated an interest – which transcends latent class boundaries – in preserving the compensatory distribution façade.

Furthermore, the displacement of the conflict zone from the class boundary to the underprivileged regions of life does not mean at all that serious conflict potential has been disposed of. As the extreme example of racial conflict in the United States shows, so many consequences of disparity can accumulate in certain areas and groups that explosions resembling civil war can occur. But unless they are connected with protest potential from other sectors of society no conflicts arising from such

[5] Offe, op.cit.

underprivilege can really overturn the system – they can only provoke it to sharp reactions incompatible with formal democracy. For underprivileged groups are not social classes, nor do they ever even potentially represent the mass of the population. Their *disfranchisement* and pauperization no longer coincide with *exploitation*, because the system does not live off their labour. They can represent at most a past phase of exploitation. But they cannot through the withdrawal of cooperation attain the demands that they legitimately put forward. That is why these demands retain an appellative character. In the case of long-term non-consideration of their legitimate demands underprivileged groups can in extreme situations react with desperate destruction and self-destruction. But as long as no coalitions are made with privileged groups, such a civil war lacks the chance of revolutionary success that class struggle possesses.

With a series of restrictions this model seems applicable even to the relations between the industrially advanced nations and the formerly colonial areas of the Third World. Here, too, growing disparity leads to a form of underprivilege that in the future surely will be increasingly less comprehensible through categories of exploitation. Economic interests are replaced on this level, however, with immediately military ones.

Be that as it may, in advanced capitalist society deprived and privileged groups no longer confront each other *as* socio-economic classes – and to some extent the boundaries of underprivilege are no longer even specific to groups and instead run across population categories. Thus the fundamental relation that existed in all traditional societies and that came to the fore under liberal capitalism is mediatized, namely the class antagonism between partners who stand in an institutionalized relationship of force, economic exploitation, and political oppression to one another, and in which communication is so distorted and restricted that the legitimations serving as an ideological veil cannot be called into question. Hegel's concept of the ethical totality of a living relationship which is sundered because one subject does not reciprocally satisfy the needs of the other is no longer an appropriate model for the mediatized class structure of organized, advanced capitalism. The suspended dialectic of the ethical generates the peculiar semblance of *post-histoire*. The reason is that relative growth of the productive forces no longer represents *eo ipso* a potential that points beyond the existing framework with emancipatory consequences, in view of which legitimations of an existing power structure become enfeebled. For the leading productive force – controlled scientific-technical progress itself – has now become the basis of legitimation. Yet this new form of legitimation has cast off the old shape of *ideology*.

Technocratic consciousness is, on the one hand, 'less ideological' than all previous ideologies. For it does not have the opaque force of a delusion that only transfigures the implementation of interests. On the other hand today's dominant, rather glassy background ideology, which makes a fetish of science, is more irresistible and farther-reaching than ideologies of the old type. For with the veiling of practical problems it not only justifies a *particular class's* interest in domination and represses *another class's* partial need for emancipation, but affects the human race's emancipatory interest as such.

Technocratic consciousness is not a rationalized, wish-fulfilling fantasy, not an 'illusion' in Freud's sense, in which a system of interaction is either represented or interpreted and grounded. Even bourgeois ideologies could be traced back to a basic pattern of just interactions, free of domination and mutually satisfactory. It was these ideologies which met the criteria of wish-fulfilment and substitute gratification; the communication on which they were based was so limited by repressions that the relation of force once institutionalized as the capital–labour relation could not even be called by name. But the technocratic consciousness is not based in the same way on the causality of dissociated symbols and unconscious motives, which generates both false consciousness and the power of reflection to which the critique of ideology is indebted. It is less vulnerable to reflection, because it is no longer *only* ideology. For it does not, in the manner of ideology, express a projection of the 'good life' (which even if not identifiable with a bad reality, can at least be brought into virtually satisfactory accord with it). Of course the new ideology, like the old, serves to impede making the foundations of society the object of thought and reflection. Previously, social force lay at the basis of the relation between capitalist and wage-labourers. Today the basis is provided by structural conditions which predefine the tasks of system maintenance: the private form of capital utilization and a political form of distributing social rewards that guarantees mass loyalty. However, the old and new ideology differ in two ways.

First, the capital-labour relation today, because of its linkage to a loyalty-ensuring political distribution mechanism, no longer engenders uncorrected exploitation and oppression. The process through which the persisting class antagonism has been made virtual presupposes that the repression on which the latter is based first came to consciousness in history and *only then* was stabilized in a modified form as a property of the system. Technocratic consciousness, therefore, cannot rest in the same way on collective repression as did earlier ideologies. Second, mass loyalty today is created only with the aid of rewards for *privatized needs*. The achievements in virtue of which the system justifies itself may not in principle be interpreted politically. The acceptable interpretation is immediately in terms of allocations of money and leisure time (neutral with regard to their use), and mediately in terms of the technocratic justification of the occlusion of practical questions. Hence the new ideology is distinguished from its predecessor in that it severs the criteria for justifying the organization of social life from any normative regulation of interaction, thus depoliticizing them. It anchors them instead in functions of a putative system of purposive-rational action.

Technocratic consciousness reflects not the sundering of an ethical situation but the repression of 'ethics' as such as a category of life. The common, positivist way of thinking renders inert the frame of reference of interaction in ordinary language, in which domination and ideology both arise under conditions of distorted communication and can be reflectively detected and broken down. The depoliticization of the mass of the population, which is legitimated through technocratic consciousness, is at the same time men's self-objectification in categories equally of both purposive-rational action and adaptive behaviour. The reified models of the sciences migrate into the socio-cultural life-world and gain objective power over the latter's self-understanding. The ideological nucleus of this consciousness is *the elimination of the distinction between the practical and the technical*. It reflects, but does not objectively account for, the new constellation of a disempowered institutional framework and systems of purposive-rational action that have taken on a life of their own.

The new ideology consequently violates an interest grounded in one of the two fundamental conditions of our cultural existence: in language, or more precisely, in the form of socialization and individuation determined by communication in ordinary language. This interest extends to the maintenance of intersubjectivity of mutual understanding as well as to the creation of communication without domination. Technocratic consciousness makes this practical interest disappear behind the interest in the expansion of our power of technical control. Thus the reflection that the new ideology calls for must penetrate beyond the level of particular historical class interests to disclose the fundamental interests of mankind as such, engaged in the process of self-constitution.[6]

If the relativization of the field of application of the concept of ideology and the theory of class be confirmed, then the category framework developed by Marx in the basic assumptions of historical materialism requires a new formulation. The model of forces of production and relations of production would have to be replaced by the more abstract one of work and interaction. The relations of production designate a level on which the institutional framework was anchored only during the phase of the development of liberal capitalism, and not either before or after. To be sure, the productive forces, in which the learning processes organized in the sub-systems of purposive-rational action accumulate, have been from the very beginning the motive force of social evolution. But, they do not appear, as Marx supposed, *under all circumstances* to be a potential for liberation and to set off emancipatory movements – at least not once the continual growth of the productive forces has become dependent on scientific-technical progress that has *also* taken on functions of *legitimating political power*. I suspect that the

[6] See my essay 'Erkenntnis und Interesse' in *Technik und Wissenschaft als 'Ideologie'*. It will appear in English as an appendix to *Knowledge and Human Interests*. [See Bibliographical References, Ed.]

frame of reference developed in terms of the analogous, but more general relation of institutional framework (interaction) and sub-systems of purposive-rational action ('work' in the broad sense of instrumental and strategic action) is more suited to reconstructing the socio-cultural phases of the history of mankind.

12

The Ethical Potential of Marx's Thought

SVETOZAR STOJANOVIĆ

I

A Marxist ethics, at least one worthy of Marx's name, has yet to be constructed. Does this problem exist because of obstacles inherent in Marx's thought itself or perhaps simply because of certain external circumstances, such as the immaturity of Marx's followers? The following lines, written by Antonio Labriola, show that some Marxists have not even understood the ethical *problem* in Marxism:

> Ethics and idealism consist henceforth in this, to put the thought of science at the service of the proletariat. If this ethics does not appear moral enough for the sentimentalists, usually hysterical and silly, let them go and borrow altruism from its high priest Spencer who will give them a vague and insipid definition of it, such as will satisfy them.[1]

An examination of the reasons which might account for the non-existence of a Marxist ethics is a precondition for any more complete evaluation of Marx's philosophy. One of the criteria for evaluating a body of thought is its capacity of embracing all the key problems of man. It is not good for it to remain powerless before the moral dimension of social life.

How could it have happened that a revolutionary movement whose goal was the realization of the most radical humanistic ideals still lacks a developed ethics? To this very day Marxists have argued more about the causes of the undeveloped state of

Excerpt from Svetozar Stojanović, *Between Ideals and Reality* (New York: Oxford University Press, 1973) pp. 137–55. Reprinted by permission of Oxford University Press.

[1] *Essays on the Materialistic Conception of History*, p. 75.

their ethics than they have worked to develop one. Two reasons are commonly put forward for this – one socio-political, the other socio-psychological.

The state of the workers' movement, social democratic as well as communist, is usually cited as the first reason. Indeed, if 'the ultimate aim of socialism is nothing, but the movement is everything,'[2] it is difficult to find a place for ethics. On the other hand, Stalinism and contemporary Maoism have made a caricature of Marxist ethics: ethical theorists become the apologists of state policy.

The second, socio-psychological factor usually advanced to explain the lack of a Marxist ethics is the tendency of Marxists to postpone the formulation of a positive programme in times of revolutionary action. To this is usually added the observation that, although in 1844 he did intend to write a book on ethical problems, Marx himself did not have enough time to work on ethics. Marx, however, used his time for what he thought was more important. But if Marx did not have the time, this surely cannot be said of many of his followers. Nevertheless, to this very day we have not come upon a satisfactory Marxist ethics. A more complete explanation, apparently, will have to be sought in certain theoretical obstacles inherent to Marx's thought itself.

Throughout the history of Marxism and Marxology there have been two conflicting interpretations of Marx – ethical and a-ethical. This writer represents the view that Marx's thought contains ethical values which can serve as a point of departure for a Marxist ethics. But Marx also gave occasion for the contrary – a-ethical – interpretation. This ambivalence creates difficulties for any Marxist-oriented philosophy of morals. In addition, however, there is one more, significantly larger obstacle, i.e. Marx's understanding of historical determinism.

II

What evidence is there for those who claim that Marx's work has absolutely no ethical content?

[2] Eduard Bernstein, *Evolutionary Socialism*, p. 202.

Marx asserted that he had emerged from the province of speculation into the domain of 'real, positive science'.[3] He was attempting to establish a scientific socialism, as opposed to the moralizing-utopian socialism which had existed previously. Partisans of the a-ethical interpretation of Marx's thought usually refer to the following or similar passages:

> Communists cannot preach any kind of *morality* at all, something that Stirner does altogether too much. They cannot pose any kind of moral demands at all to people: love one another, do not be egoists, etc. On the contrary, they know very well that egoism, just as well as self-sacrifice, *is* in specific conditions a necessary form of individual self-affirmation.[4]
>
> Communism is for us not a stable state which is to be established, an *ideal* to which reality will have to adjust itself. We call communism the *real* movement which abolishes the present state of things.[5]
>
> Law, morality, religion, are to it [the proletariat – S.S.] so many bourgeois prejudices, behind which lurk in ambush just as many bourgeois interests.[6]
>
> *Morality is 'impotence in action'*. Every time one struggles with some vice it is defeated. But Rudolph cannot even raise himself to the standpoint of independent morality, which is based at least upon *human dignity*. To the contrary, his morality bases itself upon consciousness of human weakness. His *morality* is *theological*.[7]

In his letter to Engels of 4 November 1864,[8] Marx complained that the Mazzinists had forced him to throw two phrases into the Preamble of the Statutes of the International about 'duty and right' as well as about 'truth, morality, and justice', but added that in such a place they would do no damage.

In his letter to Sorge of 19 October 1877, Marx complained about those people who wanted to 'replace its [socialism's –

[3] *The German Ideology*, 1947, part I, p. 15.
[4] 'Die Deutsche Ideologie', part III, *Werke*, 1959, vol. 3, p. 229.
[5] *The German Ideology*, part I, p. 26.
[6] *Communist Manifesto*, p. 44.
[7] 'Die Deutsche Ideologie', part III, *Werke*, vol. 3, p. 213.
[8] Karl Marx and Frederick Engels, *Selected Correspondence* (Moscow, 1956) p. 182.

Tr.] materialistic basis (which demands serious objective study from anyone who tries to use it) by modern mythology with its goddesses of Justice, Liberty, Equality, and Fraternity'.[9]

The group which interprets Marx as an a-ethical thinker includes Werner Sombart, Benedetto Croce, Karl Kautsky, Max Adler, Rudolf Hildferding, the neo-Kantians, Lucien Goldmann, among others. Some of them hold that the absence of an ethical position is a shortcoming of Marx's thought and, therefore, seek to supplement Marx through Darwin (Kautsky), Darwin and Kant (Ludwig Woltmann), or Kant (the neo-Kantians).

III

Opposed to the group described above is an entire succession of theorists who think that Marx's thought has ethical content: Eduard Bernstein, Maximilien Rubel, Karl Popper, John Lewis, Eugene Kamenka, and others. Once again I have cited non-Marxists as well as Marxists. This second group embraces both those who believe that Marx's doctrine is purely ethical and non-scientific, and those who claim that it is ethical only in one of its dimensions and scientific in the other.

They also rely upon many passages from Marx, for example:

> The criticism of religion ends with the doctrine that *man is the supreme being for man.* It ends, therefore, with the *categorical imperative to overthrow all those conditions* in which man is an abased, enslaved, abandoned, contemptible being. . . .'[10]
>
> The social principles of Christianity preach cowardice, self-contempt, abasement, submission, humility, in short, all the qualities of the *canaille*, while the proletariat, not wanting to be treated as *canaille*, needs its courage, pride, and sense of independence much more than its daily bread.[11]
>
> The standpoint of the old materialism is *civil* society; the standpoint of the new is *human* society, or socialized humanity.[12]

[9] Ibid., pp. 375–6.

[10] Marx, in Bottomore (ed.), *Early Writings* 1963, p. 52.

[11] *Karl Marx, Friedrich Engels: Historisch-kritische Gesamtausgabe* (*MEGA*) (Berlin, 1932) 1/6, p. 278.

[12] 'Thesis X on Feuerbach', in Marx and Engels, *Selected Works*, p. 30.

Marx pleaded for a society 'in which the free development of each is the condition for the free development of all'.[13] In the same document he often used ethical expressions, such as 'naked self-interest and callous cash-payment', 'oppression', 'degradation of personal dignity', 'shameless, direct, and brutal exploitation', 'inconsiderateness', 'the modern slavery of capital', 'subjugation', 'the masses of workers are slaves', and so on. Marx's *Capital* (especially chapters IV, VII, and XXIII of the first volume) is also permeated with ethically coloured formulations.

So is the following passage from *The Poverty of Philosophy* concerning capitalism: 'This is the time when the very things which till then had been communicated, but never exchanged; given, but never sold; acquired, but never bought – virtue, love, conviction, knowledge, conscience, etc. – when everything, in short, passed into commerce. It is the time of general corruption, of universal venality. . . .'[14]

In his *Critique of the Gotha Programme*, Marx compares bourgeois, socialist, and communist distribution of the social product, demonstrating the advantages of the communist mode of distribution from the principle of social equality.

But there is no need to go on referring to passages from Marx's works. With the books by Marek Fritzhand[15] and Eugene Kamenka,[16] in which Marx is quoted and analysed in detail, I think that it has been definitively proven that Marx's thought has an ethical dimension. From his earliest through his latest works, Marx wrote as an heir of the great European humanistic-ethical tradition. Many non-Marxist thinkers as well have conceded this point.

How could it have been, and still be, that in the face of so many proofs to the contrary, there have been interpreters of Marx's thought who have claimed that it is a-ethical, and furthermore that it is not accidentally so but rather a-ethical in its very essence? In this connection, as we have seen, these interpreters refer to Marx's statement about the scientific

[13] *Communist Manifesto*, p. 53.
[14] Marx, *The Poverty of Philosophy* (New York, 1963) p. 34.
[15] *Myśl Etyczna Młodego Marksa* (Warsaw, 1961).
[16] *The Ethical Foundations of Marxism*.

character of his work and some of his thoughts on morality. As final proof they usually cite Marx's understanding of historical determinism – but we shall address ourselves to this topic in the next section.

From Marx's belief in the scientific character of his own teaching, of course, it does not at all follow that this teaching was not ethically coloured. The point is that Marx did not take 'science' to mean 'value-free' intellectual activity, which is what certain Marxologists have in mind when they speak of 'science'. Marx never drew the kind of distinction between cognitive and value statements which would place the latter outside the realm of science. We can never overlook the fact that Marx was a student of Hegel, and that Hegel had rejected Kant's dualism because he was convinced of the unity of the Is and the Ought, of *Sein* and *Sollen*.

No passage quoted by adherents of the a-ethical interpretation of Marx proves convincingly that moral values remained external to the content of his thought. On the contrary, there are many passages which prove the opposite. There is not a single passage of Marx's that *must* be interpreted in such a manner as to show that he was hostile to morality, but there are quite a few which unquestionably express a strong aversion to the *preaching* of moral values. At first glance it might seem as if the following lines, which we have already quoted above, are an exception in this respect: 'Law, morality, religion are to it [the proletariat – S.S.] so many bourgeois prejudices, behind which lurk in ambush just as many bourgeois interests.' But contextual analysis shows that this passage is hostile to the bourgeoisie and its invocation of morality rather than to morality as such.

Why was Marx against the preaching of morality? This cannot be explained in terms of his personal moral qualities, as Karl Popper tries to do when he writes: 'Marx, I believe, avoided an explicit moral theory, because he hated preaching. Deeply distrustful of the moralist who usually preaches water and drinks wine, Marx was reluctant to formulate his ethical convictions explicitly.'[17] Marx, for instance, had nothing against the personal moral standards of certain utopian

[17] *The Open Society and Its Enemies*, pp. 385–6.

socialists. But he criticized them none the less, as he wanted to transcend moralizing socialism with scientific socialism.

The moral preacher, according to Marx, operates on the assumption that 'a moral command to people to change their consciousness will really change their consciousness.'[18] The preacher is the personification of 'impotence in action'. This is the reason Marx decided in favour of a scientific investigation of existing society and reliance upon those forces which are interested in changing it at its very foundations. With complete devotion, he plunged into the task of establishing the regularities of capitalism and the forces which maintain it, the possibilities and tendencies pointing toward the transcendence of capitalism, as well as the task of discovering the identity of the agent of such revolution. Not believing in the efficacy of moral preaching, Marx insisted upon the need for radical changes in the social conditions which lead to immorality. His humanism is neither moralizing nor even primarily moral, although it does contain the moral dimensions as well; instead, it is practical and revolutionary. This humanism attempts to penetrate to the causes of an inhuman social order, and is not concerned primarily with consequences, unlike utopian socialism, which remains naïve and powerless. Marx's humanism, rather than relying upon its moral appeal and influence, relies upon something else much more basic – the *interests* of the working class. The task of Marx's theory is to contribute to the awakening of the working class's consciousness of its own interests.

Marx's intellectual position is not beyond moral values; but it is antimoralistic. Every moralist gives precedence to a moral judgement (rather than an examination of reality) and expects that this judgement in and of itself will move people to change reality. Moralism in practice corresponds to ethicism in theory.

Marx did make moral judgements about capitalism. Yet what was most important to him was scientific investigation into the nature of capitalism. In contrast to moralists, Marx held no illusions about the efficacy of moral judgements which do not coincide with real social interests, and although he evaluated capitalism from a humanistic standpoint, he did not

[18] 'Die Deutsche Ideologie', part III, *Werke*, vol. 3, p. 232.

feel the need to formulate and explicate the principles upon which he had based these judgements. Marx was a critic, and an ethical critic at that, but he was not a systematic ethical theorist. Should it not be possible, however, for those people who seek to construct a Marxist ethics to try to explicate, systematize, evaluate and employ his moral principles? This task is still no more than at its first stage, and no one has done more in this respect than M. Fritzhand, whom we have already mentioned.

Marxists are heirs to the clearly antimoralistic and anti-ethicist posture of Karl Marx. A Marxist ethics cannot consider its primary task to be to urge individuals to perfect themselves in a moral sense. A Marxist ethics must be the ethics of the revolutionary movement. Such an ethics finds its hope in moral revolution, but only as an aspect of social, and even more broadly, total humanist revolution. All this demands that a Marxist ethics be differentiated from classical normative ethics. Moreover, it should be recognized that Marxists have the best prospects of making new contributions in problems of social, rather than individual, ethics. Even so, they still cannot afford to lose sight of the ethical problems of the individual, such as for instance the meaning of life, happiness, love and hate, friendship, and so on.

IV

That alongside of his understanding of historical determinism Marx also left a place for human praxis, freedom, and self-realization is demonstrated by many of his texts, of which the following are illustrative:

> Men make their own history, but they do not make it just as they please; they do not make it under circumstances chosen by themselves, but under circumstances directly encountered, given and transmitted from the past.[19]
>
> History is nothing but the succession of the separate generations, each of which exploits the materials, the forms of capital,

[19] 'The Eighteenth Brumaire of Louis Bonaparte', in Marx and Engels, *Selected Works*, p. 97.

the productive forces handed down to it by all preceding ones, and thus on the one hand continues the traditional activity in completely changed circumstances and, on the other, modifies the old circumstances with a completely changed activity.[20]

World history would indeed be very easy to make if the struggle were taken up only on condition of infallibly favourable chances. It would on the other hand be of a very mystical nature, if 'accidents' played no part. These accidents naturally form part of the general course of development and are compensated by other accidents. But acceleration and delay are very much dependent upon such 'accidents', including the 'accident' of the characters of the people who first head the movement.[21]

Still, Marx belonged to nineteenth-century science, in which the strict determinism of the natural science of the time was still the theoretical and methodological ideal for all the sciences. It should also be taken into consideration that in his philosophy of history, Marx's mentor, Hegel, treated people as instruments of the objective Spirit. All this had to have an impact upon Marx, who occasionally went to the extremes of absolute determinism:

My standpoint, from which the evolution of the economic formation of society is viewed as a *process of natural history*, can less than any other make the individual responsible for relations whose creature he socially remains, however much he may subjectively raise himself above them.[22]

But capitalist production begets, *with the inexorability of a law of Nature*, its own negation.[23]

Marx approvingly quoted one of *Capital*'s reviewers, who had written:

Consequently, Marx only troubles himself about one thing: to show, by rigid scientific investigation, the necessity of successive determinate orders of social conditions, and to establish, as impartially as possible, the facts that serve him for funda-

[20] *The German Ideology*, part I, p. 38.

[21] Marx's Letter to L. Kugelmann of 17 April, 1871; in Marx and Engels, *Selected Correspondence*, p. 320.

[22] *Capital*, 'Preface to the First German Edition', vol. I, p. 10. My emphasis – S.S.

[23] Ibid., p. 763. My emphasis – S.S.

mental starting-points. For this it is quite enough, if he proves, at the same time, both the necessity of the present order of things, and the necessity of another order into which the first must inevitably pass over; and this all the same, whether men believe or do not believe it, whether they are conscious or unconscious of it. *Marx treats the social movement as a process of natural history, governed by laws not only independent of human will, but rather, on the contrary, determining that will, consciousness, and intelligence. . . .*[24]

In the passage which follows, Marx advocates both strict determinism, according to which social laws function with 'iron necessity', but at the same time a milder form of determinism as well, which treats laws as 'tendencies': 'Intrinsically, it is not a question of the higher or lower degree of development of the social antagonisms that result from the natural laws of capitalist production. *It is a question of these laws themselves, of these tendencies working with iron necessity toward inevitable results.*'[25] And in the third volume of *Capital*,[26] Marx again puts forth the view that a law is only a tendency which can be annulled by contradictory tendencies.

And even when a society has got upon the right track for the discovery of the *natural laws of its movement – and it is the ultimate aim of this work, to lay bare the economic law of motion of modern society* – it can neither clear by bold leaps, nor remove by legal enactments, the obstacles offered by the successive phases of its normal development. But it can shorten and lessen the birth-pangs.[27]

There are, then, two interweaving and conflicting motifs in Marx's writings. While people are the subjects of the historical process, its course is independent of human consciousness and will. While man is a creative being, there is only one possible direction which history can take. While people can exert an influence upon historical events, they can exert such influence

[24] Ibid., 'Afterword to the Second German Edition', p. 18. My emphasis – S.S.

[25] Ibid., p. 8. My emphasis – S.S.

[26] Ibid., vol. III, pp. 234–5.

[27] Ibid., vol. I, Preface to the First German Edition', p. 10. My emphasis – S.S.

only upon the speed with which they take place, and not upon their general course. To be sure, this rule of blind historical forces over man was for Marx a sign that we are still in man's prehistory. In communism, associated humanity would determine the course of history.

Both as a philosopher and as a student of history, Marx had to give an account of the relationship between determinism and freedom. Experts on the history of human thought are aware that this is one of the so-called eternal philosophical problems, that the basic *types* of solutions had been outlined before the time of Marx, and that each of them has had its own powerful mode of argumentation and justification. Without being aware of it Marx continuously vacillated between two mutually exclusive positions.

Consequently, two different orientations branched off from Marx, orientations which have trailed through the history of Marxism to the present day. The majority of the Marxists of the Second International understood Marx as a theorist of strict determinism. At the same time, such a Marx had to be seen as an a-ethical thinker. Naturally, those Marxists who felt the absence of ethics to be a shortcoming had to seek a supplement to Marx's thought in other philosophies, above all in the philosophy of Kant.

Opposing himself to Western social democracy, Lenin gravitated toward the conception of Marx as a thinker of revolutionary-historical creativity. However, it must be pointed out that Lenin did not take note of the contradiction in Marx's understanding of historical determinism. Moreover, Lenin himself restated the idea that communism is historically inevitable while at the same time maintaining an activist posture. While in theory he often used severely deterministic language, in practice Lenin firmly insisted upon revolutionary consciousness and creativity. Perhaps no social movement more than the communist movement has insisted so vigorously upon the inevitability of its own goal and simultaneously upon the activism of organized fighters for that goal.

Faith in the inevitability of socialism had a diverse psychological effect upon the international workers' movement. Social democrats have rather passively expected capitalism to gradually arrive at its final crisis, while Leninists have actively pursued the destruction of capitalism with a great deal of self-confidence. Stalinists, in order to reassure their followers and render their opponents powerless, have made masterful use of the psychological effect of the concept of the inevitability of socialism. Faith in the inevitability of socialism, apparently, also fortifies the Maoists' conviction (in the spirit of indeterminism which they otherwise reject) that the determining nature of China's backwardness does not constitute an obstacle over which the organized masses cannot execute 'great leaps forward'.

V

Assuming that Marx's occasional extremely deterministic statements are true, that socialism is an historical inevitability, and that people can only speed up or slow down its advent: in that case, is a Marxist ethics possible?

The task of such ethics, among other things, would be to morally stimulate and obligate people to struggle for socialism. This effort of the ethical theorists, however, makes sense only if people can influence the course of history. Yet we have already quoted extensively from the Marx according to whom people have a weak impact upon the historical process and, therefore, bear little responsibility for the outcome of this process.

Precisely because he looked upon socialism as an historical inevitability, Marx did not feel the need to give an explicit ethical justification for it. Much less did he want to prescribe that people *ought* to try to bring about the triumph of socialism.

This has led a few interpreters – Karl Popper,[28] N. B. Mayo,[29] George L. Kline,[30] and others – to conclude that Marx took historical necessity as his ethical criterion. Since Popper's statement is the most fully elaborated, it seems most natural that his statement should be presented and evaluated here.

Popper characterizes Marx's position as 'moral positivism', or even more precisely, 'moral futurism', but immediately

[28] *The Open Society and Its Enemies.*
[29] *Democracy and Marxism*, ch. 7.
[30] *European Philosophy Today*, p. 132.

adds: 'Marx, I assert, would not seriously have defended moral positivism in the form of moral futurism if he had seen that it implies the recognition of future might as right.'[31] As evidence for his interpretation, Popper refers to the following passage from Engels: '. . . that morality which contains the maximum of durable elements is the one which, in the present, represents the overthrow of the present, represents the future: that is, the proletarian.'[32] But first of all, this passage does not prove that historical necessity was an ethical criterion for Engels. And secondly, even if it were to do so, this is Engels and not Marx. Popper did not quote Marx, and could not, because there are no passages in Marx's writings to justify such an interpretation. He read the ethical criterion implicit in Stalinism into Marx: that which triumphs in history is *ipso facto* moral.

Robert C. Tucker[33] rightly rejects Popper's interpretation, suggesting that Marx first arrived at the idea of a human society, and only later reached his convictions about its necessity. At this point we might also take note of another rather convincing counterproof offered by Tucker: it is hardly credible that anyone would be so disgusted by existing society, to the extent that Marx was, solely on the basis of the intellectual conviction that it would inevitably disappear and yield to communism. In my opinion, the idea of the humanistic foundation of communism led Marx *psychologically* to his conviction of its inevitability, and not conversely. As a great optimist he was convinced that the historical process would necessarily lead to a *human* society. However, these two matters – the historical necessity and the humanistic justification of communism – were *logically* independent of each other in his mind.

Because of its occasionally absolutely deterministic dimension, however, Marx's thought peculiarly does harm to the very cause it espouses. For a Marxist to be able to construct an ethics of revolutionary action, he must reject Marx's rigid determinism. Such determinism excludes human freedom, which is the *ratio essendi* of morality and ethics.

[31] *The Open Society and Its Enemies*, p. 393.
[32] *Anti-Dühring*, p. 104.
[33] *Philosophy and Myth in Karl Marx*, p. 21.

Many Marxists have accepted a milder variant of Marx's determinism. But it is by now high time to approach serious work on the formulation, development, and justification of this position. In Marxism this point of view has merely been reiterated, with minor variations, yet other, non-Marxist philosophers have written many significant works on the problem of historical determinism and freedom. One could not say that they have solved this problem, of course, but it is certain that they have made a considerable degree of progress in both the presentation of the problem and the argumentation of their positions.

The milder variant of determinism proceeds from the assumption that every historical situation bears within it more than one possibility. Yet possibilities are not unlimited, contrary to what Marxists who have fallen under the influence of existentialism may think, for the framework of possibilities is defined by the historical level achieved. Human freedom consists of the power to choose one of these possibilities and to commit oneself to its realization. Only when man possesses this power of choice is he morally responsible for the course of history. An ethics of revolutionary action is possible only on the basis of faith in the relative openness of the future.

However, even once one concludes that a Marxist ethics must renounce Marx's occasional absolute determinism, one need not in the least agree with Popper, who writes: '"Scientific" Marxism is dead. Its feeling of social responsibility and its love for freedom must survive.'[34] Today rigid determinism has been transcended in natural science as well as in social science. But even if science does not reveal inevitabilities in history, it is still capable of establishing historical possibilities and tendencies.

Socialism is one of these real possibilities and tendencies, but hardly an inevitability. Whether or not it will be realized depends upon human beings. Only a Marxism which sees socialism as a possibility can ethically obligate them to commit themselves to its realization.

After all the events of the past hundred years it is no longer possible to believe in the inevitability of socialism. At least two

[34] *The Open Society and Its Enemies*, p. 397.

fundamental changes have occurred since Marx's time. First, a new form of class prehistory – statism – has been created, a form which Marx did not foresee; and second, man has accumulated such destructive forces in his hands that not even the existence of humanity can be taken for a certainty, much less the movement of history in any particular direction. Today it is not only possible for mankind to pass over from prehistory into true history; it may also pass over into de-history. What if it turns out that humanity has been trying to perform a task of Sisyphus? Or even worse – what if the stone destroys Sisyphus, and thus if the disappearance of the absurd is produced only at the price of the triumph of nothingness?

VI

Marx took possession of the pre-existing store of humanistic-ethical ideas, into which, among others, the ideals of the great democratic revolutions had found their way, and then radicalized, developed and made it concrete. The humanistic-ethical basis of his work is composed of the concepts of de-alienation, freedom, social equality and justice, the abolition of exploitation, the disappearance of social classes, the withering away of the state, the creation of self-managing associations of producers, and so on. No satisfactory socio-political ethics today can steer clear of these values.

Marx's contribution to ethics must be sought in the radicalization and concretization of these values rather than in the formulation of a basic ethical criterion. To this day many Marxists have tried to find confirmation of such a criterion in Marx's writings, but to no avail.

At first the ethical criterion was sought in the abolition of exploitation and the interests of the proletariat. But one need not be very analytically-minded to see that these principles cannot fulfil this role.

Marx's concept of exploitation embraces only a small portion of the moral phenomenon, and it is for this very reason that the abolition of exploitation could not be an ethical criterion. The attempt of certain Marxists to understand exploitation in a much broader sense, as *any situation* in which one person uses another *to his own advantage*, while avoiding the above-mentioned pitfall, introduces a second, no less dangerous one – excessive vagueness. Besides, ethics, particularly a Marxist ethics, cannot simply demand that people eliminate a situation in which each takes advantage of the other, but must rather demand instead something much more, something positive.

Lenin was in the habit of saying: 'We say that our morality is entirely subordinated to the interests of the proletariat's class struggle. Our morality stems from the interests of the class struggle of the proletariat.'[35] But when suggested as an ethical criterion, the interest of the proletariat has unavoidable weaknesses. Above all, the very notion of interest is extremely vague, and even Marx himself decisively rejected all utilitarian ethics. Some theorists have sought the solution in the difference between the immediate and historical interests of the proletariat. It is generally recognized that Marx clearly discriminated in favour of the latter. For him the proletariat's immediate interest was not even an unconditionally positive ethical value, much less a fundamental ethical criterion. The history of the proletariat and the proletarian movement indeed show how right Marx was to have a critical attitude toward its immediate interest.

However, to take the historical interest of the proletariat as the ethical criterion is to be caught unawares in a vicious circle. Analysis of Marx's writings demonstrates that the historical interest, as distinguished from the immediate interest of the proletariat, includes *by definition* the realization of the humanistic-ethical values enumerated above, thereby presenting us once more with the original question: which of these is the supreme ethical value that can serve as a basis for the supreme ethical criterion?

This vicious circle is not so conspicuous as the one within which Lenin was caught when he tried to define *communist* morality as that which 'serves to destroy the old exploiting society and to unite all the working people around the proletariat, which is building up a revolutionary, a *communist* society.'[36] For decades Soviet ethicists have retraced this circle.

[35] *Works*, in English (Moscow, 1950) vol. 31, p. 266.
[36] Ibid., vol. 31, p. 268. My emphasis – S.S.

As illustration I refer to Shishkin: 'Marxism-Leninism sees the highest criterion of communist morality in the struggle for communism.'[37] But under the influence of Stalinism these ethicists went even 'farther' than Lenin by identifying the historical interest of the proletariat with the policies of their own Communist Party. They thus opened the door to the ethical degeneration of the party, as well as of the revolution.

More recently, certain Marxists have sought the supreme ethical criterion in de-alienation. This certainly represents theoretical progress, as the concept of de-alienation is more fundamental and complex than that of either the abolition of exploitation or realization of the interests of the proletariat. But this effort as well has failed to produce any satisfactory results.

In the second chapter of this book we analysed Marx's concept of de-alienation. On the formal level, de-alienation means the transcendence of the contradiction between human essence and human existence. On the level of content, the de-alienated person is creative, whole, free, sociable, and multilaterally developed. When we analyse such a complex concept as that of de-alienation, that is to say, we find multiple values contained within it, once again posing the question from which we had started: which of these values is most fundamental, so that it may serve as the basic ethical criterion?

'Creativity' and 'wholeness' even at first glance are unsatisfactory because what we need is precisely a measure by which we can judge when a person, even in his creativity and wholeness, is moral, and when he is not. Freedom, again, cannot be a moral *criterion* because it is a *presupposition* of morality. Moral judgement presupposes moral responsibility, and moral responsibility presupposes freedom. Besides, freedom itself is subordinate to an ethical evaluation (there are abuses as well as uses of freedom), and it therefore cannot be a measure for such an evaluation.

This means that only two of the above-mentioned notions remain – sociability and the multilateral development of human potentials. In his previously cited book, Fritzhand, after detailed analysis, extracts these two principles – the socializa-

[37] *Osnovy kommunisticheskoi morali* (Foundations of Communist Morality) (Moscow, 1955) p. 95.

tion and self-realization of man – as the axiological basis of Marx's work. But he did not succeed in finding one basic value in Marx which might serve as a rule of thumb when these two principles come into conflict. It is accurate to say that Marx was a sort of ethical perfectionist: he stood for the realization of every human potential which does not threaten man's social nature. But where is the border between egoistic self-realization and socialization which does not smother individuality? Where does the free development of every individual as a 'condition for the free development of all' end and the development of an individual who threatens the freedom of others begin? How can we formulate a principle on the basis of which we can distinguish obligations of the free individual toward society from sociability which threatens human freedom?

Yet if Marx cannot help us to solve the problem of the fundamental ethical criterion, he still did articulate some important thoughts concerning individual ethical values. This fact should be put to good use in the construction of a Marxist ethics. A Marxist ethical theorist, of course, cannot afford to dwell too long on the establishment and systematization of Marx's contribution to ethics. Even if he extends his scope to other great socialist thinkers, which is undoubtedly necessary, he will still be no closer to a *living* ethics. Nothing can replace a critical analysis of the moral praxis of the revolutionary movement. Especially great prospects in this respect are offered by a humanistic-ethical critique of Stalinism.

13

Labour and Human Needs in a Society of Associated Producers

AGNES HELLER

Now we can discuss the interaction between production and the structure of needs in the society of associated producers.

We have already noted that in his conception of the society of associated producers, Marx is working with an altogether new structure of needs. The primary role here is played by the need for labour (by which the whole theory stands or falls) and, as we have seen, by the need for surplus labour.

We know that the origin of the need for labour and its growth into a 'vital need' are not synonymous for Marx. In capitalism labour is a burden, (*a*) because it is performed under external compulsion, because it is alienated, and (*b*) because its specific nature offers no possibility of self-realisation:

> He [Adam Smith] is right, of course, that, in its historic forms as slave labour, serf-labour, and wage-labour, labour always appears as repulsive, always as external forced labour; and not-labour, by contrast, as 'freedom and happiness'. This holds doubly: for this contradictory labour; and, relatedly, for labour which has not yet created the subjective and objective conditions for itself . . . in which labour becomes attractive work, the individual's self-realization, which in no way means that it becomes mere fun, mere amusement, as Fourier, with Grisette-like naiveté, conceives it.[1]

Marx uses the composition of music as an example of the kind of labour that is purely intellectual.

Excerpt from Agnes Heller, *The Theory of Need in Marx* (London: Allison & Busby, 1976) pp. 118–30. Reprinted by permission of Allison & Busby.

[1] *Grundrisse*, p. 611.

In the *Grundrisse* both conditions are satisfied: alienation is overcome and labour becomes *travail attractif*. Since with the production of material goods labour in the traditional sense ceases, all labour becomes essentially intellectual labour, the field for the self-realization of the human personality. It thus becomes the vital need, a determining (even if not the most determining) human need, and hence it also assumes a dominant role in the structure of needs. In this conception, there never can arise any question about 'why' human beings work.

In the framework of *Capital*, however, only one condition is satisfied: the alienation of labour ceases (in every aspect), but labour itself does not become *travail attractif*. In this interpretation labour in the society of associated producers is not free self-activity:

> In fact, the realm of freedom actually begins only where labour which is determined by necessity and mundane considerations cease; thus in the very nature of things it lies beyond the sphere of actual material production. . . . freedom in this field can only consist in socialised man, the associated producers, rationally regulating their interchange with nature, bringing it under their common control, instead of being ruled by it as by the blind forces of nature; and achieving this with the least expenditure of energy and under conditions most favourable to, and worthy of, their human nature. But it none the less still remains a realm of necessity. Beyond it begins that development of human energy which is an end in itself, the true realm of freedom, which, however, can blossom forth only with this realm of necessity as its basis. The shortening of the working day is its basic prerequisite.[2]

Three comments need to be made here. First, since according to the quotation from *Capital* only free time is the sphere of free self-activity, Marx is attributing an even greater importance here than in the *Grundrisse* to time-economy, to the reduction of the necessary working time and to the rationalisation of production. Secondly, since labour is not itself *travail attractif*, it may be asked why people work. Thirdly, I would like to

[2] *Capital*, vol. III, pp. 799–800.

emphasize that from this point of view the project here appears just as utopian, despite the fact that its presentation is more realistic, as in the *Grundrisse*; I believe it inconceivable that there should be such a huge abyss between the activity of labour and the activity of free time. The *Grundrisse*'s noble picture of the individual active in his free time who re-enters production a changed man would lose its relevance: production does not 'need' to be performed by 'changed', 'richer' human beings.

This discussion could take us far away from our real argument, so let us return to the second question: why do people work? Assuming the structure of needs to be what it is today, the answer can only be conceived in terms of the general obligation to labour. But 'the obligation to labour' for Marx is characteristic only of a period of transition (the brief phase of the dictatorship of the proletariat). In the society of associated producers only nature can force people to do anything: no one can force anyone else (feudal lordship and serfdom are, in Marx's view, reciprocal determinations; there is no feudal lordship without serfdom and vice versa). In the first phase of communism (in which people share products according to their labour) there is naturally a form of obligation inherited from capitalism: in order to live, people must work. But when they share their goods according to their needs, and the labour time of each individual is not divided into necessary labour and surplus labour, then this form of obligation also ceases to exist. So why do human beings work? In *Capital*, Marx posits a structure of needs that is basically new, that transforms human beings into changed people, for whom 'social duty' is *not only an external but an internal motivation*: in this respect, 'Must' [*Müssen*] and 'Ought' [*Sollen*] now coincide. (I can only imagine this model in a society composed of communities. We shall see below how this hypothesis occurred to Marx.)

Only in *Capital* do we find a consistent conception of the interaction between material needs and production:

> It is only where production is under the actual, predetermining control of society that the latter establishes a relation between the volume of social labour time applied in producing definite

[3] Ibid., p. 184.

> articles, and the volume of the social want to be satisfied by these articles.[3]

And further on:

> Secondly, after the abolition of the capitalist mode of production, but still retaining social production, the determination of value continues to prevail in the sense that the regulation of labour-time and the distribution of social labour among the various production groups, ultimately the book-keeping encompassing all this, become more essential than ever.[4]

And again:

> Surplus labour in general as labour performed over and above the given requirements, must always remain. . . . a definite quantity of surplus labour is required as insurance against accidents, and by the necessary and progressive expansion of the process of reproduction in keeping with the development of the needs and the growth of population, which is called accumulation from the viewpoint of the capitalist.[5]

What then, according to this point of view, is the relationship between material needs and production?

Society produces *for* needs; hence the 'accidental' character of the market is eliminated. It is therefore possible, according to Marx, to avoid the 'waste' of material goods and productive capacities which characterizes capitalism and stems from the fact that production and needs are brought together only on the market. How are needs and production matched? The 'associated producers', as I have already indicated, will measure (*a*) needs and (*b*) their disposable labour time, and will fix (*c*) the labour time socially necessary for each activity. They will then divide up (and reallocate) the productive forces between various branches of production. They will, of course, also take into account the production that does not directly serve the satisfaction of needs (the expansion of production, insurance funds and – they are not mentioned here, but they

[4] Ibid., p. 830.
[5] Ibid., p. 799.

appear in other passages – public investments that will satisfy needs only over a period of time).

What are the needs which must be measured and for which production must be undertaken? They are the 'true social needs' which are identified with 'necessary needs'.

But how can 'true social needs' be measured? It is assumed that the needs of individuals that are directly oriented towards consumption are, both qualitatively and quantitatively, roughly equal. It is therefore extraordinarily easy to account for them: with the aid of random samples, both quality and quantity can be determined. So far so good: but human beings in communist society, in Marx's view, are characterized above all else by the fact that their needs, considered *individually*, and the needs of different individuals, will be qualitatively and quantitatively extremely varied. If this is also true of material needs, the kind of measurement given in *Capital* is simply absurd. Even if a procedure were invented – it would be indeed a complex one – to carry it out, one could assert with some certainty that such a 'production for needs' would lead to a 'waste' of material goods and productive forces much greater than that to which the production of commodities (regulation by the market) has led or can lead. We would thus be saying that Marx did not apply the individualization of needs to the field of need for material goods. Only non-quantifiable types of need would become individual (and qualitatively different); quantifiable types of need (true material needs) would not become individual. This would lead to an extremely homogeneous and almost uniform image of the individual – if, that is, one accepts that Marx regarded material needs as playing a decisive role in the structure of needs of individuals. But Marx actually thought exactly the opposite: that for individuals in the society of associated producers, material needs occupy a subordinate role in the structure of needs, so that the development of a system of individual needs becomes possible notwithstanding their qualitative and quantitative 'equality'.

This conception is based upon relatively static needs which develop very slowly (at least where material needs are concerned). It does not even take into consideration the fact that, as we have said, purely qualitative needs (which are *eo ipso* individual) also call for material production, and that this raises further difficulties in 'calculating' them.

In this conception of material needs, a kind of 'egalitarianism' predominates. It is important to underline this point because 'egalitarianism' has no bitterer enemy than Marx himself. He holds that the concept of equality belongs to commodity production: in fact commodity production is 'realized equality'. Equality and inequality are reciprocally determined: where there is equality there is inequality, and vice versa. 'Equality' as a slogan and as a demand always remains within the horizon of bourgeois society. It abstracts from the uniqueness of the individual, and quantifies what is qualitatively diverse. In the society that develops the wealth of individuality – in communist society – 'equality' is not realized: equality and inequality as reciprocal determinations become meaningless and irrelevant. In order to demonstrate that this idea is constantly present in Marx's thought I shall cite two passages: one from a work of his youth, the other from a late work. In *The Holy Family* Marx writes:

> Proudhon did not succeed in giving this thought the appropriate development. The idea of 'equal possession' is a political-economic one and therefore itself still an *alienated* expression for the principle that the object as being for man, as the objectified being of man, is at the same time the existence of man for other men, his human relation to other men, the social relation of man to man.[6]

The idea of 'equal possession' therefore articulates, in an alienated manner (i.e. within the horizon of bourgeois society and with its terminology), the real aim, which is to overcome the alienated relations. In the *Critique of the Gotha Programme* Marx does not attack the concept of equal possession but that of equal right (equal right, as we know, will continue to subsist in the first phase of communism, which therefore will still be a bourgeois society in this respect): 'This equal right . . . is therefore a right to inequality in its content, like every right.'[7] This equality is 'abstraction', because it takes account of man only as worker. At the same time it abstracts from the effective needs of

[6] *The Holy Family*, p. 60.
[7] *Critique of the Gotha Programme*, in *Selected Works*, vol. II, p. 564.

individuals, by furnishing them with equal amounts of goods from the social wealth according equal amounts of labour, whatever their needs actually are. Distribution according to needs, in contrast to distribution according to labour, overcomes both this equality and this inequality.

According to the *Critique of the Gotha Programme*, as we know, *no value* exists in the second phase of communism, and labour is not reduced to simple labour; at the same time Marx posits an extraordinary wealth of goods. Precisely for this reason there is no place for what we have called the 'egalitarian' aspect of communism. This is not the case in *Capital*, where we come across a 'saturation model' regarding material goods. In Marx's conception, this kind of 'egalitarianism' is in no way identical with the equality of commodity production (equality of possession and of rights): the matter at issue is rather the relative equality of actual needs as regards material goods. These, as we know, are only limited by other (higher) needs of individuals. We ourselves cannot imagine any social order in which the need for material goods can become saturated relatively easily and where the individuality of needs develops exclusively through non-material needs. Today, we would call the conception which appears in *Capital* 'egalitarian'. However, the fact is that it was not an egalitarian one in Marx's eyes, and that he associated this model not with 'equality' but with the complete restructuring of the system of needs.

The great importance that Marx attached to the restructuring of the system of needs also appears clearly in two observations in the *Grundrisse* (in his maturity Marx considered such a restructuring to be a *sine qua non*; on this point there is no difference between *Capital* and the *Grundrisse*). He writes about workers in capitalism as follows:

> Through excessive exhaustion of their powers, brought about by lengthy, drawn-out monotonous occupations, they are seduced into habits of intemperance, and made unfit for thinking or reflection. They can have no physical, intellectual or moral 'amusements' other than of the worst sort.[8]

The intemperance follows from the fact that no capacity for

[8] *Grundrisse*, p. 714. Marx is actually quoting Robert Owen.

physical, intellectual and moral 'amusements' can develop in the worker. In the 'society of associated producers', in which this capacity (qualitative needs) is well developed, 'intemperance' ceases. In another passage Marx expounds the problem with reference to the social whole. If society has attained a certain level of [material] wealth, then 'society [is] able to wait; . . . a large part of the wealth already created can be withdrawn both from immediate consumption and from production for immediate consumption.'[9] Let me repeat once again: for material needs, Marx is using something quite close to a 'saturation model', at least when he analyses the period after the attainment of a certain level of material wealth.

At this point the following question arises: who makes the decisions about how productive capacity should be allocated? Who decides, for example, how long the production of goods directly serving consumption can 'wait'? Marx's reply, of course, is *everyone* (this is precisely why he speaks of 'associated individuals'). But how can every individual make such decisions? Marx did not answer this question, because for him it did not arise. For us, however, in our times, it has become perhaps the most decisive question of all. The focal point of contemporary marxism is to work out models for this (or at least it ought to be).

Naturally, it is no accident that Marx did not even once formulate the question about 'how every individual can take part in decision-making'. We have already noted that in his opinion the category of interest will be irrelevant in the society of the future, and that there will therefore be no group interests, nor conflict of interests. The clear common interest of every member of society, apart from the satisfaction of necessary needs (which, as we have seen, still play a subordinate role in the structure of needs), will be the reduction of labour time. This is possible only through the maximum of rationalization. Consequently, every individual strives for the same thing, namely this maximum of rationalism; and the manner in which decision-making is carried on is of no consequence whatever. Whether the decisions are made by means of a referendum or through rotating representatives, every individual expresses

[9] Ibid., p. 707.

the needs of all other individuals and it cannot be otherwise. In 'socialized' man, the human species and the individual represent a realized unity. Every individual represents the species and the species is represented in every individual. The needs of 'socialized' human beings determine production – and this means that the human species itself makes the decisions.

To put it in hegelian terms, in Marx's society of associated producers the sphere of 'the objective spirit' goes up in smoke. We find no system of right, no institutions or politics there. What remains of the sphere of the 'objective spirit' of class society is elevated to the sphere of the 'absolute spirit'. For it is not only the pre-existing activities and objectivations (in an alienated form) of class society, such as art or philosophy, which are 'in conformity with the species for itself'. Morals too, and every human relationship, become 'in conformity with the species for itself'. To continue with the hegelian analogy: the 'world spirit' is not only recognized in art and philosophy, but in every human relationship; every individual is representative of a conformity to the species that has become real and actual, he recognizes this representativeness in every other person, and presents himself as such in relation to them. All this is very well expressed in *The Holy Family*, where Marx speaks of morality in the future:

> Plato admitted that the law must be one-sided and must make abstraction of the individual. On the other hand, under human conditions punishment will really be nothing but the sentence passed by the culprit on himself. There will be no attempt to persuade him that violence from without, exerted by others, is violence exerted on himself by himself. On the contrary, he will see in other people his natural saviours from the sentence which he has pronounced on himself; in other words the relation will be reversed.[10]

In one of Kant's hypotheses he imagined 'the ideal society' to be that in which people make a contract to proceed according to the categoric imperative. From the point of view of his own philosophy this is in effect a contradiction: if it is a case of

[10] *The Holy Family*, pp. 238–9.

making a contract, morality is changed into legality. In Marx's eyes, the same model – at least from the philosophical standpoint – appears to be posed without any contradiction. If every individual represents conformity with species for itself, then the *need* of every individual (in this case, moral need) is involved at the level of this conformity. If his own particularity transgresses this conformity, he may therefore punish himself. The conflict between morality and legality is thus surmounted, since the opposition or opposed Being between morality and legality (which for Marx is found only in class society, in alienation) disappears.

The disappearance of legality and of all institutions does not of course imply the simple disappearance of objectivation. Quite the opposite. Only in communism (in the positive abolition of private property) is individual possession properly founded. Remember: needs are always directed towards objects. These objectivations are all 'for themselves' – except the sphere of production, which is in and for itself. Since we can no longer speak of material needs, but only of needs which 'stand outside them', every objectivation belongs to the realm of the 'absolute spirit'. Non-material needs are therefore all directed to the 'absolute spirit', to their objectivations, to their objects and to the allocation of these objects.

It is precisely for this reason that in the society of associated producers the need for 'free time', for 'leisure time', has such a leading role in man's system of needs. ('Leisure time' is not necessarily synonymous with 'free time': the latter can in fact be interpreted as a negative concept, as freedom from labour. For Marx, however, free time is 'leisure time', an unambiguously positive category: time for genuinely human, high-level activities – free activities.) Furthermore, artistic activity has a leading role in free-time activities, as the work of Marx's most creative periods clearly demonstrates. Artistic activity, which even in the era of class society is already drawn towards objectivations 'for themselves' and creates them, is the simplest and most illuminating example of what preoccupies Marx: the need for objectivations which are objectivations *for themselves* and which conform to the species, is the true human need of the members of the 'society of associated producers'.

Needs for objectivations (and objects) for themselves are

purely qualitative needs, which are not quantifiable; furthermore, they are always needs to an end. This is formulated in the third volume of *Capital* as follows: beyond production 'begins that *development of human energy* which is an *end in itself*, the true *realm of freedom*.'[11] In activities which are directed towards objectivations for themselves, the true wealth of human beings develops, a universality of needs and capacities that satisfies qualitatively different (non-quantifiable) needs: 'Wealth is disposable time and nothing more.'[12]

The object for itself of needs can, as we have already noted, be not only an objectivation but also the other person. Recall the *Economic and Philosophical Manuscripts of 1844*: in his human relationships, socialized man at all times makes qualities possible only for other men, and this is an end in itself; 'rich man' is man rich in human relationships. The question here is: does need for human beings also mean 'need for community'?

The question is of significance not only for the system of needs, but also for the whole social model. We have seen that in Marx's notion of the society of associated producers there is no place for the 'objective spirit', for the system of institutions. But should this also imply that there is no place for human integration?

For Marx, community (even on the smallest scale) is justifiable and relevant only when it appears as the immediate form of conformity to the species for itself, when it is an objectivation that conforms with the species for itself. There is no interest, and no conflict of interests: community, like the individual, can only be an *immediate* expression of such conformity to the species.

In the young Marx, community and the need for community undoubtedly appear as a *leitmotiv*. Remember his thoughts on the meetings of communist workers: 'But at the same time, as a result of this association, they acquire a new need – the need for society – and what appears as a means becomes an end.'[13] In the same work he also says: 'Although communal activity and communal enjoyment – i.e. activity and enjoyment which are

[11] *Capital*, vol. III, p. 800.

[12] *Theories of Surplus Value*, vol. III, p. 255.

[13] *Economic and Philosophical Manuscripts of 1844*, p. 137.

manifested and directly revealed in real association with other men – will occur wherever such a direct expression of sociability stems from the true character of the activity's content and is adequate to its nature.'[14] Or again: 'In the same way, the senses and enjoyment of other men have become my own appropriation. Besides these direct organs, therefore, social organs develop in the form of society; thus, for instance, activity in direct association with others, etc., has become an organ for expressing my own life, and a mode of appropriating human life.'[15] 'Universal consciousness', reflection, philosophy, theory and thought must be rooted in this communal Being, and not 'grip the masses' merely after the event. 'My general consciousness is only the theoretical shape of that which the living shape is the real community, the social fabric, although at the present time general consciousness is an abstraction from real life and as such confronts it with hostility.'[16] This is why I stated earlier that, in Marx's view, not all philosophy will cease under communism, but only the philosophy which counterposes the particular to that which conforms with the species, and which counterposes appearance to essence – the philosophy built on self-realizing values. It is social science instead which, according to this conception, would seem to cease. In fact there will no longer be any fetishism; in society essence and appearance will overlap. And so social science, which owes its existence to the contradiction between essence and appearance, will in effect be superfluous under communism according to Marx's view.

The idea of community and of the need for society, which is properly central in the works of his youth, moves somewhat into the background in his later works. We can see various reasons for this. First, there is his critique of the 'community' of natural societies and its 'limitedness'. Wherever Marx speaks of community – even in his earlier works – he is thinking of something different from 'natural communities'. He conceives the communities of the future as freely chosen, as made up of individuals who freely unite, as 'purely social' relations – a consequence of the pushing back of natural limits. However, as

[14] Ibid., p. 137. Translation modified.
[15] Ibid., pp. 139–40. Translation modified.
[16] Ibid., p. 137.

Marx devotes himself with increasing intensity to his analysis of the evolution of capitalism as alienated *evolution*, he puts increasing emphasis on the positive trend which capitalism has produced – amongst other things, by dissolving the natural communities. But there is another factor to be taken into account: that the presence of communities in the future society seemed so obvious to Marx that he did not see any necessity for discussing it separately. Very often he speaks of the society of the future as the 'society of co-operatives'! The existence of the 'community' and the 'need for community' in effect pass into the background; and in the few passages where he speaks of them, they appear as a 'natural' perspective. This is how he deals with it in the third volume of *Capital*, for example. Analysing the embryos of the future which exist in the present, he speaks of Robert Owen's co-operative factories:

> The co-operative factories of the labourers themselves represent, *within the old form, the first shoots of the new* . . . the capitalist stock companies, as much as the co-operative factories, should be considered as *transitional forms* from the capitalist mode of production to the associated one, with the only distinction that *the antagonism is resolved negatively in the one and positively in the other.*[17]

In the draft of a letter to Vera Zasulic, written in 1881, Marx expresses himself in a still more broad and unambiguous manner. The Russian rural community 'finds capitalism in a crisis that will end only with its elimination, and *with the return of the modern societies* to the "archaic" type of communal property; or, as an American author has said, the new system to which modern society is tending will be a revival in a superior form of an archaic social type. There is no need to be frightened of the expression "archaic".' Furthermore, in discussing those aspects of the communities of the future which will be different from the archaic communities, he points before all else to the fact that the former will not be based upon blood ties. This conception is in no way different from the position taken by Engels in his article of 1845, 'Description of the communist

[17] *Capital*, vol. III, p. 431.

colonies that have originated in recent times and are still existing', in which he refers enthusiastically to the religious communes of the United States and predicts that they will spread. Marx was alarmed by the dissolution of the existing communities, because he recognized and treasured them as embryos of the form of intercourse and integration which in communism would become general.

In Marx's view, therefore, the 'everyday life' of man in the future society is not built around productive labour. On the contrary, productive labour occupies a subordinate position in the activities of everyday life; the centre of organization of life is represented by those activities and human relationships which conform with the species for itself. The needs directed towards these (qualitative needs-as-ends) will become man's primary needs, they will constitute his unique individuality and will limit needs for material goods. It is in this way that the personality that is 'deep' and rich in needs will be constituted.

Marx believed this change in the structure of needs to be 'natural' and 'obvious'. He took so little account of the possibility of conflicts that one thing must be repeated: although the change in Being is the decisive issue for him, there are quite a few Enlightenment aspects to be found in his conception. One will search in vain for the actual conflicts and problems of the transition which are so relevant for us and which are now a century old, but even so this 'pure' model has not lost its decisive significance for us.

Engels spoke with pride of the development of socialism from utopia to science. Today, science contains more than a few utopian elements. But as Ernst Bloch has so strikingly said, there are fertile and infertile utopias. There are many respects in which Marx's ideas on the society of associated producers and on the system of needs of united individuals are utopian, when measured against our own today and our own possibilities for action; they are none the less *fertile*. He establishes a norm against which we can measure the reality and value of our ideas, and with which we can determine the limitedness of our actions: it expresses the most beautiful aspiration of mature humanity, an aspiration that belongs to our Being.

Bibliographical References

Adler, Max, *Kausalität und Teleologie im Streite um die Wissenschaft*. Vienna: Wiener Volksbuchhandlung, 1904.

—— *Lehrbuch der materialistischen Geschichtsauffassung* (1930–2). Republished with the addition of a third volume under the title *Soziologie des Marxismus*. Vienna: Europa Verlag, 1964.

Althusser, Louis, *Lenin and Philosophy and Other Essays*. London: New Left Books, 1971.

Althusser, Louis, and Balibar, Étienne, *Reading Capital*. London: New Left Books, 1970.

Anderson, Perry, *Passages from Antiquity to Feudalism*. London: New Left Books, 1974.

—— *Lineages of the Absolutist State*. London: New Left Books, 1974.

Baran, Paul, and Sweezy, Paul, *Monopoly Capital*. New York: Monthly Review Press, 1966.

Bastide, Roger (ed.), *Sens et usage du terme structure*. Brussels: Mouton, 1962.

Bauer, Otto, 'Marxismus und Ethik', *Die Neue Zeit*, XXIV, 2 (1905–6). English trans. in Bottomore and Goode (eds.), *Austro-Marxism*.

Bernstein, Eduard, *Evolutionary Socialism*. New York: Schocken Books, 1961.

Bhaskar, Roy, *A Realist Theory of Science*. Brighton: Harvester Press, 2nd edn, 1978.

—— *The Possibility of Naturalism: A Philosophical Critique of the Contemporary Human Sciences*. Brighton: Harvester Press, 1979.

Bottomore, Tom, *Marxist Sociology*. London: Macmillan, 1975.

—— *Sociology as Social Criticism*. London: Allen & Unwin, 1975.

Bottomore, Tom, and Goode, Patrick (eds.), *Austro-Marxism*. Oxford: Oxford University Press, 1978.

Bukharin, Nikolai, *Historical Materialism: A System of Sociology*. New York: International Publishers, 1925.

Croce, Benedetto, *Historical Materialism and the Economics of Karl

Marx. London: Howard Latimer, 1913.

Ellman, M., 'Did the Agricultural Surplus Provide the Resources for the Increase in Investment in the USSR during the First Five Year Plan?', *Economic Journal* (December 1975).

Ellul, Jacques, *The Technological Society*. New York: Vintage Books, 1967.

Engels, Friedrich, *Dialectics of Nature*. Moscow: Foreign Languages Publishing House, 1954.

Forde, Daryl, and Radcliffe-Brown, A. R. (eds.), *African Systems of Kinship and Marriage*. London: Oxford University Press, 1950.

Fromm, Erich (ed.), *Socialist Humanism*. Garden City, N.Y.: Doubleday & Co., 1965.

—— *Marx's Concept of Man*. New York: Frederick Ungar, 1961.

Gehlen, Arnold, *Studien zur Anthropologie und Soziologie*, Berlin, 1963.

Godelier, Maurice, *Rationality and Irrationality in Economics*. London: New Left Books, 1974.

—— *Perspectives in Marxist Anthropology*. Cambridge: Cambridge University Press, 1977.

Goldmann, Lucien, *The Hidden God*. London: Routledge & Kegan Paul, 1964.

—— *Marxisme et sciences humaines*. Paris: Gallimard, 1970.

Gough, Ian, 'State expenditure in advanced capitalism'. *New Left Review* (July/August 1975).

Gramsci, Antonio, *Selections from the Prison Notebooks*. London: Lawrence & Wishart, 1971.

Habermas, Jürgen, *Knowledge and Human Interests*. London: Heinemann, 1972.

—— *Legitimation Crisis*. London: Heinemann, 1976.

Hahn, M., and Wiedmann, F. (eds.), *Die Philosophie und die Frage nach dem Fortschritt*. Munich, 1964.

Hilferding, Rudolf, *Finance Capital*. London: Routledge & Kegan Paul, 1981.

Jay, Martin, *The Dialectical Imagination*. Boston: Little, Brown & Co., 1973.

Kamenka, Eugene, *The Ethical Foundations of Marxism*. London: Routledge & Kegan Paul, 1962.

Kline, George L., *European Philosophy Today*. Chicago: University of Chicago Press, 1965.

Kolakowski, Leszek, *Marxism and Beyond*. London: Pall Mall Press, 1969.

—— *Main Currents of Marxism*. 3 vols, Oxford: Oxford University Press, 1978.

Korsch, Karl, *Marxism and Philosophy*. London: New Left Books, 1970.

—— *Karl Marx*. London: Chapman & Hall, 1938.

Kosik, Karel, *Dialectics of the Concrete*. Dordrecht and Boston: D. Reidel, 1976.

Kress, Gisela, and Senghaas, Dieter (eds.), *Politikwissenschaft*. Frankfurt-am-Main: Suhrkamp, 1969.

Kühne, Karl, *Economics and Marxism*. 2 vols, London: Macmillan, 1979.

Kuhn, A., and Wolpe, A. M. (eds.), *Feminism and Materialism*. London: Routledge & Kegan Paul, 1978.

Labriola, Antonio, *Essays on The Materialistic Conception of History*. Chicago: Charles H. Kerr, 1908.

Lange, Oskar, *Political Economy*. Vol. I, London: Pergamon Press, 1963.

Larrain, Jorge, *The Concept of Ideology*. London: Hutchinson, 1979.

Leach, Edmund, *Political Systems of Highland Burma*. London: Bell & Sons, 1964.

Lévi-Strauss, Claude, *The Savage Mind*. London: Weidenfeld & Nicolson, 1966.

—— *The Elementary Structures of Kinship*. London: Eyre & Spottiswoode, 1968.

—— *Conversations with G. Charbonnier*. London: Jonathan Cape, 1969.

—— *Totemism*. Harmondsworth: Penguin Books, 1969.

—— *From Honey to Ashes*. London: Jonathan Cape, 1973.

Lichtheim, George, *From Marx to Hegel and Other Essays*. London: Orbach & Chambers, 1971.

Löbl, Eugen, *Geistige Arbeit – die wahre Quelle des Reichstums*. Vienna, 1968.

Lukács, Gyorgy, *History and Class Consciousness*. London: Merlin Press, 1971.

Mandel, Ernest, *Late Capitalism*. London: New Left Books, 1975.

Marcuse, Herbert, *Reason and Revolution: Hegel and the Rise of*

Social Theory. New York: Oxford University Press, 1941.

—— *One-Dimensional Man*. London: Routledge & Kegan Paul, 1964.

Marković, Mihailo, and Cohen, Robert S., *Yugoslavia: The Rise and Fall of Humanist Socialism*. Nottingham: Spokesman Books, 1975.

Marković, Mihailo and Petrović, Gajo (eds.) *Praxis: Yugoslav Essays in the Philosophy and Methodology of the Social Sciences*. Dordrecht: D. Reidel, 1979.

Marx, Karl [In the case of Marx's writings the contributors cite various editions, and references are therefore given in footnotes.]

Mayo, N. B., *Democracy and Marxism*. New York: Oxford University Press, 1955.

Michels, Robert, *Political Parties*. New York: Free Press, 1966.

Miliband, Ralph, *The State in Capitalist Society*. London: Weidenfeld & Nicolson, 1969.

—— *Marxism and Politics*. Oxford: Oxford University Press, 1977.

Musil, Robert, *The Man Without Qualities*. Vol. I, London: Secker & Warburg, 1953.

Nadel, F., *The Theory of Social Structure*. London: Cohen & West, 1957.

O'Connor, James, *The Fiscal Crisis of the State*. New York: St Martin's Press, 1973.

Offe, Claus, *Strukturprobleme des kapitalistischen Staates*. Frankfurt-am-Main: Suhrkamp, 1972.

—— 'The theory of the capitalist state and the problem of policy formation.' In L. Lindberg et al. (eds.), *Stress and Contradiction in Modern Capitalism*. London: D. C. Heath, 1975.

Palloix, C., 'The self-expansion of capital on a world scale', *Review of Radical Political Economy*, IX, 2 (1977).

Plekhanov, G. V., *Fundamental Problems of Marxism*. London: Martin Lawrence, 1929.

Popper, Karl, *The Open Society and Its Enemies*. London: Routledge & Kegan Paul, 1945.

Poulantzas, Nicos, *Classes in Contemporary Capitalism*. London: New Left Books, 1975.

Prawer, S. S., *Karl Marx and World Literature*. Oxford: Oxford University Press, 1976.

Rose, Gillian, *The Melancholy Science: An Introduction to the Thought of Theodor W. Adorno*. London: Macmillan, 1978.

Sekine, T. Uno-Riron, 'A Japanese Contribution to Marxian Political Economy'. *Journal of Economic Literature*, XIII, 3 (September 1975).

Schelsky, Helmut, *Der Mensch in der wissenschaftlichen Zivilisation*. Cologne-Opladen: Westdeutscher Verlag, 1961.

Schumpeter, J. A., *Capitalism, Socialism and Democracy*. London: Allen & Unwin, 5th edn, 1976.

Taylor, John G., *From Modernization to Modes of Production: A Critique of the Sociologies of Development and Underdevelopment*. London: Macmillan, 1979.

Tucker, Robert C., *Philosophy and Myth in Karl Marx*. Cambridge: Cambridge University Press, 1961.

Wallerstein, Immanuel, *The Modern World System*. New York: Academic Press, 1974.

Wellmer, Albrecht, *Critical Theory of Society*. New York: Herder & Herder, 1971.

Contributors

Louis Althusser teaches at the École Normale Supérieure in Paris. His best known writings are *For Marx*, *Reading Capital*, and *Lenin and Philosophy*.

Tom Bottomore is Professor of Sociology at the University of Sussex. His writings include *Sociology*, *Elites and Society*, *Marxist Sociology*, and *Political Sociology*.

Meghnad Desai is Lecturer in Economics at the London School of Economics and has written on various aspects of Marx's economic theory.

Maurice Godelier is Directeur d'études at the École des Hautes Études en Science Sociale, Paris. His writings include *Rationality and Irrationality in Economics* and *Perspectives in Marxist Anthropology*.

Lucien Goldmann (1913–70) wrote extensively on Marxist method and on the sociology of literature. His writings include *The Hidden God*, *Recherches dialectiques*, and *Marxisme et sciences humaines*.

Antonio Gramsci (1891–1937) was one of the founders of the Italian Communist Party and its most original thinker. Arrested by the Fascist Government in 1926 he was sentenced first to internment and then to prison, where he remained for the next eight years and produced some of his most important works, subsequently published as *Quaderni del carcere*, 6 vols, Turin: Einaudi, 1948–51.

Jürgen Habermas is the most eminent thinker of the later Frankfurt School. He was Professor of Philosophy and Sociology at the University of Frankfurt and is now Director of the

Max Planck Institute in Starnberg. Most of his major works have been translated into English, including *Knowledge and Human Interests* and *Legitimation Crisis*.

ANDRAS HEGEDUS was Prime Minister of Hungary in 1955–6, and from 1963 director of the Sociological Research Group in the Hungarian Academy of Sciences. After protesting against the Soviet invasion of Czechoslovakia in 1968 he was dismissed from this post and subsequently expelled from the Communist Party. He now teaches in Australia. He has written several works on socio-economic questions, including *Socialism and Bureaucracy*.

AGNES HELLER taught at the University of Budapest until she was dismissed in 1956 after the suppression of the Hungarian revolution and is now at La Trobe University, Victoria, Australia. Her main interest is in problems of moral philosophy, and more particularly Marxist ethics, and her best-known works in English are *The Theory of Needs* and *The Philosophy of the Radical Left* (forthcoming from Basil Blackwell).

RUDOLF HILFERDING (1877–1941) was one of the principal Austro-Marxist thinkers. He became a leading figure in the German Social Democratic Party, and was Finance Minister in two governments of the Weimar Republic. In 1933 he was obliged to go into exile, and in February 1941, after being handed over to the German authorities by the Vichy government, he died in Paris at the hands of the Gestapo. His major works are *Böhm-Bawerk's Marx-Critique* and *Finance Capital*.

GAJO PETROVIĆ is Professor of Philosophy at the University of Zagreb and a leading member of the *Praxis* group. His writings include *English Empiricist Philosophy* and *Marx in the Mid-Twentieth Century*.

NICOS POULANTZAS (1936–79) was one of the leading younger members of the Marxist structuralist school in Paris. His best known works are *Political Power and Social Classes* and *Classes in Contemporary Capitalism*.

Svetozar Stojanović was Chairman of the Department of Philosophy and Sociology at the University of Belgrade and a prominent member of the *Praxis* group. His best-known work in English is *Between Ideals and Reality*.

Albrecht Wellmer was one of the leading members of the postwar Frankfurt School, and is now Professor of Philosophy at the University of Konstanz. He is best known to English readers for his book *Critical Theory of Society*.

Index

Accumulation, 191; primitive, 144; by the state, 104–5
Adler, Max, 13–14, 16, 16n, 17n, 42, 173
Adorno, Theodor W., 5n
Alienation, 28, 197; de-, 184, 185; of labour, 188–9; and possession, 193; of property, 119; and reification, 71n
Althusser, Louis, 11, 14, 17; 'Ideology and Ideological State Apparatuses', 16n
Anderson, Perry, 15n
Animals, 24, 25–6, 27
Anthropology, structural, 84, 89
Aristocracy: labour, 139; Prussian, 135; in Rhenish Diet, re freedom of press, 46–7
Aristotle, 24–5
Artistic activity, 188, 197
Asiatic mode of production, 122–3
Austro-Marxists, 2, 11, 13–14, 16–18

Bachelard, Gaston, 11, 14n
Baran, Paul, 100
Bauer, Otto, 17n, 18
Bendix, Reinhard, 117
Bentham, Jeremy, 23–4
Berlinguer, Enrico, 120
Bernstein, Eduard, 171n, 173
Bhaskar, Roy, 14n, 16n
Bismarck, Otto von, 98
Bloch, Ernst, 201
Bloch, Josef, letter to, 32n
Bolsheviks, 1, 2
Bottomore, Tom: *Austro-Marxism*, 14n; *Karl Marx*, 1n; *Sociology as Social Criticism*, 7n
Bourgeoisie, the: class fractions, 149, 150; idealist philosophy, 68–70, 93; ideology, 151–2, 155, 157, 158, 166; and nature of man, 24; private property, 111, 114–15, 117, 122–3, 124; in Rhenish Diet, re freedom of press, 47; rise of, 75–6, 133; and the state, 98, 133–4, 135–6; *see also* Capitalism, Capitalist
Bukharin, Nikolai: and dialectic, 39–41; and intellectuals, 37–8; science and system, 39; *Theory of Historical Materialism*, 29–41, 98
Bureaucracy, 48–9, 135, 136, 149

Capitalism: advanced, 159, 163–5; competitive phase, 95, 98, 99, 100, 101; development, 99, 131–2, 200; labour in, 188, 194–5; liberal, 155–6, 165, 168; Marx's model of, 95–9, applied to contemporary society, 102–9; monopoly phase, 98–103; and morality, 176–7; property and power relations, 115–18, 124; reproduction, 154; state-regulated, 156–7, 163–4; surplus product, 118–19
Capitalist mode of production, 78–9, 80–1, 142, 144–5, 147, 163
Capitalist society: class struggle and ideology in, changing, 162–9; European, composition of, 147; *see also* Bourgeoisie
Cartesians, 71, 74
Censorship, 45–6
Chamberlin, E. H., 100
China, 116, 181
Civil society, separation from state, 96–9, 109
Class, social: antagonism mediatized today, 165; categories, 149;

concepts of strategy, 150; determination, 132, 136–7, 138–54; equilibrium of forces, 133, 136; exploitation, 144–5; fractions, 139–40, 149; functions and strata, 139–40, 149; and ideology, 75–6, 140–1, 146, 162–9; instinct, 141; and modes of production, 148; position, 139–40; 'power bloc', 150; powers, 146; reproduction, 153–4; ruling, 133; and state apparatus, 150–3; and state power, 132–6
Class consciousness, 4, 132, 141
Class struggle(s), 64, 131–2, 138–9, 140, 141; and institutionalizations, 65; liberating function, 62n; and social formation, 148; and state apparatus, 150–4; and state intervention, 163–5; and state power, 130–1; *see also* Revolution
Classless society: and ideology, 76–7; and state, 129n; transition to, 62–3
Commodity: fetishism, 58; labour power as, 144; relations, 144
Commune, Paris, the, 97, 123
Communes, US, 201
Communism, 73–4; first phase, 190; second, 194; and historical determinism, 180, 182; and morality, 172, 185–6
Communities, 198–201
Competitive economy, 95, 98, 99, 100, 101; sector, 104, 105–6
Comte, Auguste, 30n
Concept, in Marxian theory, 82–3
Conflicts, social, 64–6, 164–5; *see also* Class struggle
Consciousness, 25–6, 27–8; class-, 4, 132, 141; formation of, 59–62; and ideology, 74–5; self-realization, 186–7; and social reality, 49; universal, 199; *see also* Knowledge
Contradiction, social, 63–4
Co-operatives, 124, 200
Critical theory, 4n, 8; revolutionary function of, 62
Croce, Benedetto, 11, 13n, 32n, 173
Darwin, Charles, 173
Decision-making, 160, 195–6
de Man, Hendrik, 12n, 17n, 34–5
Democracy, 106–7
Depression: UK, 102, 106; US, 106
Der Kampf (journal), 12n, 17n
Descartes, René, 69
Determinism, 49, 177–84
Deutsch-Französische Jahrbücher, 52
Development, theories of, 15
Dialectic, 39–41, 49–50; ethical, 165–6; and Hegel, 50–3; *see also* Dualism
Dialectical materialism, 40, 52–3
Dialectical philosophy, 43–5
Domination, 59–60, 64, 65–6
Dualism, 44, 49, 51, 53; Kant's, 175; overcoming, 6–8
Duty, social, 190

Economic: apparatus, 151, 152; concept of the, 79–83, 142–3; ownership in production process, 143–5; and the political, separation of, 96–9; theory, Marx' model of, 95–9; three sectors, 103–6; *see also* Capitalism, Political Economy
Economics and structuralism, 84, 87–8
Ellman, M., 95n
Ellul, Jacques, 160n
Empiricism, and idealism, 69–70
Employment, 104, 105, 106–7
Engels, Friedrich, 45, 73, 133, 172, 201; *Anti-Dühring*, 182; re communes, 200–1; concept of the state, 129n; *Dialectics of Nature*, 27; Letters, 32n
Engineers, 147
England: Civil service, 136; Industrial Revolution, 137; liberalism, 133
Enlightenment, the, 20, 44, 49, 50, 201
Epistemology, 2, 11, 14n, 126–7; *see also* Knowledge
Equality, 193–4
Ethics, 17n, 73; and determinism,

177–84; dialectic of, 165–6; and freedom, 186; future, and law, 196–7; Marxist, 12, 18, 19–20, 170–87; preaching, 175–6; Protestant, 122; and science, 171–6; and socialism, 172–3, 181–2; and technocratic consciousness, 167–8
Evolution, 31, 89; of capitalism, 200; misconception of, 63
Exchange, 90, 156, 157
Exploitation, 83, 144–5, 146, 148; abolition of, 184–5; pre-capitalist, 144; and the underprivileged, 165

Feminism, 15
Fetishism, 71n, 80, 94, 199
Feudal mode of production, 77, 144
Feudalism, 79, 96, 113, 115, 117; reciprocity, 190; *v.*, 133
Feuerbach, Ludwig, 20, 69, 128; Marx's Theses on, 43, 44, 54, 67; 'practice', 70
Fourier, F. M. C., 123, 188
France: bureaucracy, 136; Enlightenment, 20, 44, 49, 50, 201; Paris Commune, 97, 123; Revolution, 96, 97
Frankfurt School, 2, 3–6, 11, 15n
Franklin, Benjamin, 24–5
Freedom: bourgeois ideology, 76–7; and determinism, 180, 182; of expression, 45–7; and labour, 189, 198; of labour, 155; and morality, 186; realm of, 8
Free time, 189–90, 197–8
Fritzhand, Marek, 8, 174, 177, 186–7
Fromm, Erich: *Marx's Concept of Man*, 26, 27; *Socialist Humanism*, 7n, 8n, 12n
Functionalism, 84–5, 89, 94
Futurism, moral, 181–2

Galli, G., 35n
Gehlen, Arnold, 160n, 161
Germany, 96, 135; Bismarck, 98; state power, 136
Godelier, Maurice, 14, 79n; *Perspectives in Marxist Anthropology*, 15n, 16n, 17n
Goldmann, Lucien, 6n, 7n, 15n, 173
Gough, Ian, 108
Gramsci, Antonio, 2, 120; *Selections from the Prison Notebooks*, 11, 21, 29n
Greece, ancient, 89

Habermas, Jürgen, 8–10, 15n, 56–7
Hegedus, Andras, 15n
Hegel, G. W. F., 25, 44, 125, 128, 131, 152, 165, 175, 178; concept of man, 27–8; Marx's critique of *Philosophy of Right*, 52–4; of *Philosophy of the State*, 44, 50–3; politics, 96–7
Hegelians, Young, 44, 52
Heinzen, K., 114–15
Hess, Moses, 45
Hilferding, Rudolf, 17n, 21, 98, 173
Historical determinism, 177–84
Historical materialism, 13n; and ideology, 73–7; in Marx's early writing, 44, 50–2; Marx's theory of, 70–1; 'modified', 58–9, 66; and political economy, 58–9, 62–7; and sociology, 29–35, 55; and structuralism, 88–92
History: Lévi-Strauss's concept of, 88–94; Marx's concept of, and production, 52–62, 68, 127–34; materialist, conception of, 125–54; and philosophy, 126–7; and praxis, 27, 31–6, 40–1; and structure, 36–7; structure of society, 53, 54, 55
Horkheimer, Max, essays, 4
Human societies, three formations of, 73
Humanism, in Marxist thought, 2–3, 7–8, 19–20, 128; and ethics, 176–7, 184, 185; as ideology, 68–75

Idealist philosophy, 68–70, 93
Ideological relations: and class structure, 140–1, 146, 149; and

state apparatus, 150–2
Ideologies, Lévi-Strauss's theory of, 90, 92, 93
Ideology, 17, 31, 155–69: bourgeois, 151–2, 155, 157, 158, 166; class function, 75–7, 149; and consciousness, 74–5; criticism of, 58–62; humanism as, 68–75; just exchange, 156–7; and knowledge, 71–3; and science, 57, 66–7, 73; and state intervention in economic system, 155–9, 163–6; technology and, 155, 159–63, 166–8
Imperialism, 2, 98, 149
Incomes: derived, 137; level, and class division, 142; *see also* Wages
Inflation, 106; class perspective, 107–8; and state expenditure, 102
Inheritance of property, 119
Institutional framework, of social class, 151–2, 162, 169
Intellectual labour, 188–9
Intellectuals, 37–8, 137, 149

Jay, Martin, 3n, 4n
Joint stock companies, 117, 124
Jurisprudence, and property, 112–13

Kalecki, M., 100
Kamenka, Eugene, 173, 174
Kant, Immanuel, 14, 17n, 18, 69, 173, 180, 196; neo-Kantians, 14, 173
Kautsky, Karl, 173
Keynesian economics, 106–7
Kinship theory, 90–2
Kline, George L., 181
Knowledge: of the absolute, 27–8; dialectic, 39–41, 49; epistemology, 2, 11, 14n, 126–7; and ideology, 71–3; and science, 16–17, 126–7; sociological theory of, 47–9; *see also* Consciousness, Positivism
Kolakowski, Leszek: *Main Currents of Marxism*, 8–9, 11n, 14n; *Marxism and Beyond*, 18–19
Korsch, Karl, 2–3, 4–5, 42; *Karl Marx*, 11n; *Marxism and Philosophy*, 3; 'Ten Theses on Marxism Today', 6
Kruschev, N., 1
Kühne, Karl, 15n

Labour: alienation, 188–9; as commodity, 144; in economy sectors, 104–5; free, emergence of, 96; intellectual, 188–9; in monopoly sector, 105, 106; 'the naked worker', 144; and needs, 188–201; object of, 26; obligation to, 188, 190; productive, 103, 145; social, 56–7; social division of, 137, 145–7; surplus, 144, 191; time, 189–91, 195; *see also* Production
Labour contract, 155
Labour power, 78, 155; value of, 98, 103
Labour process, 23, 142–6
Labriola, Antonio, *Essays* . . ., 170
Landowners, 132, 136; feudal, 113, 117
Lange, Oskar, *Political Economy*, 111, 113
Language: and new ideology, 167–8; philology, 32–4
Larrain, Jorge, 17n
Law: and morality, 196–7; natural *v.* social, 49, 50; and power, 128–30; and production relations, 77n, 78, 128; and social transformations, 48
Leach, Edmund, 86, 87, 89; *Political Systems of Highland Burma*, 85n, 89n, 94n
Leisure time, 189–90, 197
Lenin, V. I., 98, 139, 141; determinism, 180; ethics, 185–6; revolutionary social democracy, 120; *What is to be Done?* 54
Lévi-Strauss, Claude: *Elementary Structures of Kinship*, 89; *From Honey to Ashes*, 86, 88–9; history, 88–94; structuralism, 14, 17n, 84, 85–6, 88
Lewis, John, 173

Liberalism, English, 133
Liberty, 46–7; *see also* Freedom
Lichtheim, George: *From Marx to Hegel*, 3n, 4
Löbl, Eugen, 160n
Locke, John, 69
Loewy, Michael, thesis of, 53n
Lukács, Georg, 2, 4–5, 11, 42, 44, 58, 140; *History and Class Consciousness*, 3, 4

Man: /citizen, 96; essence of, 69–70; Marx's concept of, 8, 18, 22–8; problematic of, 69; religious concept of, 173; *see also* Humanism
Management, 117, 118–119
Mandel, Ernest, 99, 103, 104, 105–6; *Late Capitalism*, 100–2
Maoism, 171, 181
Marcuse, Herbert, 4, 4n, 155, 156, 159
Marković, Mihailo, 7n, 10
Marx, Karl, Works: *Capital*, 23–4, 71n, 109, 131–2, 192, 194; Pref. to 2nd ed., Vol. I, 57n; Vol. I, 23, 87n, 94, 174, 178–9; Vol. II, 101, 154; Vol. III, 77, 101, 189, 190–1, 198, 200; *Class Struggles in France*, 137; *Contribution to the Critique of Political Economy*, 87n; Preface to, 37, 64, 125; *Critique of the Gotha Programme*, 174, 193–4; *Critique of Hegel's Philosophy of Right, Introduction*, 44, 52–4; *Critique of Hegel's Philosophy of the State*, 44, 50–3; *Economic and Philosophical Manuscripts*, 12, 17n, 22, 25–6, 198–9; *1844 Manuscripts*, 71n; *Eighteenth Brumaire*, 137, 177; *German Ideology*, 23, 43, 44, 63–4, 66, 67, 176, 177–8; *Grundrisse*, 188, 189–90, 194; *The Holy Family*, 193, 196; letters, 1877, 92n, 172–3; letter to V. Zasulik, 200; *Moralising Critique and Critical Morals*, 111, 114–15; *The Poverty of Philosophy*, 110, 111–12, 174; Preamble of the Statutes of the International, 172; *Revelations about the Cologne Communist Trial*, 62n; articles in *Rheinische Zeitung*, 44, 45–50; *Theories of Surplus Value*, 198; *Theses on Feuerbach*, 18, 43, 44, 54, 67, 69
Materialism, 40, 67; *see also* Historical materialism
Materialist conception of history, 125–37
Mayo, N. B., 181
Mazzinists, 172
Michels, Robert, 30n, 34, 35, 35n
Mikhailovsky, N. K., 92n
Miliband, Ralph, 15n
Monarchy, 133, 135
Monetarists, 106
Money, 71, 72n
Monopoly: phase of capitalism, 98–102; sector of economy, 103–4, 105–6
Morality, *see* Ethics
Mosca, G., 35n
Murdock, G. P., 91
Musil, Robert, *The Man without Qualities*, 20
Mythology, 88–9, 92, 93

Nadel, F., 85
Naturalism, 19–20, 128
Natural law and morality, 49, 50
Needs: material, 190–5; moral, 196–7; objectivation, 197–8; for society, 198–200; structure of, 188–201
Neurath, Otto, 16

Objectivation, 26, 59; of needs, 197–8
Objective spirit, 196, 198
Obligation, 188, 190
O'Connor, James, 15n, 103–6, 108
Offe, Claus, 15n, 158, 163–4
O'Malley, Joseph, 96n
Organization theory, 152
Overlordship, 48
Owen, Robert, 200
Ownership, *see* Property

Palloix, C., 109n
Pareto, Vilfredo, 30n, 35n
Peasants, 137; expropriation of rights, 48
'people', the, 150
Petrović, Gajo, 8
Philology, 32–4; language, 167–8
Philosophy: under Communism, 199; constructing a Marxist, 11–20; of praxis, 11, 29–41; and science, 16–17, 68–70, 125–7; and sociology, 42–55; *see also* Ethics, Positivism
Piaget, Jean, 54
Plato, 35, 76, 196
Plekhanov, G. V., 37
Political economy, 70, 95–109; criticism of, 58–9, 62–3, 155–8; revival of Marxist, 15; state interventionism, 155–9, 163–6; *see also* Capitalism, Production
Political formation *(Gestaltung)*, 77–8
Political power, legitimation of, 157–9
Politics: and economy, 156–9; and sociology, 31–4, 68; and technology, 162; *see also* State
Popper, Karl, 173, 175, 181–2, 183
Positivism, 31, 42; critique of Marx's 56–67; moral, 181–2; recent criticism of, 8–9
Positivists, 17; concept of man, 24
Possession, 110n, 113, 119, 121; in communism, 197; equal, 193; in production process, 143–4
Poulantzas, Nicos, 14, 15n
Power: and class, 146, 150, 152; and law, 128–30; legitimation of political, 157–9; and property, 114–18, 119, 121; state, 129–30, 132–6, 152–3; structure, capitalist, 164
Prawer, S. S., 12n
Praxis (journal), 7–8, 10
Praxis, 10–11, 55; constituent parts of, 35–6; and determinism, 177; the dialectic, 39–41; man as, 25–8; Marx's concept of, 59–62, 70; sociology and, 29–41; structure and historical movement, 36–7
Preaching, moral, 175–6
Pre-capitalist societies, 95n, 144
Prices, 105; *see also* Values
Primitive societies, 80
Production: Asiatic mode of, 122–3; Capitalist mode of, 80–1, 142, 144–5, 147, 163; and communism, 74; contradiction with forms of intercourse, 63–5; in Marx's concept of history, 56–60, 125–6, 127–9, 131; and material needs, 190–1; mode of, and social formation, 147–54; ownership of means of, 111–13, 116–18, 122–4; and political formation, 77–80; pre-capitalist modes of, 144; and property relations, 119–21; society of associated producers, 188–201; and structuralism, 87–8; *see also* Labour
Production, relations of, 64–5, 77n, 78–83, 127–31; and class, 131–4, 142–8; and new ideology, 168; structure of, 81–3
Profits, 87, 100–1; *see also* Surplus value
Proletariat, 96; interest and ethics, 185–6; as revolutionary force, 52–3; *see also* Working class
Property: and economic ownership of means of production, 143–5; and forces of production, 119–21; inheritance and alienation of, 119; Marx's concept of, 96; in Middle Ages, 48; and power, 14–18; private, abolished, 121, 122–3, 124; society based on, 48; and surplus product, 118–19; *see also* Capitalism
Property relations: and bourgeois private property, 122–4; and relations of production, 77n, 145; and social relations, 110–13; sociological analysis of, 110–24
Prussia, state power in, 135
Public-sector employees, 103
Punishment, 196–7

Radcliffe-Brown, A. R., 85
Radicalism, democratic, 45, 49
Rationalism, 11, 14, 44–5, 49, 50
Reason, 25; activity of, 8–10, 18
Reductionism, 32n
Reification, theory of, 48, 71n
Religion: history of, 94; Marx criticizes, 173; and science, 73
Reproduction, social, 60, 65; of capitalism, 154
Revolution, 10, 60, 62–3, 64–5, 124, 126, 132, 152–3; French, 96, 97; October, 120; and proletariat, 52–3
Ricardo, D., 83
Rose, Gillian, 5n
Rousseau, J. J., 75–6, 96
Rubel, Maximilien, 173

Scheler, Max, 24
Schelsky, Helmut, 160n
Schematism, 120
Schumpeter, J. A., 13n
Science: and determinism, 178, 183; and ideology, 57, 66–7, 73; Marxism as, 12–20; Marx's concept of, and value, 174–5; Marx's new, 68–83; and philosophy, 16–17, 68–70, 125–7; social, 12–20, 33–4, 199; and system, 39; and truth, 67; USSR official, 120; *see also* Technology
Scientific socialism, 172, 176
Self-realization, 186–7; in labour, 188–9
serfs, 113, 117, 144; *see also* Feudalism
Shishkin, A. F., 186
Smith, Adam, 83, 97, 188
Social capital, 105
Social categories, 149
Social class, *see* Class
'Social Contract', UK, 107–8
Social formation: and mode of production, 147–9; and state apparatus, 150–4
Socialism: bringing about, 63; and ethics, 170–3; inevitability of, 180–1, 183–4; and property relations, 110–13, 115, 120–4; and schematism, 120; Stalinist, 120
Socialist revolutions, 10, 120, 124, 152–3
Socialization of man, 186–7, 196
Social relations, and property relations, 110–13
Social science, 12–20, 33–4, 199
Social structure, 85–6
Sociologism, 42
Sociology: laws of, 35; Marxism as scientific, 13–18; and Marx's conception of history, 125; and philosophy, in Marx's early writings, 42–55; and the philosophy of praxis, 29–41; and property relations, 110–24
Sombart, Werner, 42, 173
Sorge, F. A., letter to, 172–3
Soviet Union, official science, 120
Spencer, Herbert, 170
Stalinism, 2, 182, 186
Stalinists, 1, 181
State: accumulation by, 104–5; authoritarian, 2, 162; autonomy of, 104, 107; and civil society, 95–9, 109; and economic development of nations, 97–9, 109; expenditure by, 102–5, 106–8; intervention in economy, 155–9, 163–6; in Marx's early articles, 45; modern, creation of, 133–4; power, 129–30, 132–6, 152–3; property, 117–18, 123–4; sector of economy, 104–6; social classes and, 138–54; *see also* Politics
State apparatuses, 133–5, 150–4
Statism, 184
Statistics, laws of, 33–5
Stojanović, Svetozar, 8, 12
Structuralism, 14–18, 84–94
Suffrage, 95n
Surplus product, disposition over the, 118–19
Surplus value: concept of, 82–3; distribution of, 118–19; forms of, 87; and labour, 144, 159–60; and

profits, 100–1, 102–4; and technology, 159–60
Sweezy, Paul, 100
Systems analysis, 84–5, 161–2

Taxation, 103, 104
Taylor, John G., 15n
Technicians, 139–40, 147
Technocratic: consciousness, 166–8; ideology, 160–2; misconception, 63
Technology, 61, 102, 104, 145, 155–6, 158–9; scientization of, 159–62
Theft, 48
Third World, 165
Togliatti, Palmiro, 120
Totality, 3, 82
Trade unions, 95n, 104, 107
Transformation: of economic basis, 64–6; of men, 62; perpetual, 77; social, 88, 89
Truth, 67
Tucker, Robert C., 182
Tylor, E. B., 89

Underprivileged groups, 164–5
Unemployment, 104, 105, 106–7
United States, bureaucracy, 136
Uno-Riron, T. Sekine, 96n
Utilitarianism, 23–4, 185
Utopias, 73, 175–6, 201

Value judgements, 6–7, 16n, 50–1
Values, 18; economic categories, 97, 103; humanistic-ethical, 184, 185; and science, 175; *see also* Surplus value
Vico, Giambattista, 32n
Vorländer, Karl, 42

Wage contract, 95
Wages, 105, 145–6; and inflation, 106; and social welfare, 103
Wallerstein, Immanuel, 15n
Weber, Max, 9, 16n, 30n, 114, 150, 155; power, 114, 152; value theory, 16n, 18
Welfare, social, 98, 107; costs, 103, 104
Wellmer, Albrecht, 9n, 12
Women, 15, 146
Working class: awakening of, 176; class consciousness, 131–2, 141; in revolution, 152–3; and technicians, 139–40; wages, 145–6; *see also* Labour, Proletariat
World War I, 98, 106
World War II, 102

Yugoslavia, 7, 10

Zasulich, Vera, letter to, 200